THE GROWTH OF BULBS

APPLIED BOTANY

A Series of Monographs

CONSULTING EDITOR

J. F. Sutcliffe

School of Biological Sciences, University of Sussex, England

THE GROWTH OF BULBS

Applied aspects of the physiology of ornamental bulbous crop plants

A. R. REES

Glasshouse Crops Research Institute,
Littlehampton, Sussex, England

1972

ACADEMIC PRESS – London and New York

ACADEMIC PRESS INC. (LONDON) LTD.
24–28 Oval Road
London NW1

United States Edition published by
ACADEMIC PRESS INC.
111 Fifth Avenue
New York, New York 10003

Library of Congress Catalog Card Number: 72–189933
ISBN: 0–12–585450–1

Printed in Great Britain by
Butler & Tanner Ltd, Frome and London

323752

Editor's Foreword

The cultivation of crops is rapidly becoming a highly organized and increasingly efficient branch of industry. In order to produce the amounts of food and other plant products which are required by the growing world population, agriculturalists, horticulturalists and foresters are depending more and more on the results of scientific research. These are published in a large number of journals, some of which are not readily available, and even with the help of the abstracting services it is not always easy to get the information required.

The purpose of the Applied Botany Monographs is to bring together our knowledge of selected aspects of crop science for the benefit of growers, research workers, and those students who are being trained for careers in agriculture, horticulture and forestry. By drawing attention to gaps in our knowledge the monographs may also help to direct the course of future research towards areas where it is most needed.

J. F. SUTCLIFFE
Consulting Editor
Applied Botany Series

Preface

"A familiarity with palms at once explains the corm and
bulb so mysteriously storage in the perennial introduction
to botany." E. J. H. Corner, 1963

Bulb crops have been studied for many decades, especially in the Netherlands which are so closely associated with bulb flowers. Much of the early
information was published in Dutch, in journals now often difficult to
trace and obtain. The more applied aspects of these early studies have
been assimilated into bulb growing throughout the world, but the scientific
basis is often well buried. A few reviews in English have appeared, but these
are brief and again some are not easily obtained. Continued work on flower
bulb physiology has led to some modifications of the original recommendations, and new aspects of bulb growth have been investigated recently. It
is certainly true that there is currently more active research work in progress
on ornamental bulbs than at any time past, and this work is being done
all over the world.

These changing methods, growing areas and plant materials used have
led to a reassessment of some aspects of bulb growing. Traditional methods
are being reconsidered and new methods introduced which are more in
keeping with present-day mechanization of crop growing. It is timely,
therefore, to consider the present state of knowledge of bulbs and bulb
growing.

My aim was to prepare an account of ornamental bulbs as plants and as
crops, with emphasis on scientific aspects of bulb growing, bulb treatment
and bulb forcing. Inevitably the account will be biased towards British
bulb growing, but I have attempted to introduce as much as possible of
bulb growing in other parts of the world, especially in the Netherlands, the
U.S.A., Israel and Japan. I did not feel qualified to write a detailed account
of pests and diseases, but a brief account of these is included; and reference
is made to the machinery, stores and other hardware of bulb growing only
where necessary for an understanding of the plant or crop response.

The survey of the literature was completed in mid-1971. Some references
from the First International Symposium on Flowerbulbs held at Noordwijk/
Lisse in 1970 which was published late in 1971 have, however, been
included.

Acknowledgements

It is a pleasure to acknowledge the help and encouragement of colleagues concerned with bulb growing. Particular mention should be made of the Directors of Rosewarne and Kirton Experimental Horticulture Stations of the Agricultural Development and Advisory Service, Mr. J. Eaton and Mr. G. Baines, who have always gone out of their way to be helpful. Staff at Kirton E.H.S. who have co-operated in bulb research are Mrs. E. D. Turquand, who introduced me to the intricacies of bulb forcing, and her able successor Mr. J. B. Briggs. At Rosewarne Mr. L. W. Wallis proved most knowledgeable on bulb growing in the South West, recognition of which has led to his appointment as Regional Specialist (Bulbs). Mr. N. D. Goodway has co-operated on many aspects of bulb growing on the Isles of Scilly and contact with Rosewarne is being maintained through the good offices of Mr. A. A. Tompsett.

At the G.C.R.I. I am more than grateful for the friendship and encouragement of my bulb colleagues, Mrs. J. McD. Gilford who has worked with me for a number of years, Mr. A. A. Brunt and Dr. D. Price, with whom I share many memories of bulbs and bulb fields. Thanks are due to my colleagues in the Physiology Department, G.C.R.I., who read and commented on the manuscript and to Mr. J. J. Hesling, Mr. A. A. Brunt and Dr. D. Price for much needed assistance with Chapter 10. The responsibility for all errors and omissions is, however, mine.

Finally, thanks are due to the growers—without whom there would be no crop and no research—in the bulb-growing areas of the South West and eastern England. They have always been ready to discuss aspects of bulb growing, and not only those related to profit, and give much time and material readily and willingly in the cause of science.

April, 1972   A. R. REES

Contents

For Mo, David and Sian

Chapter 1 ══════════════════════════════

Bulbs as crop plants: their origins and present distribution

> "It is artificial to try to establish hard-and-fast distinctions
> between bulbs and other subterranean forms of reserve-
> containing shoots."   A. Arber, 1925

I. World production of bulbs

Bulbous plants grow in probably every country in the world, because even if the climate is unsuitable for wild plants, the cultivated form can be treated so as to flower in a wide range of environments.

Few countries are, however, of importance as bulb producing areas, and these are mostly in the cool temperate areas, although some are within the tropics at high altitudes. Table 1.1 gives such data as are available on the global distribution of bulb growing. The statistics are incomplete, but the importance of the Netherlands, the United Kingdom, the U.S.A. and Japan is unquestionable. The data for miscellaneous crops probably includes in a number of cases plants which do not have true bulbs, e.g. *Freesia*, *Begonia* and *Gladiolus*.

Confining this consideration to true bulbs, the largest area of any bulb crop is that of *Tulipa*, followed by *Narcissus* and then *Iris*, *Hyacinthus* and *Lilium*. For individual countries, however, this order is not always maintained; British *Narcissus* areas are double those of *Tulipa*, and individual countries "specialize" in some crops (e.g. the Netherlands produce 95% of the world's hyacinths).

1

Table 1.1

World production of bulbs. Numbers of hectares devoted to the various crops (data mainly from Gould (1967) and Schenk 1969).

		Narcissus	Tulipa	Hyacinthus	Iris	Lilium	Miscellaneous	Total
Australia	1966						324	324
Belgium	1968		16				45	61
Canada	1962	168	25		4		5	202
Denmark	1967	115	357	15			34	521
England and Wales	1968	3561	1781		207		283	5832
France	1964	70						70
Germany E.	1962		150?					150
Germany W.	1966		400?				54	454
Ireland	1964	16						16
Israel	1967						10	10
Italy	1968	66	200?				71	337
Japan	1967	47	750	24	164	319	165	1469
Netherlands	1968	1418	5562	855	510	156	1802	10,303
Scotland	1968	160	22				2	184
U.S.A.	1967	902	119	6	414	305	450	2196
U.S.S.R.	1968		150					150
New Zealand	1966						90	90
Total		6523	9532	900	1299	780	3335	22,369

There are considerable fluctuations in acreages of bulb crops, but the area of land devoted to flower bulbs is generally increasing. In some countries the increases have been rapid, e.g. Japan's tulip area more than trebled in the decade to 1965, whilst that of the Netherlands and Britain increased by about 70%. Tulip production in the U.S.A. fell markedly, due probably to increased competition from Japan but this trend now seems to have levelled off. Trends in areas of *Narcissus* are much less dramatic than for tulips, with the industry expanding by about 20% a decade in Britain and Holland, and remaining fairly static in Japan and the U.S.A. Britain grows more than half the world's area of *Narcissus*, with the Netherlands and the U.S.A. second and third.

Bulbs are also exported in large numbers from the producing countries, the Netherlands especially. Gould (1967) quotes U.S. imports for 1965 as 288·4 million bulbs and about £3·5 million is spent on bulb imports (about 200 million bulbs) to Britain, largely from the Netherlands. Imports into Britain expressed as a percentage of total bulbs used is, however, falling. For *Narcissus* 70% of bulbs in 1965 were home produced compared with only 45% in 1958 and 55% of tulips were home produced in 1965, compared with 38% in 1958.

It would be futile to try and assess the value of the World bulb industry because of the shortcomings in the data on areas of crops. The British industry is valued at about £16 million.

II. Parent species and classification of important bulb crops

Many of the currently important bulb species have been highly developed by decades of selection and breeding, so that they are very different from the original wild form or forms from which they were derived. Others, however, are very similar to their wild ancestors which still grow wild in their original habitats. Information on the development of modern cultivars is, therefore, somewhat uneven in quantity and also quality; some genera and species have been looked at in detail, others have not. The important genera are therefore considered separately.

A. *Narcissus*

The horticultural forms of *Narcissus* have been derived from wild species either unchanged as in many of the smaller species commonly grown in rockeries, or by hybridization of native species. In general, *Narcissus* species cross with great facility, and many spontaneous hybrids occur. *Narcissus* is a genus of the northern hemisphere, centred on Spain and Portugal, and occupying within this geographical range a range of habitats, from exposed mountain sites up to 2000 m to sheltered valleys and lowlands. The most important species is probably *N. hispanicus* which occurs through northern Spain and south-west France along the Pyrenees but has been cultivated in Britain for over 300 years as *N. maximus* or *N. maximus superbus*, a tall trumpet daffodil. Many species have a localized distribution (Table 1.2).

Table 1.2

The distribution of some of the important species of *Narcissus*, with chromosome numbers and indications of ploidy. (After Jefferson-Brown (1969) and Fernandes (1967).)

N. hispanicus n = 7 (2n–6n)	N. Spain, S.W. France.
N. bulbocodium n = 7 (2n–6n)	Spain, Portugal, S.W. France, N. Africa.
N. jonquilla n = 7 (2n)	Spain, Portugal, N. Africa.
N. triandrus n = 7 (2n)	Spain, Portugal, Iles des Glenans.
N. pseudonarcissus n = 7 (2n)	France, Belgium, Switzerland, N. Italy.
N. poeticus n = 7 (2n, 3n)	S. Europe from Spain to Greece.
N. tazetta n = 10 (2n)	Spain and N. Africa in a narrow band as far east as Japan and China.
N. cyclamineus n = 7 (2n)	Portugal.

Many cultivated forms are closely related to the wild species and although the *Narcissus* did not become an important bulb crop until the end of the nineteenth century, the parents of the present cultivars had been known for hundreds of years (Doorenbos, 1954). *Narcissus* is classified into a number of divisions where the divisional characteristics are described as having the characteristics of the appropriate group either "clearly evident" or "without admixture of any other group". This applies to *N. triandrus, N. cyclamineus, N. jonquilla, N. tazetta* and *N. poeticus*. The yellow trumpet daffodils are derived from *N. hispanicus,* and the white trumpets, apparently, from *N. moschatus, N. albestris* and *N. albescens*. Initial crosses between trumpet forms and *N. poeticus* species and varieties were the origins of the large-cupped narcissi which are now the largest division of modern daffodils and the most important commercially. The origin of the small-cupped narcissi is more complex: *N. poetarum* has been important as a source of red-cupped flowers and *N. exertus ornatus* and *N. hellenicus* have contributed to the paler forms. These forms and their progeny crossed with large-cupped flowers gave the first of the small-cupped flowers.

The Royal Horticultural Society has been appointed as the International Registration Authority for narcissi and periodically publishes a *Classified List and International Register of Daffodil Names*. The classification into divisions is largely artificial but is of useful descriptive value:

1. Trumpet narcissi of garden origin.
2. Large-cupped narcissi of garden origin.
3. Small-cupped narcissi of garden origin.
4. Double narcissi of garden origin.
5. Triandrus narcissi of garden origin.
6. Cyclamineus narcissi of garden origin.
7. Jonquilla narcissi of garden origin.
8. Tazetta narcissi of garden origin.
9. Poeticus narcissi of garden origin.
10. Species and wild forms and wild hybrids.
11. Split-corolla narcissi.
12. Miscellaneous narcissi.

The divisions are subdivided according to other features such as colour (1, 2 and 3) or corona length (5, 6, 7). The classified list contains nearly 10,000 names, and commercial catalogues contain many hundreds. Commercial growers use relatively few cultivars; it was recently reported that the largest forcer of narcissi in the U.K. used only three cultivars.

The cytology of the genus has been studied for many years at the University of Coimbra, Portugal (Fernandes, 1967). Chromosome numbers of 7 and multiples thereof, especially 14, 21, 28 and 42 are most frequent, but a group based upon 5, with frequent occurrences of 10 and 11 exists, and Fernandes has classified the genus into two subgenera, the first, *Hermione* (including only *N. tazetta* of the species mentioned so far) having numbers based on 5 and its derivatives 10 and 11 and a second larger subgenus *Narcissus* based on 7 and its derived 13 chromosome numbers.

Present-day plants of specific status have probably evolved from extinct ancestral forms with 14 chromosomes by gene mutation, hybridization, polyploidy and chromosomal alteration or loss. Fernandes lists over 60 full species with an additional large number of varieties. The situation is complex; Jefferson-Brown (1969) lists 19 pages of specific names which have been used at one time or another.

The most frequently grown cultivars arose from only a few species: *N. pseudonarcissus*, *N. poeticus* and *N. tazetta*. The trumpet narcissi arose from *N. pseudonarcissus* with 14 chromosomes, but triploids and tetraploids have been found in the wild. 'King Alfred' is thought to have been the first commercial tetraploid cultivar of the trumpet group although diploid and triploid cultivars are also known (Doorenbos, 1954).

B

The popularity of *Narcissus* cultivars is not closely related to their attractiveness; early forcing quality, suitability for use as cut flowers or garden plants, and high flower numbers per weight of bulbs planted are criteria important for growers.

B. *Tulipa*

The garden tulip complex largely forms the Gesnerianae (Hall, 1940), although the natural origin of the garden tulip is unknown. It was, however, first known to western Europe about the middle of the sixteenth century, although clear evidence exists of previous cultivation and breeding in Turkey and Persia where the species was greatly prized. Even in the seventeenth-century Dutch paintings and in the early herbals, both short cupped and long pointed flowers and "broken" forms were common. Only "broken" forms were prized together with the "mother" plants of plain colours which produced "broken" progeny. It was centuries before the virus cause of the "broken" condition was recognized. The interrelations of the complex that make up the genus are discussed in detail by Hall (1940), whilst other authorities state that species segregation which is still occurring in the native habitat of Turkey and Iran makes part of the genus very difficult to study.

The genus is Asiatic in the main with a centre in the hilly regions of Asia Minor, the southern Caucasus, Turkistan and Bukhara, gradually dying out in north-east Asia but persisting into China and Japan and occurring westwards along the northern Mediterranean as far as Portugal and in the Atlas mountain foothills from Morocco to Tripoli. Generally the genus is found in hilly country, up to 4000 m in the Himalayas. The extreme climate in these areas is closely tied in with the tulip's physiology. Winters are extremely cold but summers are hot and dry.

A classified list of registered names was published in 1929 by the Royal Horticultural Society and the Dutch General Bulb Growers' Society. This list is revised and added to from time to time, and is published as *The Classified List and International Register of Tulip Names*, available from either of the above Societies. An indication of the range of tulip types can be obtained from the following classification, which follows that of the most recent list.

Early flowering

1. DUC VAN TOL TULIPS   Very early flowering single tulips, seldom taller than 15 cm.

2. SINGLE EARLY TULIPS

3. DOUBLE EARLY TULIPS

Mid-season flowering

4. MENDEL TULIPS — Chiefly result of crosses between Duc van Tol and Darwin Tulips. Single, seldom taller than 50 cm.

5. TRIUMPH TULIPS — Chiefly results of crosses between Single Early and Late (May-flowering) tulips. Single, stouter plants than Mendel tulips and sometimes taller than 50 cm.

Late or May-flowering

6. DARWIN TULIPS — Single, tall, lower part of flower usually rectangular in outline.

7. DARWIN HYBRID TULIPS — Single, result of crossing Darwin tulips with *Tulipa fosteriana* and its varieties.

8. BREEDER TULIPS (AND OLD ENGLISH BREEDER TULIPS) — Single, flowers oval or cup-shaped.

9. LILY-FLOWERED TULIPS — Single, flowers with pointed reflexed petals.

10. COTTAGE TULIPS (SINGLE LATE TULIPS) — Single, flowers often long or egg-shaped.

11. REMBRANDT TULIPS — Broken Darwin tulips.

12. BIZARRE TULIPS — Broken Breeder and Cottage tulips. Single, dark colour on yellow ground.

13. BIJBLOEMEN TULIPS — Broken Breeder and Cottage tulips. Single, dark colours on white ground.

14. PARROT TULIPS — Tulips with laciniate petals.

15. DOUBLE LATE TULIPS (PAEONY-FLOWERED TULIPS)

16–23. SPECIES, HYBRIDS AND THEIR VARIETIES.

The division of tulips into these groups is largely artificial, being based on the time of outdoor flowering, the division into early and late cultivars following the classification of Clusius who studied the genus in the late sixteenth century.

Petrova and Silina (1966) refer to 5544 modern varieties, of which 3454 are of commercial importance, according to the classified list, but Zeilinga and Schouten (1968) in their study of chromosome number could obtain and report on only 614 cultivars in the Netherlands, and a few of these were no longer cultivated (Table 1.3). Most cultivars are diploid but of the cultivars and their sports described by Zeilinga and Schouten, only four were tetraploid and 85 were triploid. Bochantseva (1962) (quoted by Petrova and Silina, 1966) examined 46 species of tulip and found polyploids in the divisions *Leiostemones* (3 out of 26 examined) and *Eriostemones*

(5 out of 16). Polyploids are apparently found on the edges of the high-altitude distribution of the species, and are usually auto-polyploids. Southern (1967), from his study of species relations in the *Eriostemones* section of *Tulipa* concluded that the evidence relating to the ploidy relationships within the section is inconclusive.

Petrova and Silina emphasize the importance of polyploidy in the

Table 1.3

Summary of polyploids found in tulips of various classes by Zeilinga and Schouten (1968)

Class	No. of cultivars and sports examined	No. of diploid (2n = 24)	No. of triploid (3n = 36)	No. of tetraploid (4n = 48)
Duc van Tol	16	16	0	0
Single early	59	54	4	1
Double early	35	35	0	0
Mendel	34	32	2	0
Triumph	148	131	17	0
Darwin	81	76	5	0
Darwin hybrids	25	1	24	0
Breeder	9	8	1	0
Lily-flowered	26	25	1	0
Single late	63	43	18	2
Rembrandt	4	4	0	0
Bizarre	2	2	0	0
Bijbloemen	1	0	1	0
Parrot	20	18	2	0
Double late	12	12	0	0
Kaufmanniana hybrid	17	17	0	0
Greigii hybrid	25	23	2	0
Fosteriana hybrid	24	20	3	1
Greigii var.	1	1	0	0
Fosteriana var.	4	4	0	0
Gesneriana var.	4	1	3	0
Kaufmanniana	1	1	0	0
Holland Breeder	1	1	0	0
Lily-fl. × *greigii*	1	0	1	0
Unknown	1	0	1	0
Total	614	525	85	4

evolution of many crop plants, especially as it is frequently connected with an increase in plant height and size of parts as well as complete or partial sterility. Hall (1937) and others refer to species of *Tulipa* from Europe and Asia Minor which form polyploid series e.g. *T. clusiana* 2n = 24, 36, 48 and 60, *T. orphanidea* 2n = 24, 36 and 60; species with diploid and tetraploid forms e.g. *T. chrysantha* 2n = 24, 48; species with triploid forms, e.g. *T. saxatilis* 2n = 24, 36, and species existing only as polyploids e.g. *T. aleppensis* 2n = 36. Because polyploidy in tulips is mainly auto-polyploidy, it has played only a minor role in the evolution of the genus (Upcott and La Cour, 1936).

Central Asian tulip species (*T. fosteriana*, *T. greigii*, *T. ingens* and *T. kaufmanniana*) have played an increasingly important role in tulip selection, thus Petrova and Silina state that in 1952 only 3% of the commercial tulip cultivars were derived from Central Asian species but by 1966 the figure had risen to 14%, largely because of the use of *T. fosteriana*, *T. greigii* and *T. kaufmanniana*. The *T. fosteriana* commercial variety 'Mme. Lefeber' is the paternal parent of the Darwin hybrid group which have large stems, leaves, flowers and bulbs and early flowering and a high tendency to mutate to give bud sports. The triploid nature of all but one (cv. 'Spring Song') of these Darwin hybrids is the cause of their complete sterility which prevents their use for further hybridization.

Petrova and Silina (1966) regard the present-day selection using central Asian species of *Tulipa* as taking two directions, firstly the development of cultivars which retain the external form of the wild species but which possess some features of cultivated plants (e.g. the capacity for vegetative multiplication, uniform morphological characteristics and gregarious flowering). These are being bred by the selection of decorative forms, interspecific hybridization and crossing species with varieties. Many wild qualities will be retained and polyploidy will be only of secondary importance. Secondly there is a creation of cultivars possessing both the basic character and habit of the cultural tulip e.g. tall, with strong flowering shoot, a single large flower and bulbs which propagate well. The only characteristics of the wild tulips that are retained are the isolated ones of brightness of flower colour, resistance to disease, etc.

Remote hybridization of the better cultivated tulips in combination with polyploidy using Central Asian species produces valuable new commercial cultivars, and this method is one of the most promising for future tulip selection. For commercial acceptance one of the main requirements is that the tulip can be forced early and easily, and the number of cultivars in this group is relatively small. In 1954 Doorenbos reported that 72% of the whole tulip acreage in Holland was occupied by only 20 cultivars and their sports.

Few countries keep sufficiently good national statistics on the relative quantities of different cultivars, so that for assessing the popularity of cultivars, data from the Netherlands are normally used. There is a danger, however, that by doing this the local or national preferences in other countries are overlooked. 'Rose Copland', for instance, appears to be more popular in the U.K. than in the Netherlands, and it seems that the modern red colour of 'Apeldoorn' has very little appeal in Japan where the most widely grown cultivar is 'William Pitt'.

C. *Hyacinthus*

There are about 30 species of *Hyacinthus* which are mainly of Mediterranean origin but a few species are native to tropical and southern Africa. Few species are in cultivation, and there is only one of horticultural importance. This is *H. orientalis* from which has been developed the familiar hyacinths so widely grown as house plants in the winter. This species is indigenous to Asia Minor and was imported into western Europe before 1568 when it was illustrated in Dodonaeus's herbal. At that time blue, white and purple forms were known, and double flowers were described in 1612 (Doorenbos, 1954).

The diploid form has 16 chromosomes of five different types, and there are triploids (3n = 24) and a large number of heteroploid, e.g. 'L'Innocence' (27), 'Ostara' (25) and 'City of Haarlem' (23), and all possible chromosome numbers between 16 and 31 have been found except 18. No true tetraploid (4n = 32) has been described.

D. *Iris*

The origins of cultivated *Iris* are uncertain, but modern cultivars are based on *I. xiphium* (Spanish *Iris*), *I. tingitana* and *I. filifolia*. *I. reticulata* is also of increasing importance. The Dutch *Iris* are the most widely grown; these are based on selections and crosses from *I. tingitana* and *I. xiphium* and include the well-known cultivars 'Golden Harvest', 'Imperator', 'Professor Blaauw', 'H. C. van Vliet', 'Wedgwood' and 'White Excelsior'. The most widely grown *Iris* cultivar is 'Wedgwood' because of its early flowering and response to storage treatments; it is derived from a cross between *I. xiphium praecox* and *I. tingitana* and a cross between *I. xiphium* and *I. xiphium lusitanica* ('Cajanus'). The favourable early flowering is apparently derived from *I. tingitana*. Cultivar 'H. C. van Vliet' is another offspring of the same parents, but at a later date (Kamerbeek, 1963). Because of the uncertainties of the origin of many *Iris* cultivars, they are referred to by name rather than their parent species.

The original habitats of the various species are:

I. filifolia   S. Spain, N.W. Africa.
I. reticulata   Asia Minor and N. Persia.
I. tingitana   Nr. Tangiers and in Morocco.
I. xiphiodes   Central and W. Pyrenees, N.W. Spain.
I. xiphium   Portugal, Spain, S. France and N. Africa.

E. *Lilium*

The three major countries producing lilies are, in the order of import-ance, Japan, the U.S.A. and the Netherlands (Gould, 1967). Small areas of lilies are grown in a large number of other countries.

Lilies grow wild throughout Europe, northern Asia and North America, and the genus is a large one of 80 or more species which is normally classified using the artificial grouping adopted by the Royal Horticultural Society and the North American Lily Society:

DIVISION 1   The Asiatic hybrids
         2   The Martagon hybrids
         3   The Candidum hybrids
         4   Hybrids of American species
         5   The Longiflorum hybrids
         6   The Trumpet hybrids
         7   The Oriental hybrids
         8   Other hybrids
         9   True species and their botanical forms.

Probably the most important group is the longiflorum lilies, *L. longi-florum* Thunb., the Japanese Eastern Lily, Long-tubed White Lily or Trumpet Lily. More than 7·5 million of these bulbs are grown in coastal northern California and southern Oregon, which represents about 75% of the lily bulbs grown in the U.S.A. for use as potted plants and cut flowers (Miller and Kofranek, 1966). This species is endemic to LiuChiu (south of Japan) and was first commercially grown for bulb production in Bermuda in the late nineteenth century. Most of the production in the U.S.A. is in Florida, Louisiana, Mexico and Oregon, using bulbs imported from Japan or grown in the west coast of U.S.A., Florida and Bermuda. The commonest-grown cultivars are: 'Creole', 'Croft', 'Georgia', 'Nellie White' and 'Slocum's Ace' usually referred to as 'Ace'.

Other species widely grown in the field or glasshouse for florists' use, as potted plants or for gardens, are *L. speciosum*, a native of Japan, *L. regale* from western China, *L. formosanum* from Formosa and *L. candidum*, which is assumed to be a native of southern Europe and south-west Asia although there is doubt whether it has been found in the wild.

III. The bulbous habit

A bulb can be described as an organ consisting of a short stem bearing a number of swollen fleshy leaf bases or scale leaves, with or without a tunic, the whole enclosing the next year's bud. This definition suffers from the limitation that it gives little indication of the geographical or botanical occurrence of the habit or the diverse types of bulbs found in nature. Arber (1925) said that it is difficult to establish a hard-and-fast distinction between bulbs and other subterranean forms of reserve-containing shoots. For example, some species of *Allium* have rhizomes, whilst others have bulbs, but the rhizomes are no more than the bulb axes of many years' growth.

The bulbous habit is found almost exclusively in the Monocotyledons, but it is not generally realized that true bulbs also occur in the Dicotyledons e.g. *Oxalis*. Galil (1967) has recently described the growth of *Oxalis* bulbs which bear no roots but produce a thread-like shoot, bearing roots, which forms a rosette of leaves at ground level. There is no obvious reason why the bulbous habit should not have arisen more widely in the Dicotyledons.

A consideration of bulbs leads inevitably to analysis of growth forms in the Monocotyledons. Holttum (1955) emphasized that the absence of the cambium is a fundamental feature of the Monocotyledons, although a few have developed a cambium (almost all in the *Agavales* but also *Aristea* (Iridaceae), indicating at least two lines of development). Holttum postulated that the lack of a cambium led to a continuous vegetative growth (sympodial growth) in the moist tropical climate where higher plants first evolved. A sympodial branching habit is almost universal in Monocotyledons. With the start of colonization of areas with a climate with some unfavourable periods—whether this was due to an extension of an original habitat or to a change in climate—the sympodial growth form proved particularly adaptable to the production of resting organs. This allowed the spread of cambiumless plants to seasonal climates. Other workers, Sargant (1903) in particular, have regarded the absence of the cambium in the Monocotyledons as being due to its loss from an ancestral form with a cambium, because this loss would facilitate the production of perennating organs. In a consideration of plant form, bulbs could be regarded as "trees without wood".

Despite the absence of cambium, monocotyledonous plants have localized groups of cells which remain meristematic. These frequently occur at nodes (in the grasses), at the junction of the basal sheaths and the long flat blade of narcissus foliage leaves (Chen, 1966) and just below the flower in the tulip (Sachs, 1962). Adventitious buds can also develop from epidermal and subepidermal cells in hyacinths, and not from pre-formed meristematic tissue as might have been expected. There is, however, no zone of cells which continues division indefinitely and no formation of additional vascular tissue once the growth in width of a stem is completed. In monopodial forms, which are the exception rather than the rule in the Monocotyledons, growth is concentrated at the apex, but in sympodial plants, extension growth is frequently due to the enlargement of cells formed previously in the life history and requiring some external stimulus for enlargement (such as the cold requirement of tulips) or is due to the activity of a subapical meristem (Sachs, 1962) and much of the plant form occurs as compressed axes with short internodes.

A consequence of the general localization of meristematic cells to nodes is that adventitious structures such as lateral buds and roots occur only at nodes. The diameter of the primary root is too small to supply the water requirement of an extended shoot, and because of this size limitation imposed by the overall dimensions of the embryo and the absence of a cambium it must be supplemented by other roots. These other roots are adventitious, and therefore arise at nodes. Stem growth is limited by the number of roots which can be borne by the lower nodes of the stem; short internodes in the basal parts of the stem are necessary for producing the large numbers of roots essential for the maintenance of a large leaf area. To accommodate the increase in diameter of the embryo stem-meristem to an adult size, the base of the stem is an inverted cone due to the development of a "primary thickening meristem" which widens the internodes before elongation preponderates, a process which is often extended over a number of years. This process may also be considered as a predomination of radial growth which deforms a potentially conical apex into a bowl-shaped one (Rees, 1964). The inverted cone is supported by roots growing from the nodes, and for vertical stability the cone must be vertically as short as possible, if it is at or near the soil surface. If the structure at this time in the life of the plant is underground, stability is less important than is a means of ensuring a subterranean position. In bulbous plants there are at least two ways of achieving this. In the tulip, "dropper" formation occurs in seedlings and in certain circumstances in adult plants of tulip and *Erythronium* (Robertson, 1906; Ogura, 1952). These structures are a form of stolon where the extended portion is a continuation of the base of a foliage leaf, the morphology of which is partly foliar and partly axial. In other genera, contractile roots pull the bulb down into the soil (Wilson and Honey, 1966).

The basic sympodial pattern of monocotyledonous growth envisaged as developing in an even tropical climate would exhibit some periodicity because the lateral basal buds which invariably develop at the lower nodes would be suppressed by apical dominance exerted by the terminal shoot and flower. This periodicity would not be in phase with any external factor, but should the environment change to include dry periods, it is easy to envisage the development of resting periods between the death of shoots and the replacement by basal buds. This could perhaps occur by the death of the mother axis root system and the failure of the daughter bulbs to establish a new root system until soil moisture conditions improved. The adaptations necessary for this are that each new growth should arise from an underground lateral bud, and that the underground part should develop adequate storage tissue to enable survival during the unfavourable period. The replacement of aerial parts of limited height and duration by basal shoots tends to give clumped or tufted growth.

Good (1966) commented on the relative frequencies of monocotyledonous and dicotyledonous plants (the latter have 2·5-4 times as many species) and stated that the Monocotyledons are found outside the tropics only as relatively small plants which die down below ground level at the onset of winter. He attributes this to their inability to produce secondary protective tissues against the dangers of frost. This vulnerability of the normally watery plant body of the Angiosperms to frost seems to leave little room for doubting that the group originated and evolved for a long period under conditions where this hazard did not exist, namely in the tropics, and by an extension of the same reasoning probably the equatorial belt where seasonal climatic variation is at its lowest.

Presumably later in the migration from the tropics, adaptations to allow regrowth only after the end of a cool period would allow the plants to be dormant over winter. The summer dormancy mechanism allied to a cold requirement allows bulbous plants to grow very successfully in Mediterranean-type climate in many parts of the world. Non-periodic forms are still found in areas where no unfavourable period prevents growth.

As long ago as 1925, Arber stated that it is not known why one organ rather than another becomes loaded with food and suffers a distortion of form; we must confess to being in the same position now with regard to bulbs.

Bulbous forms occur in the following families:

Amaryllidaceae	*Leucojum, Galanthus, Narcissus, Hippeastrum*
Iridaceae	*Iris*
Liliaceae	*Lilium, Fritillaria, Tulipa, Lloydia, Gagea, Ornithogalum, Scilla, Endymion, Muscari, Allium* Urginea, Dipcadi, Leopoldia

Bulbous plants occur in a wide range of habitats from tropical forests to open grassland scrub and desert. The bulbous habit must therefore confer a measure of success to the plant, especially, it seems, as a means of enduring extremes of arid climates.

There are a number of physiological considerations of the bulbous habit. For the developing plant the possession of a bulb is in some ways equivalent to growing from a large seed. The bulb allows the formation of a large shoot before this is exposed to the rigours of the outside environment, and the subsequent growth of the shoot and the roots is independent of current photosynthesis. This allows growth early in the spring in temperate latitudes where incoming radiation is low.

The food reserves in bulbous plants allow the plants to survive extended periods when growth is not possible, such as in cold winters and hot dry summers. These advantages of the bulbous habit probably account for the greatest development of the bulb flora in areas with a Mediterranean climate. Burns (1946) stressed that the majority of corm-and-bulb-producing species occurred between 23–45°N and 23–45°S latitude, and suggested that climate and medium day-length may have been the most important factors in the evolution of the geophytic habit. Savos'kin (1960) considers that the regular onset of a hot dry climate is of fundamental importance in the evolution of bulbous geophytes, and that the development pattern is caused by the Mediterranean climatic rhythm of warm, wet winters and hot, dry summers. Holttum's (1955) work does appear to favour a tropical origin for bulbous plants, despite their greater frequency in the Mediterranean areas, which must reflect the advantages of the bulbous habit in unfavourably dry climates.

A third physiologically important feature of the bulbous habit is in propagation. Daughter bulbs are produced at frequent or infrequent intervals in the axils of bulb scales, foliage leaf bases or in other positions and are responsible for the occurrence of clumps of plants derived from the same parent bulb, although these clumps are seen more commonly in temperate gardens than in the natural habitat, where solitary plants are more usual.

Many of the plants which have become horticulturally important are derived from parents growing originally in Mediterranean climate areas, e.g. *Narcissus*, *Tulipa*, *Hyacinthus* and *Iris*, and still possess a number of features adapting them to a winter and a hot dry summer, despite a great deal of hybridizing which has been done for centuries. The possession of summer dormancy and a cold requirement encouraged the development of storage temperature treatments allowing controlled flowering. The dormant bulb forms a very convenient stage for handling, transport and treatment. No special lighting is required, because the bulbs are not photosynthesizing so that the early Dutch work on effects of temperature on flowering can be described as the first controlled-environment studies of whole plants. The early work on temperature treatment for early flowering has been greatly extended in more recent years, greater precision is now possible in bulb growing, newer varieties are available and completely new techniques for promoting early flowering have been developed. It is useful, however, to consider these horticultural modifications in the light of the original habitats of the parents of present-day cultivars.

Chapter 2 ⸻⸻⸻⸻⸻⸻⸻⸻⸻⸻⸻

Bulb structure, morphology, development and periodicity

"Sous un mode de vie apparement uniforme, les plantes bulbeuses cachent une grande diversité." P. Chouard, 1931

Hitherto bulbs have been referred to as if there was only a single common structure. This is not the case. There is a range of bulb types, and three will be considered in some detail, as representative of the range.

I. The *Hippeastrum* bulb type

The simplest type is represented by *Hippeastrum*, whose bulb is composed entirely of leaf bases. The plant grows in regions of low environmental variation and corresponds with the hypothetical ancestor of bulbous plants which developed in a tropical non-periodic climate. The genus *Hippeastrum* occurs in tropical and subtropical America from Mexico and the West Indies southwards to Chile and southern Brazil, and the species from which the commercial hybrids were derived occur in areas both with and without a marked dry season (Blaauw, 1931). In both situations there is a single flowering season, although occasionally flowers appear at other times. Commercially *Hippeastrum* is grown in northern Europe (mainly in Holland), and outdoors in Florida, southern California and South Africa.

17

Externally the plant shows typical characteristics of the Amaryllidaceae with 6–12 emerged leaves 30–60 cm long borne on a mature bulb. These emerge all through the year, in succession, so that the plant is evergreen. The bulb is composed of leaf bases only, there are no scales as in many other bulbs, and the flowers do not emerge from the centre of the leaves as in periodic species. The bases of old inflorescence stems do not become swollen and store food reserves.

Dissection of a large bulb reveals that the bulb is a sympodial branching system, each unit of which is composed almost invariably of four leaves and a terminal inflorescence. The innermost leaf of the four has a semi-

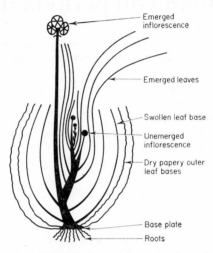

Fig. 2.1 Diagrammatic representation of a *Hippeastrum* bulb. Emerged parts are shown much reduced compared with the bulb.

sheathing base, unlike the other leaf bases which completely encircle the apex. At the time of flower initiation, a lateral growing point is formed on the side of the apex away from the last leaf. This then carries on growth and its first leaf is on the same side as the inflorescence. The emergence of the inflorescence from the bulb is much delayed in comparison with the leaves, so that it appears lateral to leaves which were initiated, later, on another unit of the sympodium (Fig. 2.1). The leaves present at any time belong to different units in the sympodial branching system, although this is not apparent until the bulb has been dissected. A large mature bulb is made up of about six units, two of which have no living aerial parts, two have emergent leaves and two units have not emerged, although there are some seasonal differences. Typically it is the fourth inflorescence from the centre which emerges and flowers.

Observations on leaf and inflorescence production in a glasshouse in south-east England at 18°C showed that about 12 leaves are produced annually, and that there is a seasonal pattern of leaf production, leaf death and date of anthesis (Fig. 2.2). The plastochrone is about 30 days and on average three inflorescences are initiated every year. Few leaves emerge in winter, but leaf death is also suppressed, so that leaf number remains constant or nearly so at a low number from December to March, when

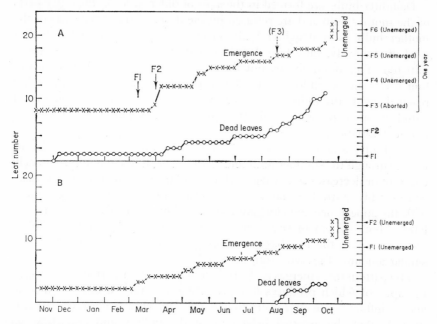

Fig. 2.2 Structure and periodicity of (A) mature and (B) immature *Hippeastrum* bulbs as shown by observations over a year of leaf emergence and death and of inflorescence emergence (F). At the end of the year the bulbs were dissected, and unemerged parts recorded.

new leaves begin to emerge. Leaf number reaches a peak in June–July, after which there is a gradual decline as emergence slows down and the death rate increases. Inflorescences emerge in March–April and a second inflorescence frequently emerges after 2–4 weeks, often before the first has died down. The second inflorescence may be followed by a third emerging in September, but this often aborts. For an inflorescence to be capable of normal, rapid emergence it must have grown to 2–3 cm in length in the bulb; once emerged a growing inflorescence increases in length by as much as 6 cm a day, to a full height of 40–60 cm.

Dissection of the recorded bulbs after a year gave an indication of the numbers of unemerged parts within the bulb. Unemerged leaves were very variable in number between three and eight, with an indication of higher numbers during the later winter. Usually three unemerged inflorescences were present within the bulb. It was deduced that the time between the initiation and emergence of a leaf was 3–8 months, and that of an inflorescence 11–14 months. The time from emergence of an inflorescence to anthesis is 3–4 weeks.

Daughter bulbs are formed in the axils of older scales in the outer parts of the mother bulb and are released by the death of the outer parts of the mother bulb. New daughter bulbs produce only leaves initially, until a total of, typically, nine have been formed, and then an inflorescence is initiated. This often aborts, but the sympodial pattern is then set up of four leaves and an inflorescence. When the emerged leaf complement has reached eight, the oldest leaves senesce and this number is maintained with leaf emergence and leaf death approximately balanced, but with some seasonal variation.

The bulb starts to increase in circumference during February and continues through the summer until mid-September; it remains approximately constant or decreases somewhat until the end of November, then decreases considerably until February. The decrease in circumference coincides with the appearance and elongation of the stems, and this loss is made up later. About 12 cm of scales are lost from the outside of the bulb by senescence and the leaf bases becoming papery, and are replaced by a similar amount of growth from the inside.

The pattern that emerges is of a bulb of basically non-periodic behaviour, the apex of which produces leaf primordia at a rate of one per month, and an inflorescence after every fourth leaf. In a very uniform climate it is possible that the external behaviour of the bulb would also show no seasonal differences, but in the varying light climate of south-east England leaf and flower emergence are affected so as to give some appearance of a seasonal pattern of behaviour.

The horticulturalist in temperate climates attempts to simulate the tropical conditions of the plant's original habitat by using high temperatures in glasshouses; superimposed upon this is a drying out of the bulbs and the loss of leaf and root to allow the production of a marketable product, the dry bulb. There is, however, no indication of a requirement for a rest period without the presence of active leaves, and some plants have been grown at the Glasshouse Crops Research Institute for many years without any drying and imposed rest. Advice is frequently given to stop watering in October, to remove offsets, and to keep the bulbs dry until the start of inflorescence emergence. If the bulbs are then planted and watered, inflorescence emergence and growth is rapid and anthesis is reached by the time a few short green leaves have emerged. This results in a more attractive plant than one grown with no imposed rest period where many large old leaves together with those of the offset bulbs surround the inflorescence.

II. The tulip bulb type

The tulip bulb, in contrast to that of *Hippeastrum*, is composed entirely of scales. (There is some confusion in the literature about the term "scale". Here it will be restricted to those leaf-like organs which make up the bulb *other* than true (i.e. photosynthetic) leaf and inflorescence bases. True scales may produce aerial green parts in exceptional circumstances but in the tulip these structures are initiated as scales, quite distinctly from foliage leaves.)

The tulip bulb is a simple structure, made up of concentric scales separated by very short internodes (Fig. 2.3). Lateral bulbs are borne in

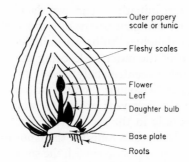

Outer papery
scale or tunic

Fleshy scales

Flower
Leaf
Daughter bulb

Base plate
Roots

Fig. 2.3 Diagrammatic representation of a tulip bulb at planting time.

the axils of these scales, which enclose an axis bearing leaves and terminating in a flower. Each mother tulip bulb planted in the autumn dies and is replaced by daughter bulbs produced within the bulb in the axils of the scales.

The bulb is composed of scales only; this follows from the fact that the tulip plant has an erect emergent stem bearing leaves. When the stem is fully emerged the green leaves are carried well clear of the bulb. The scales fit concentrically around one another and each scale has a sub-terminal hole, through which the shoot eventually grows. The outer scale or "tunic" starts life by being white and fleshy like the other scales, but shortly after the senescence of the above-ground parts it darkens and becomes tough, brown and papery. There is evidence that during this process, much of the starchy food reserve materials is transferred to the outermost daughter bulb or bulbs in the axil of the tunic. Large bulbs are usually flat on one side, and to this flat side is attached the remains of the flower stalk of the previous season. The large lowest leaf on the shoot grows out of this side of the bulb.

Usually each scale has a single daughter bulb in its axil, but there is a tendency for the outer, larger, scales to have more than one daughter bulb (Rees, 1968). In the cultivar 'Rose Copland' 93% of 218 bulbs examined had six scales including the tunic, the remainder had seven. In the sample examined, each mother bulb would have been replaced on average by 7·2 new bulbs; this figure is an over-estimation of what really occurs because some of the smaller daughter bulbs die. There are varietal differences in the number of daughter bulbs produced; the more modern Darwin hybrid, 'Apeldoorn', for instance, produces fewer mature daughter bulbs than 'Rose Copland'.

The life span of a tulip bulb depends somewhat on its date of initiation, and it may be up to 2·5 years. The mother bulb at planting time has a full complement of daughter bulbs, and by the following February these daughter bulbs will start initiating their own daughter bulbs. For part of the year, then, there are two generations of bulbs within the mother bulb. The third generation daughter bulbs are initiated from February until July, those in the axil of the outer scale being the first formed, followed progressively by the others centripetally.

This also affects later behaviour, because an outer daughter bulb frequently has a leaf in the first year of its life, whereas leaves are usually found on other bulbs only in the second (and final) year. When mature, these tunic daughter bulbs are rounder than normal bulbs and have a tattered tip to the tunic in comparison with the smooth tip of normal bulbs. They are called "pears" or "maidens", on account of their shape and the fact that they did not flower in the year before lifting. These daughter bulbs frequently have a flower a whole year before the other daughter bulbs initiated in the same season. This is not solely a result of their larger size; possibly it is due to their distance from the mother bulb which flowers at the same time. Daughter bulbs are sometimes found in the axils of the leaves, well above ground, but these are exceptional occurrences of unknown cause.

The first part of a daughter bulb to be formed is the outer scale; successive scale formation then occurs at intervals until about October, when all the scales are present. The apex of the bulb which splits off new organs is then quiescent until April, when it renews its activity by starting to form new leaves. Leaf formation continues in the larger bulbs until early July and is terminated by flower initiation. Small bulbs do not flower, and their development ceases with the formation of a single leaf, whose base encloses, and later forms the tunic of a daughter bulb. Flowering is determined shortly after the first leaf is formed; if a second leaf is produced, the bulb goes on to flower.

The tulip is periodic in its behaviour, its life cycle being closely related to the climate of its native habitat, in the mountains of Iran and Turkey, with a cold winter and hot dry summer. Floral initiation is related to the time at which the mother generation dies, and the development of the shoot continues during the "dormant" period. For extension growth to occur, however, there is a well-defined cold requirement. This prevents the growth of shoots in the autumn. By the end of the winter the cold requirement is satisfied and growth rates and flowering date outdoors are controlled by prevailing spring temperatures.

Because of the temperate origin of the tulip, horticultural practice is little different from the life cycle in the plant's natural habitat. The above-ground parts senesce early in the season compared with most outdoor crops, and the timing of this senescence is closely related to bulb yield. A hot dry early summer results in early senescence and low yields and a wet season gives late senescence and higher yields. A large number of daughter bulbs of a range of sizes is produced; for commercial reasons these bulbs are lifted annually when the tops have died down for grading, storage treatment, followed by forcing, sale or replanting.

The bulb forcing industry is based on a modification of the periodicity of the bulbs by giving low-temperature treatment out of season, starting as soon as the flower parts are completely formed. This treatment at 9°C is usually given for six weeks, the bulbs are then planted and kept outdoors under moist straw, peat or ashes to keep down the temperature (see Chapter 6). After some weeks the bulb boxes are taken into glasshouses at 16–18°C; some experience is necessary to judge readiness to house. A newer method which is gaining popularity is to treat dry bulbs at 5°C for about 12 weeks and then to plant the bulbs in the glasshouse border.

Bulb size is important in the tulip because not only do small bulbs fail to flower, but larger bulbs produce larger shoots and larger flowers. For display purposes, it is also important to obtain uniform-sized bulbs; these give uniformed-sized flowers.

III. The *Narcissus* bulb type

The third bulb species to be considered is *Narcissus*, whose bulb is made up of both scales and leaf bases. The mature, large *Narcissus* bulb is a branching system made up of a number of annual increments, which can be called bulb units. (This is to distinguish them from the separate entities of the tulip bulb type which are shorter lived.) Each apical meristem produces one bulb unit annually, and a unit comprises two, three, or four scales and two or three leaves, then the inflorescence. The number of combinations of leaf and scale is high; 22 occurred in 'Fortune' and 24 in 'King Alfred' in a study of bulb morphology (Rees, 1969c). The commonest four combinations of scale and leaf in 'Fortune' were (3 + 3), (4 + 4), (2 + 3) and (2 + 2); together they accounted for 74% of the total. Curiously, the commonest combination in 'Fortune' (3 + 3), did not occur once in 'King Alfred'. This suggests that there are differences between cultivars, and common experience that some cultivars are, for example, more leafy than others, would lead one to expect differences. There are, however, no extensive quantitative data on varietal differences in scale and leaf numbers.

Scales never have laminae, although their semi-transparent membranous distal parts extend above the soil and enclose the leaves early in the growing season. A scale may be distinguished from a leaf base which has lost its lamina because the latter has a thicker tip and a scar where the lamina was attached. After flowering, the base of the inflorescence stalk becomes flattened and contains reserve materials.

The flower is stated by some authorities to be terminal in *Narcissus*, whilst other authors are equally convinced that the apex which produces the scales and leaves produces next a lateral flower initial and itself becomes dormant until after anthesis. Whether the flower is terminal or lateral, the flower primordium rapidly dominates the apex and the quiescent vegetative apex plays an insignificant part in the apical region until later. The inaccessibility of the apex for experimentation makes the direct resolution of the question by marking techniques almost impossible. The arguments used for and against the sympodial growth pattern are as follows:

The *Narcissus* branching system has been described as monopodial and sympodial. In the former interpretation the flower is axillary and the main axis continues vegetative growth; in the latter the flower is terminal and the main axis grows sympodially. Both viewpoints are sufficiently supported to be quoted in botanical text-books. Authorities favouring monopodial growth include Gay (1858), Church (1908), Chan (1952) and Fritsch and Salisbury (1944), whilst a sympodial interpretation is preferred by Huisman and Hartsema (1933) and Priestley and Scott (1950).

Investigations on the daffodil cultivar 'Helios' by Denne (unpublished) are illustrated in Fig. 2.4. Denne dissected and sectioned a large number of apices during flower initiation and the growth of the inflorescence, paying particular attention to the small vegetative apex alongside the inflorescence. Denne bases her conclusion of a sympodial structure on the absence of a rudimentary bud in the axil of the *second* leaf. A rudimentary bud was, however, usually observed between leaf 1 and the flower, a situation which would not be expected if the flower itself were axillary to leaf 1. On two occasions, a well-developed axillary bud was found in this position.

The main argument advanced in favour of monopodial growth is the position of the first leaf of the new main shoot. There are indisputable axillary buds in the axils of lower leaves or scales, and the first leaf of each of these has its back towards the main axis of the bulb (i.e. is addorsed), but the first leaf of the new shoot faces the main axis. Denne, however, argues that the condition in an axillary bud away from the apex is different from that near the apex where the vegetative and floral primordia are

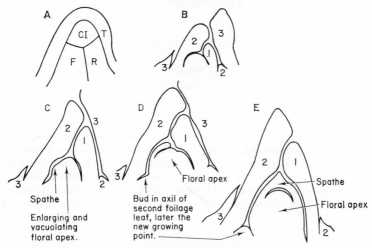

Fig. 2.4 (A) Plan of longitudinal section through a *Narcissus* apex. (After Denne, 1959.) T = tunica; CI = corpus initials; R = rib meristem; F = flank meristem. CI, F and R together form the corpus.
(B–E) Radial longitudinal sections through *Narcissus* apex, (B) in early May (C, D, E) in early June. × 35. (After Denne, unpublished.)

growing together, and Huisman and Hartsema (1933) argue that the possibility exists that the first addorsed leaf sometimes occurs as the first leaf and sometimes is lost, as in *Amaryllis belladonna*.

A further point in favour of sympodial growth is that early in floral initiation the main apex has enlarged and is vacuolated near its base, thus appearing to be "pre-floral" with no organized vegetative apex between it and leaf 2. When an apex fails to produce a flower, the *same* vegetative apex starts forming the scales and leaves of the next generation, yet in the axil of the last foliage leaf but one, a new lateral bulb unit develops, exactly as if a terminal flower had been initiated. The question will be finally resolved only by using some marking technique, such as the small carbon particles used by Soma and Ball (1963).

Clearly there are strong reasons for believing either theory. The most recent investigation was that of Denne (unpublished) who made serial sections at intervals of a population of bulbs which appeared to illustrate that the flower was terminal. The present author also inclines to this view.

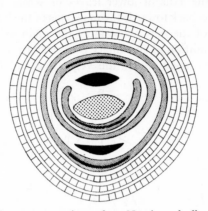

Fig. 2.5 Diagrammatic representation of a *Narcissus* bulb unit in transverse section. Three scales (cross-hatched) enclose three foliage leaves (stippled), the innermost of which has a semi-sheathing base subtending the inflorescence (dotted). Alongside the flower is a terminal bud (future bulb unit) and in the axil of the third leaf from the centre is a lateral bud (black). The positions of the leaf laminae are indicated in black on the stippled area which represents leaf base (Rees, 1969c).

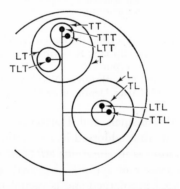

Fig. 2.6 Diagrammatic representation of a large "double-nosed" *Narcissus* bulb showing the interrelation between terminal (T) and lateral (L) bulb units and the code used to describe the various bulb units (Rees, 1969c).

Within the branching system of bulb units, further order may be seen (Figs 2.5 and 2.6). Bulb units may be terminal or lateral, i.e. may occur alongside an inflorescence or in the axil of a leaf base or scale elsewhere in the bulb unit. It is convenient to visualize the terminal inflorescence in the axil of the semi-sheathing base of the innermost leaf, the terminal bulb unit in the axil of the next leaf and the lateral bulb unit in the axil of the third leaf from the centre.

Because the bulb is a four-year-old entity (or a four-season branching system) there can be distinguished a number of classes of bulb, depending on whether they, or their parents, grandparents etc. were themselves terminal or lateral. A coding system, using T for terminal and L for lateral, shows the range of types available:

Generation	1st	2nd	3rd	4th
	T	TT	TTT	TTTT
	L	TL	TTL	TTTL
		LT	TLT	TTLT
			LTT	LTTT
			LTL	LTTL
				LTLT
				TLTT
				TLTL

All these bulbs are not readily identifiable, because by the time the 4th generation bulbs are all initiated, much of the 1st generation material cannot be identified since the outer scales dry out and become papery.

The description of single terminal and lateral bulb units at each apex is an oversimplification, but it can be considered as the basic structure which may be modified by the production of extra lateral bulb units or the failure of the normal single lateral bulb unit. Only in very exceptional circumstances, however, do lateral bulb units contain lateral bulb units. Each terminal bulb unit contains another terminal bulb unit and a lateral bulb unit. This rather idealized situation would lead, by repetition of this pattern, to a Fibonacci series of bulb number with succeeding generations (Rees, 1969c). There is evidence that daughter bulb units may be suppressed under non-ideal conditions, and commercial grading of material for sale prevents this situation occurring.

The relation between flowering and scale and leaf numbers was examined in the two cultivars 'Fortune' and 'King Alfred' (Rees, 1969c). Data for 'Fortune' are shown in Table 2.1. Flowering related to position in the branching system is shown in Table 2.2.

For 'Fortune', fewer parts were present in the lateral bulb units than in terminal ones, and this difference was reflected in their flowering; almost all terminal bulb units flowered, compared with only a small proportion of laterals. Terminal bulb units with four or more leaves did not generally flower (only 4 in 20 in 'Fortune'), otherwise almost all bulb units in the terminal position flowered, irrespective of scale and leaf number; 899

Table 2.1

The occurrence of different combinations of scale and leaf in bulb units of *Narcissus* 'Fortune' and their flowering behaviour (Rees, 1969c).

		Bulb unit number							Flower number					
		0	1	2	3	4	5		0	1	2	3	4	5
Leaf number	6				1							0		
	5			1	1	1					2	0	0	
	4		8	5	9	3				3	1	2	0	
	3	1	131	222	302	243	15		1	23	149	298	238	15
	2		89	276	48	46	2			6	106	41	44	2
	1		2	7	3					0	0	0		
	0													

Scale number — Bulb unit total 1416

Scale number — Flower total 931

Table 2.2

Mean scale and leaf number in bulb units of *Narcissus* 'Fortune' related to the bulb unit position and to flowering (Rees, 1969c).

Position	Code	Year of initiation	Mean scale + leaf number	% produced flowers	No. of bulb units used for estimating part no.	flowering
Terminal	T	1964	3·5 + 2·9	99	230	252
	TT	1965	3·6 + 2·9	98	252	252
	TTT	1966	3·3 + 2·9	98	61	61
Lateral	L	1964 + 1[1]	1·7 + 2·4	13	253	271
	LT	1965 + 1[1]	1·5 + 2·2	0	228	228
Terminal in lateral parent	TL	1965	2·1 + 2·5	96	272	272
	TLT	1966	2·4 + 2·8	91	54	56
Terminal in lateral grand-parent	TTL	1966	3·2 + 3·1	80	66	66
Total					1416	1458

[1] Laterals are initiated some months after the terminal bulb units in the same mother bulb.

flowered out of a total of 935 terminal bulb units. Lateral bulb units behaved very differently; none of the LT bulb units flowered, and only 13% of the L bulb units flowered. The total number of lateral bulb units flowering was only 32, so that it is only possible to draw the tentative conclusion that flowering in laterals is more likely with higher leaf numbers, especially three and above. There was evidence of an association between generations in 'Fortune' of similar scale- and leaf-number combinations greater than expected by chance.

Differences in bulb unit size, in scale and leaf number, and in flowering related to position in the branching system are probably due to the initiation of lateral bulb units some months after terminal ones. This affects the growth and behaviour of the laterals and the daughter bulb units borne by these laterals in the next generation. Initiation and growth of bulb units will be considered more fully later.

Narcissus bulbs are formed of the bases of foliage leaves and scales. Little is known, however, of the causes of the differences between the two kinds of foliar structure produced by the same apex (see below). In both tulip and *Narcissus*, there is a long period of apical inactivity between the formation of scales primordia and those of the leaves, and there is a tendency for leaf blades to be produced on the outer scales of some tulip daughter bulbs (especially that in the tunic axil) in normal circumstances, or following treatments which kill the leaves. These morphogenetic effects are, however, very poorly documented and understood. The loss of lamina whilst the leaf base is persistent has been described as a very curious temporary delimitation of senescence in a single organ (Carr and Pate, 1967).

IV. Morphology of above-ground parts, *Narcissus* and tulip

A. *Narcissus*

Just as there are differences in bulb structure between the well-known bulbous plants, there are differences in their aerial parts. *Narcissus* in common with all other members of the Amaryllidaceae, has linear leaves which grow by the activity of a meristem at the junction of the leaf and the leaf bases which form part of the bulb. The stem apex and leaf growth in *Narcissus pseudonarcissus* has been described by Denne (1959, 1960). The apex of cultivar 'Helios' is shown in Fig. 2.4; Denne explained how this apex was similar to the generalized description given by Stant (1954) for a range of Monocotyledons, including *Narcissus*. The flank meristem is usually cylindrical, but in *Narcissus* the flank is restricted to the side of the apex where the next primordium is about to be formed, and later extends around the apex to encircle it. By this time the next primordium has been initiated. As the same apex produces both scales and leaves, it was thought that scale production might be related to the small size of the newly-formed apex (as the inflorescence is terminal the vegetative apex is newly-formed and small when scale formation starts). However, Denne's investigations (1959) showed that apex size was not the factor controlling whether the apex produced a scale or a leaf. This explanation could, how-ever, be the reason for the differences in blade width observed between leaves on main and lateral bulb units.

The mature foliage leaf consists of a basal sheath and a long flat blade; the sheath is usually tubular and the blade is a prolongation of one side of the tube. The mature scale also has a prolongation which is like that of the mature foliage leaf but is much shorter, nearly colourless and shorter

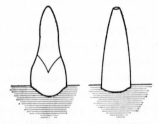

Fig. 2.7 Pre-emergence differences between a foliage leaf (left) and a scale (right) in *Narcissus*. The structures are about 1·5 cm tall. After Okada and Miwa (1958).

lived. All the primordia are externally similar until they are 1 mm long, but when they are three times this length there are obvious differences in the proportions of sheath and blade between scales and foliage leaves, as illustrated by Okada and Miwa (1958) for 'King Alfred' (Fig. 2.7). Leaves grow in length from initiation until the following February/March at a fairly constant rate of about 2 mm week^{-1}, with some decrease in rate during the winter months. Growth in leaf length after February/March follows a sigmoid pattern until June, when it ceases (Denne, 1960). There is evidence that the leaves continue to grow very slowly after this date, depending a great deal on weather. When the scales and foliage leaves are similar in appearance (up to 1 mm length) they also show a similar uniform distribution of cell division and cell length and a similar development of a vascular system. Later their growth becomes localized; in the scale, active cell division is restricted to the base of a leaf, whilst in a foliage leaf active cell division occurs in the sheath and there is also an intercalary region of more rapid cell division in the blade. The active intercalary division occurs until the leaf is about half its final length. The rate of division of all cells is the same in the basal 5 mm but just above this region (5–40 mm above the base of the blade) cell division is more rapid in the palisade layers than in the epidermis or the central parenchyma cells, so that the palisade cells are shorter than those of other tissues. Cell elongation ceases about 50 mm from the base of the blade, and intercalary cell division slows down when the leaf is more than half its final length. Further increase in leaf length is a result of cell elongation at the base of the blade.

The *Narcissus* inflorescence may have a number of flowers (*N. tazetta*) or a solitary terminal flower (*N. pseudonarcissus*) on an erect scape. Morphologically the scape is a single internode between its base and the spathe, it is lemon-shaped in transverse section and is slightly smaller in cross-section inside the bulb than outside. The aerial portion is green and ridged along its surface; the subterranean part is smooth and whitish (Chan, 1952).

When the flower bud emerges, and during its early growth, the scape is straight and vertical, but nearer anthesis a bend is formed just below the ovary so that the flower is held horizontally. After fertilization, when the floral parts above the ovary wither, the receptacle curves in the opposite direction to the previous movement, so that the fruit ripens in a vertical position.

Before the curvature of the flower stem the floral parts are enclosed in a spathe which is green initially but dries and becomes brown and papery before the final growth of the flower releases it from the spathe. Early in its development the spathe is seen to be a distinctly two-keeled tube with a vascular strand along the median line of each keel. The spathe is interpreted by Chan (1952) as a structure formed by the fusion of two prophylls, and in this opinion she is supported by Church (1908) and earlier workers. Other authorities suggest a monophyllous origin to the spathe. In *N. tazetta* the inflorescence is a double helicoid cyme (Huisman and Hartsema, 1933); here the spathe is almost certainly formed by an early fusion of two leaves. In *N. pseudonarcissus* with a uniflorous cyme (phylogenetically developed from a *N. tazetta* type of inflorescence) the spathe behaves like a single structure but the presence of two transverse tops is probably reminiscent of an originally double structure.

The flower consists of two whorls of three perianth parts, two whorls of three anthers, a tricarpellate inferior ovary containing two rows of anatropous ovules in each of the three loculi, and a paracorolla, corona or trumpet. This is the last part of the flower to be formed but is positioned between the perianth parts and the androecium. The paracorolla, which is an unusual structure, but a constant feature of the genus, has been used by the horticulturalist for classifying *Narcissus* cultivars into trumpet, large-cup and small-cup types and these divisions are further subdivided according to the colours of the perianth parts and the paracorolla. Such a division, although botanically very artificial, is nevertheless useful in describing groups of plants of similar characteristics. The morphological interpretation of the paracorolla has led to further controversy. Some authorities regard it as a prolongation of the receptacle; perhaps the most satisfying explanation is to regard it as a separate structure, an outgrowth having no relation to the primary formation of the floral tube (Church, 1908), but some affinity with the adjuncts to the filaments in many Liliaceous plants, e.g. *Brodiaea*.

The floral biology of the wild *N. pseudonarcissus* has been described by Caldwell and Wallace (1955). The flowers are homogamous, the anthers dehiscing as the perianth expands, and the stigmatic lobes are simultaneously receptive. The introrsely-dehiscing anthers form a close ring around the style, the whole being a rigid central axis in the flower. The corona and perianth tube form a narrowing passage leading to the nectaries which occur between the filaments. The flowers appear to be pollinated by bumble bees, not honey bees, and there is little evidence for pollination without insect visitation. Pollination is frequently poor, probably because of infrequent visitations in the cold wet weather of early spring. In the absence of information on other species and common cultivars, it must be assumed that this account is generally applicable.

Flowers are pollinated in mid-April in south-west England, and the fruits attain full size as ovoid green pods in about a fortnight. By early June they are mature dry capsules which dehisce by three valves in a manner typical of epigynous Monocotyledons (Caldwell and Wallace, 1955). During the development of the pods the axis straightens so the pod is held vertically, and the shiny black round seeds are scattered over a somewhat restricted area, by the divergence of the valves of the drying capsule in hot sunny weather.

B. Tulip

The nature of the above-ground parts of the tulip depends on whether the plant is a flowering one or not. Above a certain critical bulb size, flowering plants are formed but some large bulbs also fail to flower, presumably because of some accident either at the time of flower initiation or shortly afterwards. A non-flowering plant has a solitary leaf—an occurrence which is certainly most unusual, if not unique, in the plant kingdom. This leaf is large and broader than those of flowering plants and has a well-defined basal part or petiole, which emerges from the apex of the bulb. The base of this leaf encloses a maiden bulb.

The flowering bulb has, in contrast, an emergent stem which may be up to 40 cm or more long bearing a number of simple, entire lanceolate leaves. The leaf number may be three or more, depending upon species and cultivar, but the lowest is the largest and the others form a series of decreasing area. Frequently the smaller leaves appear bifid; this is probably the result of fusion of two leaves early in their development. The flowers are usually single and terminal, but some species (e.g. *T. praestans*) consistently have a terminal inflorescence of two, three or more flowers each on its own pedicel growing from the axil of a leaf. It is likely that the solitary terminal flower is a reduction from a basically multiflowered condition. In certain ill-defined circumstances in some large bulbs of the more vigorous cultivars, normally solitary flowers are replaced by well-developed inflorescences, and in others rudimentary flowers occur in leaf axils.

The flowers comprise six perianth parts in two equal whorls, six anthers in two whorls and a superior tricarpellate gynoecium. In the cultivars there is a very wide range of flower size, colour and form, a result of the hybridization which has been pursued for centuries.

The ovary is either columnar with three prominent angles or expands a little from the base and tapers to a narrow neck. The stigmatic surfaces are spreading and usually tri-partite, with fringed edges when open. These fringed edges become moist and sticky when the flower is mature. All species are protandrous, the stigmatic surface unfolding two or three days after the anthers dehisce. The seed capsule is borne erect and is approximately cylindrical with three ridges generally blunted at the top but some species have a terminal prolongation up to a centimetre long. When ripe the capsule splits from the top into three segments, each of which is separated by a septum into two cavities in which the flat seeds are arranged like piles of coins. The seeds are roughly triangular in outline, very thin and flat. The embryos are clearly visible in viable seeds (Hall, 1940).

Although up to 300 seeds can develop within one ovary, usually the number is much smaller than this, especially in inter-specific crosses where abnormal growth of pollen tubes within the embryo sacs of numerous ovules frequently prevents fertilization. The optimum temperature for fertilization in most cultivars is 14°C (Kho and Baër, 1971).

V. Structure of other bulbous plants

A. Hyacinth

The mature hyacinth bulb has been described by Blaauw (1920). A longitudinal section of a mature bulb at lifting time shows the dead inflorescence stalk surrounded by the bases of six foliage leaves whose aerial parts have recently died and, outside these, two fleshy scales (Fig.

2.8B). Surrounding these are the bases of the foliage leaves of the previous year and outside these again the two scales of the corresponding annual cycle. All these scales and leaf bases are fleshy and white and swollen with storage materials. These become surrounded by still older leaf bases and

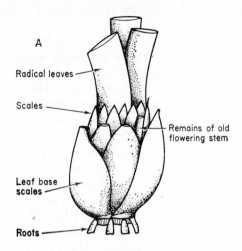

A

Radical leaves

Scales

Remains of old flowering stem

Leaf base scales

Roots

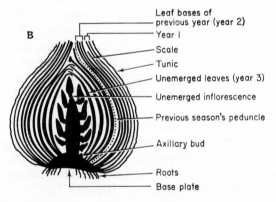

Leaf bases of previous year (year 2)

Year I

B

Scale

Tunic

Unemerged leaves (year 3)

Unemerged inflorescence

Previous season's peduncle

Axillary bud

Roots

Base plate

Fig. 2.8 (A) Bulb of *Lilium candidum*. (B) Diagrammatic longitudinal section of hyacinth bulb.

scales which are less swollen with food reserves and the outer ones are thin, leathery or papery and pigmented either purple or brown. Near the base of the inflorescence stalk is the new axillary bud which consists of two scales and five foliage leaves.

Shortly after lifting, the sixth foliage leaf is formed and the flower is initiated. The first change is an elevation of the normally flat apex, a number of flowers are produced on the elevated apex and develop into the familiar inflorescence emerging in spring. The flower spike ends blindly.

Few daughter bulbs are formed naturally and hyacinths are normally encouraged to increase daughter bulb production by the removal of the base plate (called "scooping") or by incising the base of the bulb with deep cuts which penetrate the base of the young shoot (called "cross-cutting"). This artificial removal of apical dominance results in the formation of numbers of daughter bulbs at the cut edges of the scales.

B. *Iris*

The *Iris* bulb is made up of scales and leaf bases (Blaauw, 1935; Aoba, 1967). A number of brown fibrous tunics enclose the bulb at lifting time; these are the bases of the previous season's leaves. Within these are white swollen scales, usually four in number, which do not completely encircle the bulb as in the tulip, but whose edges just meet. The innermost scale is called a half-scale. Within these are the sheath leaves, which may be two or three in number, and which later emerge above soil level with green tips, but are distinct from the true leaves which they enclose. The number of leaves is variable; normally three are present at lifting time and if the bulb is small or does not initiate a flower, either three or sometimes four leaves is the total number. A plant which will initiate a flower (later, after the bulb is planted) does produce up to eight more leaf primordia, depending on when flower initiation takes place. Two spathes are produced before the apex becomes floral.

Food reserves are stored in the scales, especially the outermost one. Daughter bulbs occur regularly in the axils of every scale, sheath leaf and the basal leaf. When the shoot grows, the insertions of the leaves, except the lowest ones, are carried up out of the bulb. A plant which does not flower has a central bulb enclosed by the bases of the three leaves. These bulbs become the so-called "round" bulbs of commerce, whereas the innermost daughter bulb of a flowering plant which grows adpressed to the shoot has a distinctly flat side and is called a "flat" commercially.

Iris flowers are actinomorphic, large and showy, enclosed in a spathe usually with scarious margins. Six perianth segments are joined together by a short tube above the ovary; the outer whorl (called falls) grows horizontally or partly erect and then turns vertically downwards about a third of the distance from the tip; the inner whorl (called standards) is smaller and often erect, usually with a well-marked limb and claw (or haft). The three anthers are inserted at the base of the outer perianth parts, between these and the style-branches which are broad, petalloid, bifid at the tip and have a crest-like appearance. The stigmatic surface is a transverse lip near the end of the split of the tip. The ovary is trilocular with axile placentation and the capsule is trigonous.

Leaves are ensiform, sometimes very narrow and often distichous and folded so that the adaxial surfaces, which are silvery, are together.

C. Lily

The lily bulb is covered with densely-crowded spirally-arranged thick scale leaves which are not concentric as in many other bulbs (Fig. 2.8A). Leaves of two kinds are produced, the first appear in the autumn at the base of the rudimentary flower stem of the following year, the other leaves are borne on the emergent, tall, flowering stem in summer. The radical leaves die down, but their bases remain as scales, each of which has a blunt tip where the emergent blade was attached. Within these are true scales which have pointed tips, and within these again are the radical leaves of the current season, whose bases later become swollen. In the axil of the innermost radical leaf, at the base of the young flowering stem is a tiny daughter bulb which becomes the next season's bulb and shoot. *L. martagon* has no radical leaves and all the scales are true scales, with no leaf-base scales.

The leaves are lanceolate, without petioles, but with bases that embrace about a third of the stem's circumference. The flowering stem does not branch but buds occur in the axils of the leaves—these may develop into aerial bulbs which can be used for propagation, but the capacity to which this is expressed depends on the species and variety.

In the genus *Lilium*, the flowers are borne in a terminal raceme, each flower is stalked and subtended by a bract. The perianth is composed of two whorls of three parts, the whole being large and attractively coloured and frequently marked in white, yellow or orange. The six versatile anthers dehisce introrsely and produce orange-coloured pollen which adheres to and discolours the perianth parts making them unattractive commercially. Anthers are often removed before flowers are sold because of this behaviour.

After pollination, the ovary becomes transformed into a large, dry capsule which dehisces by three longitudinal splits each corresponding to the middle of a carpel, to reveal the flattened seeds arranged like six piles of coins.

The most important lily in commerce is the Easter lily, and Blaney and Roberts (1966) have made a detailed study of its growth and development. The bulb is concentric with closely imbricated scales each of which bears an axillary bud. On its lower surface basal roots are borne; stem roots also occur on the below-soil part of the stem above the bulb. Small bulbs, called stem-bulblets, are produced in the underground part of the flower stem, and these are called bulblets during the next season—the second year of their life but their first year of independent existence. At the end of the second year and during the third year they are called "yearlings" in grower terminology, and when harvested at the end of the third year are sold for glasshouse forcing.

The Easter lily belongs to the subgenus *Eulirion*, the true or trumpet-lilies. The ovaries are borne above and free from the six isomorphic perianth segments, each of which has nectar furrows near its base. A stamen is more or less attached opposite each segment near its base, and the trilocular ovary contains large flat seeds in two rows in each loculus. The plant produced for sale can be modified considerably by treatment. Stem height and leaf number depend on when flower initiation occurs, and the number of flowers per stem can also be controlled within limits from a few up to eight or more. Flower number is sacrificed for early flowering provided a reasonable saleable product is produced.

VI. Apical structure

The structure of apical meristems of bulbs has received less attention than other morphological features of bulb structure.

Tulip apices have been described by Sass (1944) in the vegetative state and during flower differentiation. The vegetative apex of the principal axis is deeply buried in the bulb just above the base plate, and is 2–3 mm long and 1–2 mm wide. The apex is a short, broad smooth dome 100–125 μm high and 300–375 μm broad approximately semicircular in longitudinal section. The tunica consists of a single layer of cells; this is particularly apparent when numerous mitotic figures are visible, and during periods of slow mitotic activity it appears that at least three layers contain cells which are dividing anticlinally (Fig. 2.9).

Leaf primordia result from the division of cells in the first layer of the corpus and rapidly involve a zone three or four cells deep. The tunica of the primordium and leaf retains its single-layer identity. The floral apex is, however, two layered, with cell division being strictly anticlinal in the outer layer and predominantly so in the second layer. The gradual shift to a two-layered tunica becomes evident at the time of anther initiation. Procambial strands prominent in the second and third nodes can be followed upwards until they become obscure in the zone of leaf initiation, although there is evidence for strand formation close to the zone of leaf initiation.

The behaviour of the apex of *Lilium candidum* is similar to that of the tulip (Rivière, 1963), but three superficial layers or tunicas can be

D

distinguished by their poor staining in the vegetative state. Just prior to floral initiation the three tunic layers and the superficial corpus layers form a meristematic cover, and the lower cells of the corpus become vacuolated. During vegetative growth the leaf primordia are formed by cell division in the second tunic layer. At the end of March the plastochrone rhythm of leaf formation ceases and the bracts are formed; on the internal faces of the bracts the floral primordia are produced by the periclinal divisions of the third tunica layer.

The apex of *Endymion non-scriptus*, like the tulip, has a uniseriate tunica

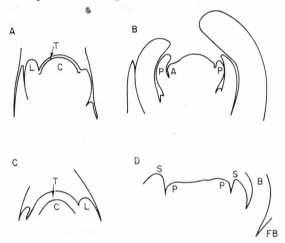

Fig. 2.9 Outline drawings of median longitudinal sections of apices of tulip and lily. (A) Vegetative apex of tulip 'Pride of Haarlem' July 15. ×60. (B) Initiation of another primordia of tulip 'Pride of Haarlem' July 20. ×48. (C) Vegetative apex of *Lilium candidum*. ×80. (D) reproductive apex of *L. candidum*. ×90. (A) and (B) after Sass (1944), (C) and (D) after Rivière (1963). T = tunica; C = corpus; L = leaf primordium; P = perianth primordium; A = anther primordium; S = sepal primordium; B = bract primordium; FB = floral bract.

of almost cubical cells (Turner, 1967) which was clearly differentiated three weeks after germination, when the hemispherical apex was 150 μm wide. In the mature plant a small residual meristem is seen at the base of the scape on the side of the youngest leaf in August. The first primordium or dorsal prophyll is formed shortly afterwards.

The vegetative *Iris* shoot apex has a two-layered tunica enclosing a central zone of larger cells. The rate of cell division is very low and the first sign of transition from the vegetative to the flowering state is an increase in cell division in the rib meristem about 10 cells below the median tunica. This activity spreads over the whole apex and the zonation pattern disappears (Rodrigues Pereira, 1962).

Although it has been suggested that flower part number can be related to apical size (see Chapter 5), little information exists for bulbous plants on the relationships between apical size and morphogenetic aspects of growth, especially following inductive treatments. For longiflorum lily 'Ace', however it has been known for some time that large bulbs produce more leaves and flowers than small ones, the Kohl (1967) observed a close correlation between bulb size and apex diameter. More recently, a study of shoot apex size and flower initiation in 'Ace' lily after vernalization for 0, 6 and 8 weeks at 4·4°C showed negative correlation between leaf and flower number and the duration of vernalization, and between apex diameter and the cold treatment (Wang *et al.*, 1970). The question whether apex diameter or cessation of initiatory activity limits flower number in the indeterminate Easter lily is still unresolved.

VII. Root systems

Root systems of mature bulbous plants are entirely adventitious, the primary root of the seedling being lost at an early stage, during the first season's growth.

In periodic bulbs, roots are initiated and emerge from the base plate in late summer, whilst in stored bulbs root emergence is generally prevented by low humidity; the emergence of roots during storage is disadvantageous because they are easily damaged during planting. In bulbs without periodicity, it is thought that roots are produced throughout the year.

Little information is available on the numbers of roots produced by bulbs, but tulips below flowering size normally have between 50 and 70. Schuurman (1971) found that root initiation in tulip 'Apeldoorn' ended shortly after sprouting of the bulb, and that root number and weight increased with bulb size but was independent of bulb shape (degree of flattening). A mean number of 32 roots per bulb was reported in studies of root production by hyacinth 'Queen of the Blues', and it was observed that no new roots were formed after mid-November under field conditions (Versluys, 1927). This confirms impressions with other bulbous plants that the roots are formed over a short period of time and emerge more or less together. Damage to the root system at this early stage cannot be made good by the formation of new adventitious roots.

Narcissus, tulip and hyacinth roots are unbranched; they bear a prominent root cap but have no root hairs. *Iris*, *Hippeastrum*, lily, *Nerine* and *Zephyranthes* roots branch and have second-order lateral roots. There is little knowledge of the normal depth of rooting, which varies with soil type, aeration, etc., but tulip roots are limited to about 65 cm even in good conditions, whilst *Narcissus* roots usually penetrate to about 80 cm.

Contractile roots are found in *Narcissus*, hyacinth and *Iris* and a number of investigations of their structure and mode of action have been made. The histological details of root contraction vary considerably in different plants, but a sinuous contraction of the stele has frequently been observed. In a recent investigation, Chen (1969b) described how all the tissues in the contractile region become adjusted to the shortening of the root which is brought about by vertical contraction and radial expansion of the inner cortical cells. The outer cortex and the exodermis are lifted passively in large horizontal wrinkles over the surface, while the vertical walls of cells in the stele become undulated or indented, as also occurs in the vessels. Contractile roots are shorter than normal roots. The contractile roots are normally 3–7 cm long in March and over a 4–5 week period decrease in size by 7–8 mm. The contraction occurs near the base of the bulb.

The mechanism for the radial expansion and axial contraction of the roots is still unknown, although it is believed that hormonal changes may affect the water balance of the cortical cells. Wilson and Honey (1966) have shown that the contraction is a growth process because it occurs in turgid tissue and is partly reversible by plasmolysis, and because the radial walls of the cortical cells concerned increase in area and the cells increase in volume. Wilson and Honey (1966) also observed that in hyacinth grown in soil, all the roots of some bulbs were observed to contract, but that similar bulbs grown in "bulb fibre" did not show universal root contraction.

Ecological implications of contractile roots and other structures are considered by Galil (1961). In *Muscari* and *Bellevalia*, contractile roots move bulblets horizontally in plants growing at normal depth, thus ensuring a vegetative dispersal. Mature bulbs of *Scilla* and *Allium* develop only weak contractile roots which do not appreciably change the bulb depth in the soil, although an ability to change bulb depth significantly is present in immature bulbs.

VIII. "Droppers" in tulip

Mature tulip plants do not have contractile roots, but bulb depth is adjusted by the formation of "droppers" or "sinkers" which have been investigated by a number of workers, notably Robertson (1906), Hagiya and Amaki (1959 and earlier papers) and Ogura (1952). Droppers are stolon-like structures which are hollow and contain near their tip a daughter bulb. They usually grow downwards vertically or nearly so, so that next year's bulb occupies a lower level than its mother bulb.

Droppers are formed when conditions are favourable for growth, especially when the mother bulbs are not deeply buried. Other favourable conditions include wet soil, low water table, high soil-CO_2 content and soil pH near neutral. Experimental conditions which do not affect dropper formation include increased soil nutrients and photoperiod (Hagiya and Amaki, 1959).

Some tulip species and cultivars (e.g. *T. edulis* and *T. latifolia* and cultivars 'Kansas', 'Keizerskroon' and 'Inglescome Yellow') regularly and frequently produce droppers, others do so only rarely, but this seems unrelated to horticultural groupings, to earliness of flowering, to soluble materials in the bulb or to root number. Droppers are difficult to recognize

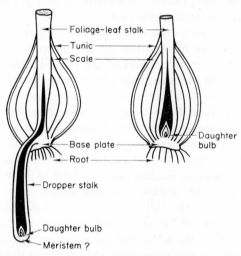

Fig. 2.10 Diagrammatic representation of, left, a tulip bulb with dropper in section, compared with, right, a normal non-flowering tulip bulb. The central foliar cavity is shaded. (After Hagiya and Amaki, 1959.)

at an early stage but tend to show asymmetric development in the scale axil, which leads to the formation of an outgrowth which penetrates the surrounding scales into the soil. The morphology of the dropper stalk is similar to the basal part of the leaf stalk of non-flowering tulip bulbs, and its central cavity is continuous with the hollow petiole of the leaf. Some vascular bundles run through the dropper stalk to the base of the daughter bulb in its tip. These bundles originate in the leaf and also from the mother bulb base plate (Fig. 2.10). The dropper grows mostly in the zone just behind its apex, as has been shown by Indian ink markings (Robertson, 1906).

Occasionally branched droppers occur, each of the branches of the dropper containing a daughter bulb. In *Tulipa chrysantha*, horizontal "droppers" occur, but this is apparently unusual.

IX. Development and periodicity

Bulb flowers are traditionally associated with spring, the flowers reaching anthesis in temperate climates when the warm weather of spring allows rapid growth to anthesis. There are, however, examples of bulbous plants growing in the tropics where there is no spring period. Their flowering is related to some other feature of the environment, such as rainfall in the case of *Pancratium* and *Zephyranthes* (Holdsworth, 1961; Kerling, 1941). These species, like *Hippeastrum*, in a relatively non-periodic environment, flower irregularly throughout the year.

It is likely that the temperate forms are derived from a tropical archetype by the development of mechanisms which allowed them to become dormant during the unfavourable part of the year. The major unfavourable features of the Mediterranean areas where bulbs flourish best are the dry hot summer followed by a cold winter. Such species as grow wild in areas of higher latitude than these Mediterranean areas (such as the British *Narcissus*) must be assumed to have evolved from those adapted to such hot, dry summers. However there are *Narcissus* varieties such as 'Grand Soleil d'Or' which have a smaller cold requirement than most cultivated narcissi and in favourable localities like the Isles of Scilly these can flower *before* the winter period, or early in a mild winter.

In general, however, the cultivated *Narcissus*, tulip and *Iris* under outdoor conditions flower in the spring and early summer; this active period is followed by death of the leaves and a perennation through the rest of the summer and winter before emergence and growth in the following spring. Flowering is an annual event and the plant has built-in mechanisms to prevent flowering at other times of the year.

The original habitat of the tulip, as far as can be ascertained, is in the mountainous areas of Iran and Turkey. Here the summers are hot and dry and the winters are cold (Fig. 8.1). The summer extremes are avoided by summer dormancy which is present in our commercial cultivars.

Some time after the flowering of a plant the leaves senesce and die rapidly, the flower stem also dries off together with the seed pod, and the living parts of the plant, the daughter bulbs, exist below ground in a condition where water loss is reduced to a minimum. In this condition the bulb is "dormant", although flower initiation can take place then and is followed by the growth of the shoot (leaves, flower and stem) at the expense of the stored material in the bulb. In the autumn, root growth occurs when soil water again becomes available, but the cold requirements of the plant prevent much extension growth or emergence above ground in the autumn, when the shoot would be vulnerable to the extremes of low winter temperatures. The net result of these two processes of summer dormancy and cold requirement is a growth pattern that is closely related to the environment and one in which the growing season is very short.

Little is known about the factors affecting the senescence of the above-ground parts. There is some evidence that the process is triggered by high temperature; the process is irreversible and a period of high temperature sets it in motion even if cooler conditions follow. There are no active above-ground vegetative apices present at the time of senescence, so that the cessation of protein synthesis in the leaves when they reach mature size may prevent the attraction of growth-promoting substances and

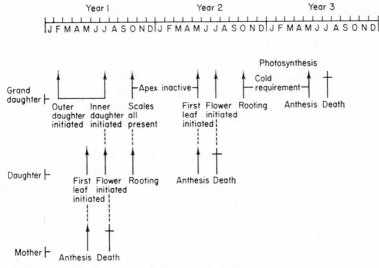

Fig. 2.11 Periodicity of growth of three generations of tulip.

carbohydrates to the leaves, which then start to die. There is some circumstantial evidence that senescence is delayed in seasons or in situations where low temperatures persist longer. It must be confessed, however, that little is known about many aspects of senescence in bulbous plant leaves. Attempts to delay senescence will be discussed in Chapter 4.

The low-temperature requirement of dormant bulbs has been studied, largely in connection with attempts to modify flowering behaviour. It will be considered in further detail later, but it is sufficient here to say that the optimum temperature for rapid development and good flower quality is about 10°C and the bulbs must be subjected to this temperature for many weeks, about 12–16 being typical figure for both narcissus and tulips, although it is known that there is a wide variation between cultivars. In some parts of the world where temperatures do not fall naturally below this level, the growing of *Narcissus* and tulip is not possible without a long period of artificial cold storage, usually of the dry bulb, before planting in the field.

In addition to the obvious periodicity exhibited by the parent plant in its emergence, flowering, senescence and death, there are further features showing periodicity, such as the timing of initiation of daughter bulbs and their growth, and of the initiation of leaves and flowers within the bulb. A good, well-illustrated account of the periodicity of the tulip is given by Mulder and Luyten (1928).

Figure 2.11 shows diagrammatically the relationship between some periodic processes in the tulip; death of the mother plant coincides with the initiation of the flower in the daughter bulb during the dormant phase, and the initiation of the innermost grand-daughter bulb within the daughter bulb. Following the initiation of scale primordia in the grand-daughter, the apex becomes inactive whilst the roots are growing on the daughter bulb. Activity is resumed by the formation of leaf primordia immediately after anthesis in the daughter bulb. The significance of these coincidences and of the inactive periods of the apices between scale and leaf formation is not known, but a considerable measure of internal control of growth of parts is implied.

A similar drawing has been made for *Lilium candidum* where the time between the formation of a new vegetative apex and anthesis is about 21 months. In this species two generations of axes bearing foliage leaves and three generations of bulb scales occur together (Herklotz and Wehr, 1969).

Similar observations have been made for Easter lily, and coincidence or perhaps correlations noted between anthesis of the mother plant and the cessation of scale initiation by apices of stem bulblets and the daughter bulb (Blaney and Roberts, 1966a).

Growth and productivity

"The proper study of the Monocotyledoneae is the monocotyledonous method of growth." P. B. Tomlinson, 1970

Studies on the productivity of flower crops, and bulb plants in particular,
have been made only fairly recently, but the limitations of the relatively
short growing season to dry-matter production have long been recognized.

I. General aspects of growth

Because of the importance of some aspects of morphology to productivity, it is worth repeating some of these. Firstly the bulb plant in
miniature is present, complete, within the planted bulb of narcissus, tulip
and hyacinth, and after emergence in the spring no active aerial apices are
present to produce new shoots or leaves, so that the plant lacks plasticity to
respond to changes in competition pressure. Secondly the bulb contains a
large amount of stored food reserves, sufficient in many species to allow a
"normal" plant to develop even under conditions of severe competition.
Finally, bulb size is important because the size of the plant produced can
depend, as in the tulip, on the size of the bulb planted. In *Narcissus* this is
also applicable but a large bulb will, because it is a branching system, have
a number of apices, each of which produces aerial leaves and/or flowers.
In *Iris* and the lily, leaves are produced by the apex until floral initiation
occurs, but no active aerial vegetative apices are present after floral
initiation.

A. Tulip

The general picture of tulip growth in south-east England, expressed as a change in plant dry weight, is shown in Fig. 3.1 (Rees, 1966a). From planting in the autumn there is an overall loss of total dry weight which extends from early October until mid-March. The tulip mother bulb weight falls to near zero by the end of the growing season.

Leaf emergence occurs in January or earlier, depending on the season, but leaf growth is initially slow and does not become rapid until the warmer conditions in April. Leaf area increases until the end of May and then falls rapidly. This general pattern of leaf growth has been observed with a number of cultivars in a number of seasons; all show a rapid growth in leaf area followed by a slowing down of growth followed in turn by a rapid senescence and loss of leaf area until none remains. Figure 3.2 shows a detailed study of leaf growth in 'Rose Copland' grown in Lincolnshire. The leaf area increase can be described by a Gompertz curve until the peak is reached, after which the decrease in leaf area is linearly related to time. Total plant dry weight increases over a 13-week period. The mother bulb dry weight falls to near zero during the growing season and is replaced by a number of daughter bulbs. The total dry weight of the daughter bulbs increases rapidly until leaf senescence starts and only slowly thereafter. Most of the dry weight increase is accounted for by these new bulbs, the harvested weights of which were found to be 1·6–2·0 times as great as the planted weight of the mother bulb, depending on cultivar (Fig. 3.1). At the planting densities employed (174 cm^2 per plant) the 11-cm bulbs planted produced maximum leaf area index (L) values of 1·7–2·4 depending on cultivar, and the leaf area durations (D) were 18–25 weeks.

The data obtained in this study also allow the assessment of the partition of dry weight between the various plant parts. Initially about 80% of the dry weight is in the mother bulb, but this falls to nearly zero by the end of the growing season, by which time the greatest percentage is in the new bulbs. The proportion of the total dry weight in both leaves and flowers increases initially then falls later in the season as these parts senesce and die (Fig. 3.3).

From the curves of dry weight and leaf area change with time the net assimilation rates (E) and crop growth rates (C) were calculated for the three cultivars over the growing season; these are shown in Fig. 3.4. These smooth curves show that E rises from about 2 g m^{-2} day^{-1} in late March to a peak of 9–10 g m^{-2} day^{-1} 5–7 weeks later and falls to zero at the end of June. Curves for C show similar peaks in May of 17–23 g m^{-2} day^{-1}. These values are similar to those obtained with a range of other temperate

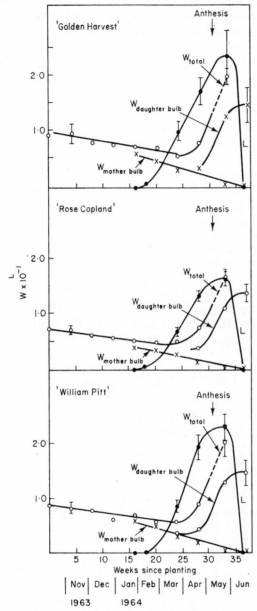

Fig. 3.1 Changes in leaf area index (L) and dry weight (W) in three tulip cultivars in the 1963–4 growing season. Vertical lines are 95% confidence limits for the means (Rees, 1966a).

crop plants such as kale, sugar beet, gladiolus, wheat, barley, grass sward and potato. Integrating C over the growth period from the time of the minimum total dry weight (mid-March, see Fig. 3.1) gives values of 9·5,

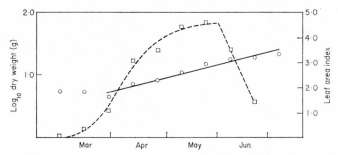

Fig. 3.2 Changes in dry weight (circles) and leaf area index (squares) of tulip 'Rose Copland' grown in Lincolnshire. The sigmoid part of the leaf area index line is described by $y = 0·203 + 4·448 \ [- \exp \ (2·322 - 0·976x)]$ where $x =$ (sample number $- 1$). Leaf area decline is linear with time and plant weight is described by $\log y = 0·716 + 0·007x$ where x is time in days.

8·3 and 9·1 kg $\times$ 10³ ha⁻¹ annum⁻¹ for the three cultivars 'Golden Harvest', 'Rose Copland' and 'William Pitt' respectively. In comparison with other crop data, these figures are low, and this must be attributed to the short period of active growth. About 90% of the total integrated dry-

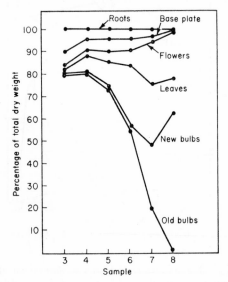

Fig. 3.3 Partition of dry matter between the parts of the tulip plant; data for three cultivars combined (Rees, 1966a).

matter production is represented by new bulb weight; this appears very high until it is realized that C was integrated from the time of minimum total plant dry weight, by which time a considerable part of the growth of the leaves and flowers had occurred.

The loss in dry weight from planting continues for about 20 or 25 weeks to the time of minimum total plant dry weight, and can be represented by a linear regression, with a slope of between 0·017 and 0·021 g dry weight

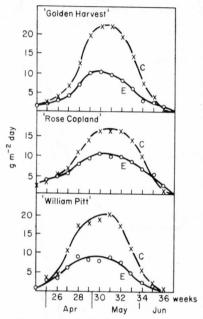

Fig. 3.4 Changes in tulip net assimilation rate (E) and crop growth rate (C) computed from smoothed curves of leaf area index and plant dry weight (Rees, 1966a).

bulb^{-1} day^{-1}. Over the whole period more than a third of the dry weight of the planted bulb is lost. Expressed as a (negative) relative growth rate, all three cultivars had an identical weight loss of 0·0023 g g^{-1} day^{-1}. Similar data were collected in a subsequent season for 'Rose Copland' grown commercially in Lincolnshire at higher densities.

B. *Narcissus*

Parallel studies on three *Narcissus* cultivars have also been made. These results are shown in Fig. 3.5. Basically they are similar to the tulip, except that the mother bulb does not die but loses weight until photosynthesis

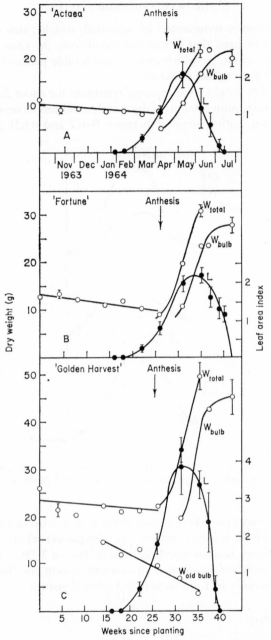

Fig. 3.5 Changes in dry weight and leaf area index of three *Narcissus* cultivars in the 1963–4 growing season. The vertical lines are 95% confidence limits for the means.

re-starts in the spring and then increases in weight again. The growing season for the *Narcissus* is longer than for the tulip—as every gardener knows, *Narcissus* leaves persist (untidily) far longer than those of tulips.

Round bulb of the two cultivars 'Fortune' and 'Actaea' were grown, with double-nosed bulbs of 'Golden Harvest'. The larger size of the 'Golden Harvest' bulbs resulted in many differences in behaviour when comparisons were made with the other two cultivars. It is believed that these differences are more related to bulb size than to varietal differences. From planting time until about 22 weeks later total plant dry weight fell, and the weight loss was described by fitting the following linear regressions:

'Fortune'	$y = 13 \cdot 4 - 0 \cdot 13 \, (\pm \, 0 \cdot 02) \, x$
'Golden Harvest'	$y = 23 \cdot 2 - 0 \cdot 08 \, (\pm \, 0 \cdot 08) \, x$
'Actaea'	$y = 9 \cdot 3 - 0 \cdot 08 \, (\pm \, 0 \cdot 03) \, x$

For 'Golden Harvest' the regression coefficient is not significantly greater than zero, but as it is not significantly different from those of the other two cultivars either, it is probably real. The high variability in 'Golden Harvest' is probably due to the larger sized bulbs which averaged 3·6 shoots per bulb compared with 2·0 for 'Fortune' and 1·8 for 'Actaea'. This figure for the shoot number in 'Golden Harvest' being far from an integer implies a mixed population of three- and four-nosed bulbs, which would add to the variability normally encountered. Only in 'Golden Harvest' was it conveniently possible to separate "new" bulb material from "old" because these larger bulbs had flowered previously and the old flower shoot formed a convenient boundary for separating the previous year's tissues. W_{bulb} of Fig. 3.5 refers to both old and new parts of the bulb. The old bulb dry weight decreased through most of the growing season.

The "falling weight" phase from planting until the minimum total plant dry weight persisted until the leaf area index reached about 1 in 'Fortune' and 'Actaea' and between 1·5 and 2·0 in 'Golden Harvest', and was followed by a period of rapid dry weight gain.

The general form of the curve of growth after the point of minimum total dry weight is probably sigmoid, although the long periods between samples did not allow accurate assessment. As in the tulip the curve of bulb growth runs approximately parallel to that of total plant dry weight. The curves of leaf area index in 'Fortune' and 'Actaea' attained peaks of over two and that of 'Golden Harvest' almost four from planting densities of 174 cm² per plant. These peak values were reached slowly, there was no long plateau of high leaf area index, and the fall to zero took about eight weeks. The timing of rapid leaf growth in the spring suggests that all three cultivars are affected by the same external factor in the environment, probably temperature.

The slopes of the dry weight increase curves are linear or nearly so between weeks 28 and 34 (late April to early June) and represent growth rates of 0·39, 0·53 and 0·23 g plant^{-1} day^{-1} for 'Fortune', 'Golden Harvest' and 'Actaea' respectively. Crop growth rates derived from these figures are 22, 30 and 13 g m^{-2} day^{-1} respectively. Net assimilation rates showed peak values of 12 and 9 g m^{-2} day^{-1} for 'Fortune' and 'Golden Harvest'. No reliable estimate could be made for 'Actaea'.

These results agree in general with those described by Grainger (1941) in his study of naturalized 'King Alfred' *Narcissus* plants grown from small bulbs (each initially only just over 2 g dry weight). However, there was no evidence with any of the above three cultivars that weight loss until March was anything but linear, whereas Grainger indicated a slow loss in weight until mid-November followed by a more rapid loss.

The work considered so far has dealt with the growth of six cultivars from material which was not infected by disease nor infested by any pests in soil where the mineral status was not limiting, i.e. comparable with a commercially-grown healthy crop. The results obtained may be considered as a basic pattern which is capable of being modified by a range of factors both internal to the plant such as different varietal behaviour, and external in terms of weather, climate and disease incidence.

It is clear that the general pattern of growth exhibited by the bulbous plants of Mediterranean and temperate areas is an inefficient one from the point of view of energy conversion and dry-matter production, because of the short growing season. It is also advantageous for dry-matter production if the peak leaf area index coincides with the peak incoming solar radiation. This is near mid-summer day, in an average season, although Milthorpe (1963) has indicated that week-to-week variations in net assimilation rate about the average curve are as great as the maximum differences in the range of values shown between early May and late August, and records at G.C.R.I. show that more radiation can be received in a single clear day near the shortest than on a very dull day near the longest day. In general, however, bulb plants, especially tulips, suffer a loss of potential dry-matter production because of their short growing season and early senescence. The crop growth rates of the three tulip cultivars described earlier in this chapter were examined (Rees, 1965) in comparison with an estimate of potential rate derived from de Wit (1959), and it was concluded that as the peak crop growth rates occurred early in May, earlier than the peak potential rate, and then fell, the relatively poor efficiency of the tulip plant on an annual basis was due to inefficient dry-matter production during the growing season. At the peak rates the efficiency of energy fixation was near the potential rate and just below 4% of incident radiation between 400 and 700 nm wavelength.

These studies quantify the features of bulb growth which are well known qualitatively: the early growth and early senescence result in a short growing season which limits yields. It is only by recognizing the problems fully that an attempt may be made to improve matters.

II. Effects of various factors on growth

A. Flower removal in *Narcissus*

Kalin (1954) investigated the effects of flower removal on bulb production in *Narcissus* 'King Alfred'. Flowers were removed as in commercial flower harvesting, or half the peduncle was left, or flower heads only were removed (deheading), and the effects of these treatments were compared with control plants where flowers were left undisturbed. Mean lifted bulb weight was highest following the deheading treatment (13·7 g bulb^{-1}) whilst flower harvesting, even when done more carefully than in commercial practice, reduced bulb yield to 12·2 g bulb^{-1}. Further work showed that the removal of flowers as soon as the peduncle had grown long enough to enable this to be done was only marginally better than deheading (Kalin, 1956).

It was concluded, as other workers, have observed, that the peduncle is an important site for photosynthesis which would be retained for most efficient bulb production, and that deheading improves bulb yield.

B. Effect of virus infection on *Narcissus* growth rates

Investigations in southern England have shown how the seasonal pattern of growth can be modified. The effect of virus infection on *Narcissus* growth was studied by Rees (1966b). Bulbs of the trumpet cultivar 'Minister Talma' infected with either narcissus mosaic virus (NMV), or with narcissus yellow stripe (NYSV) together with tobacco rattle virus (TRV) were investigated in a comparison with healthy (symptomless) plants. These stocks were obtained by indexing naturally-infected plants and propagating together those with a similar virus content for several years in isolation to prevent contamination.

The virus-infected bulbs were generally smaller than the healthy ones, but similar-sized bulbs were selected for planting. Infection had no effect on flower number or flower size but the peduncles were shorter, and the NMV-infected plants produced slightly blemished flowers and three-quarters of those from the NYSV + TRV-infected flowers were of poor quality.

E

Growth before anthesis was assessed from height measurements made weekly until early June. Values obtained in early February and mid-March show that plant height was nearly identical for the healthy and the NMV-infected plants and significantly greater than that of the NYSV + TRV-infected plants. The difference was, however, an indication of the rate or timing of leaf growth rather than of final leaf length, although the leaves of the healthy plants were longer. The leaf areas of infected plants were also lower than those of the healthy plants early in the season but later this difference disappeared; this trend was also reflected in leaf dry weight. The healthy plants had a considerably larger leaf area than the

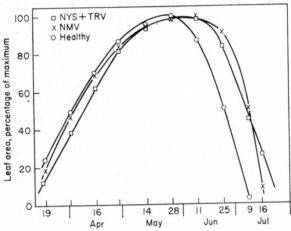

Fig. 3.6 Changes in the leaf area of *Narcissus* 'Minister Talma' expressed as percentages of maximum values for healthy, mosaic-infected (NMV) and narcissus yellow stripe virus (NYSV) + tobacco rattle virus (TRV)-infected plants. Each point a mean from 5 plants (Rees, 1966b).

infected ones by mid-March, reached their maximum leaf area about two weeks before the infected ones, and also died down about two weeks earlier. Virus infection in *Narcissus* apparently shifts the leaf area curve forward by about two weeks (Fig. 3.6). There were no effects of virus infection on the total bulb weight lifted at the end of the experiment. Early in the growing season the NYSV + TRV-infected bulbs had lost less weight than the healthy bulbs; they were 25% heavier. Virus infection may have affected translocation from the bulb; a similar effect of leaf-roll virus on decreasing translocation from leaves to tubers has been described in potato (Watson and Wilson, 1956). Alternatively, the effect could be due to a loss of apical dominance, also found in potato leaf-roll virus (Watson and Wilson, 1956).

The absence of differences in final bulb yield despite virus infection are probably due to the counterbalancing of early leaf development in the healthy plants by their earlier senescence. The possession of active green leaves later in the season by the virus-infected plants compensated for other effects due to infection. The failure to detect small differences in bulb weight does not necessarily imply, however, that these do not exist, and are not important over several years. The reduction in yield due to virus infection was, however, considerably less than earlier papers have led one

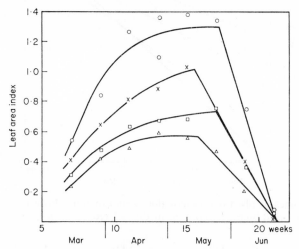

Fig. 3.7 Leaf area development and decline in plants grown from different-sized bulbs of tulip 'Rose Copland', circles, 12 cm; crosses, 10 cm; squares, 8 cm; triangles, 6 cm (Rees, 1969b).

to believe (van Slogteren and de Bruyn Ouboter, 1941), and differences in net assimilation rate between healthy and virus-infected plants, if any, were small.

C. Effects of bulb size on tulip growth

The effect of bulb size on growth pattern was investigated for tulip cv. 'Rose Copland' using 6, 8, 10 and 12 cm grade bulbs planted at standard spacing (Rees, 1969b). Similar patterns of leaf area increase and decrease were obtained with plants from all four bulb grades, but the peaks were higher in the plants from large bulbs (Fig. 3.7). There was some variation in the negative relative growth rates from planting until mid-March but they showed no trend related to planted bulb size and were similar to those found in earlier work. Plant dry weight increased logarithmically until the start of the decline in leaf area. The relative growth rates calculated from the fitted lines of Fig. 3.8 show a decrease with increasing bulb size; 0·030, 0·023, 0·017 and 0·014 g g^{-1} day^{-1}, each figure being significantly different from any other except its immediate neighbours.

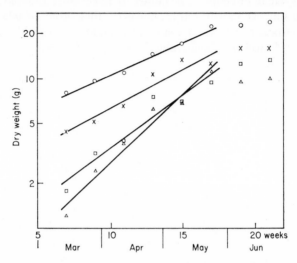

Fig. 3.8 Changes in plant dry weight (log. scale) of tulip 'Rose Copland' grown from different-sized bulbs. Symbols as in Fig. 3.7 (Rees, 1969b).

D. Effects of cultivar on tulip growth

Some effects of tulip cultivar on growth pattern have already been described; 'Golden Harvest' was more productive of dry matter than 'Rose Copland' or 'William Pitt'. To investigate varietal effects further, four contrasting cultivars were grown from 9-cm bulbs. These were 'Apeldoorn', 'Weber', 'Golden Harvest' and 'Boule de Neige', selected on the basis of a commercial spacing trial as being highly productive, of medium productivity or low productivity respectively.

Leaf area development is shown in Fig. 3.9, together with total plant dry weight. There is little evidence for differences in the timing of leaf area development, nor in the time at which senescence starts or ends. There are considerable differences however in the amount of leaf produced, that of 'Apeldoorn' being more than twice that of 'Boule de Neige', with the other two cultivars intermediate. Similarly, the plant dry weight changes, were also in the order expected with 'Apeldoorn' clearly the superior variety although its bulbs at planting were, by chance, slightly the smallest.

These differences between cultivars were also found in the growth of daughter bulbs; these will be considered more fully later.

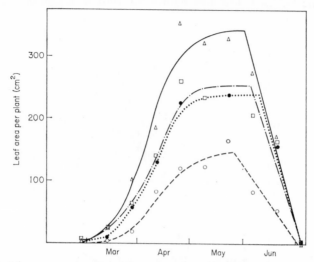

Fig. 3.9 Changes in leaf area during the growing season for four tulip cultivars, triangles, 'Apeldoorn'; squares, 'Golden Harvest'; filled circles, 'Weber'; open circles, 'Boule de Neige' (Rees, 1971).

E. Leaf damage

In preliminary work on the effects of removing leaf area of tulips on subsequent yield, reductions of 10–40% have been obtained. When whole blades were removed before flowering, yield was reduced by up to 80% after flowering the reduction was about 50% (Timmer and Koster, 1969b).

III. Environmental effects

Although there are known to be wide differences in growth pattern in the two main bulb growing areas in the U.K. (Lincolnshire and the south-west), such as earlier emergence, earlier flowering and early senescence, together with lower bulb yields, in the milder south-west, little work has been done to compare growth patterns in a quantitative manner. For *Narcissus* 'Fortune' some data for leaf area and total plant dry weight are shown in Fig. 3.10. Identical material was grown at Kirton (Lincolnshire) and Rosewarne (Cornwall) in the 1966–7 season; the latter was found to be an earlier location by two weeks to a month, and produced a higher peak leaf area. Senescence was also earlier in Rosewarne, but it is difficult to say by how much, because no Kirton data was collected after the start of senescence. The two seasons 1965–6 and 1966–7 were very similar in the patterns of leaf area development, but the first season showed an earlier decline. The G.C.R.I. leaf area figures for 1963–4, which are very high

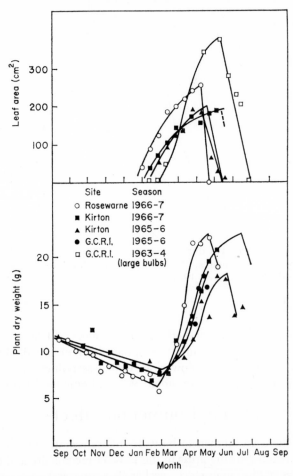

Fig. 3.10 Leaf area (above) and plant dry weight (below) changes in *Narcissus* 'Fortune' at three sites and in three seasons. In 1963–4, bulbs were larger than in other years. The graphs illustrate differences in timing rather than of magnitudes.

because large bulbs were used, showed a very late leaf growth and decline. This season followed the very severe late winter, and indicates how a single season's figures are unreliable as an indication of "normal" behaviour. G.C.R.I. is normally between Rosewarne and Kirton in emergence date, flowering and senescence.

Similar trends are detectable in the curves of total plant dry weight. The falling weight phase from planting to the time of minimum plant dry weight is similar in Rosewarne and Kirton, but the rate of dry weight loss is more rapid at Rosewarne, possibly because of higher soil temperatures (see Fig. 7.1) allowing higher rates of respiration, faster development and therefore higher rates of weight loss. The timing of the minimum plant dry weight was at the end of February at Rosewarne but at Kirton this occurred 2–3 weeks later. Weight increase occurred earlier at Rosewarne than Kirton and was also more rapid.

Although the data are not very comprehensive, it is clear that differences do exist in leaf area expansion and senescence and in dry-matter production, apparently both from site to site and season to season. Little information exists from other parts of the world, but it would be reasonable to expect differences larger than those encountered in the two major bulb growing areas of U.K. which are only a few hundred miles apart, and where differences in temperature are only a few degrees.

IV. Respiration in the field

Field methods of measuring rates of photosynthesis or of dry-matter production assess these as net processes. For some purposes it is useful to know rates of respiration as well, so an attempt to do this using the methods developed by Watson and Hayashi (1965) was made on the tulip crop. Experimental plants were shaded with opaque cardboard boxes every other day, every third day or were unshaded, the treatments being started late in April and continued for four weeks. Samples of plants were taken at weekly intervals and oven-dried at 80°C. Regression lines were fitted to the points of each of the three treatments, and the regression coefficients were plotted against the light received, expressed as a proportion of that of the unshaded plants. The intercept of this line with zero light indicated a respiration rate of 0·27 g dry matter plant^{-1} week^{-1}, equivalent to 2·2 g m^{-2} day^{-1} on a land area basis or 20% of the gross rate of dry-matter production in full light (Rees, 1967). This estimate is very similar to that of Wassink (1965) who obtained data on the weight loss of the tulips grown in total darkness. Here the dry weight loss was 0·30 g plant^{-1} week^{-1}.

These results may be criticized because the shading treatment does not give a true assessment of the rate of respiration which would occur in light; a number of reports on a range of crop plants describe higher rates of evolution of carbon dioxide in the light than in the dark. The results are, however, close to other estimates of crop respiration rates.

V. Spacing and competition

Commercial field crops of narcissi grown in the U.K. were until recently traditionally spaced 1·5–2 bulb diameters apart in rows 20–30 cm apart, giving populations ranging from 500,000 to 3,000,000 ha⁻¹ depending on the size of bulb being planted. In more recent years mechanical lifting and planting have changed the traditional spacings, and *Narcissus* bulbs are now grown in ridges 71 or 76 cm apart and about 30 bulbs m⁻¹ run of ridge. The change-over from bed to ridge systems has introduced much controversy about optimum planting densities, encouraging the experimental investigation of a number of planting densities. An early experiment, on small offsets of *Narcissus* 'King Alfred', used one of the spacing layouts developed at the National Vegetable Research Station, U.K., and described by Nelder (1962) as a simple log-log grid set at 45 degrees to the side of the plot. Contours of constant density and constant regularity (the ratio of the between-row to the within-row distances) are the two sets of lines parallel to the sides of the plot and both quantities change exponentially with distances from the origin. By using the grid with the square arrangement across the centre, plants with a given rectangularity of spacing are found at two positions equidistant from the centre, but orientated at right angles to each other. The design enables the main effects of plant density, rectangularity and row orientation and their interactions to be studied separately.

The experiment, planted at Rosewarne in 1961 included the following treatments (Rees, *et al.*, 1968).

Density (plants m⁻²)	Rectangularity	Orientation
23	1 : 1	square
46	1·5 : 1	E–W
67	2·5 : 1	N–S
91		
108	4 : 1	
130		
151	6 : 1	

Planting density had no effect on flowering date, but high densities increased stem length by over 20%. Flower number increased almost linearly with increasing density, but flower number per bulb decreased from unity to 0·87 at the highest density.

Lifted bulb weight increased with increase in planting density following the equation proposed by Bleasdale and Nelder (1960):

$$w^{-\theta} = \alpha + \beta\rho$$

where w is the mean weight in g per emerged bulb, ρ is the planting density (bulbs m^{-2}), and α and β are constants for any one set of data where density is the only variable. The best fitting values to the constants were:

$$\theta = 1, \alpha = 0{\cdot}01099 \text{ and } \beta = 0{\cdot}000{,}064{,}45$$

and the fitted line is shown in Fig 3.11. The line shows little indication of approaching an asymptote within the range of densities employed, and when the weight increase (wt lifted − wt planted) is derived, this also shows little tendency to reach an asymptote. There were, however, marked

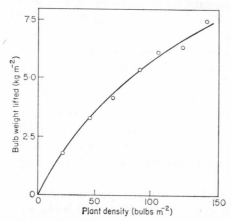

Fig. 3.11 Relation between bulb yield and spacing in *Narcissus* 'King Alfred' after two years (Rees *et al.*, 1968).

effects of density on grading of the lifted bulbs. The largest grade (double-nosed) showed marked levelling off above a planting density of about 100 bulbs m^{-2}, whilst there was a corresponding increase in the weight of round bulbs.

The results of this experiment are relevant when a *Narcissus* crop is grown from small bulbs largely for flowers with bulb yield only of secondary consideration. The bulbs were also left in the ground for two years. There are, however, clear advantages to flower production from closely-planted bulbs; flower production is hardly affected and the flower stems are longer. Even at the highest densities, the yield of bulbs was more than sufficient to provide adequate material for replanting, and, in fact, was still increasing rapidly above the highest density (160 m^{-2}), where bulb yield was over four times the planted weight.

Tulip

Experimentation in Lincolnshire on tulips (Rees and Turquand 1969b) involved a range of five planting densities and two cultivars, 'Apeldoorn' and 'Rose Copland'. Row orientations N/S and E/W were used but no effects due to orientation were observed. The experiment was repeated in two consecutive seasons (1966–7 and 1967–8) but an outbreak of cucumber mosaic virus in the second-season 'Rose Copland' depressed yields, leaving two comparisons for 'Apeldoorn' in two successive seasons and 'Apeldoorn' with 'Rose Copland' in a single season. The following were the major findings:

Leaf area index increased proportionally to the density of planting so that plant leaf area was nearly independent of spacing, within the ranges used which gave peak values of L of over 8 in both cultivars. 'Rose Copland' showed a small but significant reduction (8–10%) in leaf area per plant at high planting densities near the time of maximum leaf area (May and June). Leaf senescence occurred more rapidly in 'Apeldoorn' at higher planting densities; 22% of leaf area at peak L had been lost by mid-June at the highest density, compared with only 8% at the lowest density.

Flower stems were larger at higher planting densities, in both cultivars. The increase with density from 48 to 258 bulbs m^{-2} was from about 40 to 45 cm with 'Apeldoorn' and about 45 to 55 with 'Rose Copland'.

From the reciprocal yield law

$$w^{-1} = \alpha + \beta\rho$$

Where w is mean weight per plant, ρ is planting density and α and β are constants, the total bulb weight lifted per unit area, ρw, is given by

$$\rho(\alpha + \beta\rho)^{-1}$$

If the mean weight per planted bulb is v, then the bulb weight planted per unit area is ρv, and the increase in bulb weight per unit area is

$$\rho(\alpha + \beta\rho)^{-1} - \rho v$$

The interrelations of yield and density for the two cultivars in the 1966–7 season are shown in Fig. 3.12. Maximum weight increase was obtained at ρ values of 94 and 110 bulbs m^{-2} for 'Apeldoorn' and 'Rose Copland' respectively when the lifted weights were 3·6 kg m^{-2} for both cultivars, and the weight increase above that planted was 2·1 and 1·7 kg m^{-2}, respectively. Density affected bulb numbers in the same experiment, suggesting that the development of a number of daughter bulbs was suppressed; up to a third failed in 'Apeldoorn' and up to a quarter in 'Rose Copland'.

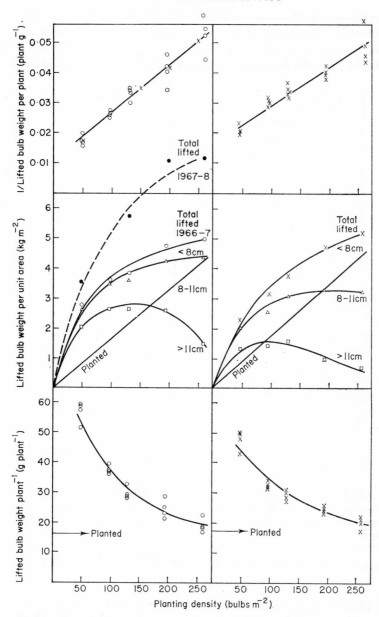

Fig. 3.12 Effect of planting density on lifted bulb weight in two tulip cultivars, left 'Apeldoorn', right 'Rose Copland'. The three bulb size grades which make up the total bulb weight are shown in the centre figures, together with the total weight curve for 'Apeldoorn' in the following season (Rees and Turquand, 1969).

Regression analysis was also used to describe the bulb grades, especially the numbers of bulbs larger than 11 cm grade, described as "forcing-size". With 'Apeldoorn' the numbers of forcing-sized bulbs was linearly related to planting density, but with 'Rose Copland' the quadratic component was

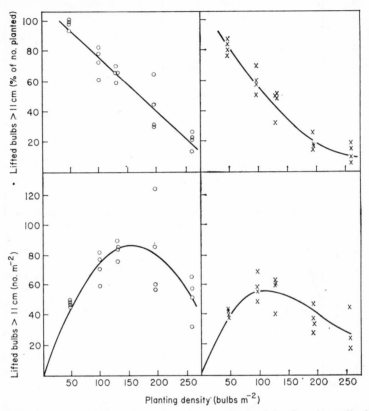

Fig. 3.13 Effect of planting density on the numbers of forcing-size tulip bulbs (>11 cm), expressed (above) as a percentage of those planted and (below) as numbers per square metre. Left 'Apeldoorn', right 'Rose Copland' (Rees and Turquand, 1969).

significant. The numbers of forcing-sized bulbs per unit area is given by

$$\rho(a + b\rho + c\rho^2)/100$$

The planting densities given maximum numbers of forcing-size bulb and the numbers of bulbs at this density were obtained for 'Apeldoorn' (87 bulbs at $\rho = 155$) and 'Rose Copland' (56 at $\rho = 112$) (Fig. 3.13). The bulb size spectrum of each cultivar as related to planting density was also obtained; with increase in planting density, the mean bulb size decreased and the strongly bimodal distribution of sizes at low densities tended to disappear, and the peaks moved to smaller bulb sizes.

Figure 3.12 shows how the two cultivars differ in their partition of daughter bulb weight between bulb grades. At the lowest planting densities used, 'Apeldoorn' partitioned about 80% of bulb weight into bulbs 11 cm grade and above, compared with only about 60% in 'Rose Copland'. The below 8 cm grades were only about 6% of the total at the lowest planting density with 'Apeldoorn' but twice this with 'Rose Copland'; with increase in density these percentages increased to 12 and 36% respectively.

One striking feature of the experiment was, however, the very large difference in production of 'Apeldoorn' bulb weight in two successive seasons. This difference was greater than that between 'Apeldoorn' and 'Rose Copland' in the same season. For total daughter bulb weight, the value of α are properties of the plant, the small difference between $1/\alpha$ for the two seasons being explained by small differences in mean planting bulb weight. The major factor affecting year-to-year variation is therefore, β (the slope of the regression line); in a more favourable year β is lower, resulting in higher yield at high densities but not when ρ tends to zero. Similarly, the numbers of forcing size bulbs are unaffected by season at low planting density but more are produced at higher values of ρ in a good growing season. Because the growing seasons 1967 and 1968 were drier and warmer, and wetter and cooler respectively than the long term averages, the optimum planting density for 'Apeldoorn' lies between the optimum of these two seasons, and planting densities higher than those giving the best results in 1967 would be best on a long-term basis.

The results obtained in this study were also compared on a financial basis, assessing the wholesale values of all the bulbs lifted and planted and thereby ascertaining the most profitable densities of planting, assuming constant costs of planting, lifting, management, etc. Profit was near zero at $\rho = 8$ plants m^{-2} (where growing costs were balanced by returns) and at $\rho = 163$ and 145 plants m^{-2} for 'Apeldoorn' and 'Rose Copland' respectively. Maximum profit was obtained for these two cultivars at $\rho = 65$ and 45 bulbs m^{-2} respectively, where profits were £3500 and £2800 per hectare respectively.

The effect of planting density on the yield of saleable bulbs per unit area can be resolved into its effects, through competition, on (i) total lifted bulb weight per unit area and (ii) the proportion of this bulb weight which is saleable. The maximum bulb weight produced per plant, as ρ approaches zero and inter-plant competition becomes negligible, is given by $1/\alpha$ where α is the constant in the equations of the equations of the straight lines shown in Fig. 3.12 ($\alpha = 0.0109$ for 'Apeldoorn' and 0.0162

for 'Rose Copland'). For the two cultivars, the maximum lifted weight per plant was 92 and 62 g respectively, so that 'Apeldoorn' showed the greater yield potential. Whether this was due to more efficient net photosynthesis or to the more effective partition of photosynthate between new daughter bulbs and the remainder of the plant is uncertain. 'Apeldoorn' was, however, more responsive to competition, so that the higher total daughter bulb yield with 'Apeldoorn' at low planting density was lost about $\rho = 178$ bulbs m^{-2} when 'Rose Copland' outyielded 'Apeldoorn'.

These tulip results, obtained from square-planted material without paths or other access, are artificial in comparison with normal commercial practice where access is essential.

Little information is available from other countries on optimum planting densities for tulips. Rasmussen (1964) in a consideration of a number of cultivars over a few years found highest yields from fifty 10 cm bulbs m^{-2} (his highest density), but concluded that as yield differences, and especially the numbers of forcing bulbs, between 40 and 50 bulbs m^{-2} was very small, 40 bulbs m^{-2} would be most economic for bulbs of the common varieties. Dutch recommendations (Anon, 1967) for 10 cm bulbs are for planting densities of 83 bulbs m^{-2}, and Bakker (1970) has recently suggested that for relatively good seasons, a planting density of 76 bulbs m^{-2} was best irrespective of seasonal differences in climate.

When *Endymion hispanicus* was grown at a range of densities between 200 and 1000 plants m^{-2} the rate of dry-matter production fell from 17 to -10 g m^{-2} day^{-1} with increasing density, although the leaf area index rose from 2 to 36. Net assimilation rate and relative growth rate both fell, from 4 g m^{-2} and 0·017 g g^{-1} day^{-1}, respectively, to negative values with increasing density (Blackman, 1962). Maximum crop growth rate (21 g m^{-2} day^{-1}) occurred at about 300 plants m^{-2}, at a leaf area index of 9·5.

A. Crop growing in ridges

Further work on *Narcissus* and tulip crops grown in ridges using different bulb sizes has also been done at Kirton (Lincolnshire) and Rosewarne (Cornwall) and effects on bulb yield and flower production recorded. In all cases where bed-planting and ridge-planting have been compared, the former has been more efficient in terms of land utilization. However, the high cost of labour has led to increasing areas of ridge planting by machine. The resulting lost yield has been considered inevitable. The loss is due to the better light interception by the regular planting pattern of the traditional bulb bed compared with the ridge, where high density of leaf area is concentrated in the ridge with low densities between ridges.

Narcissus

In a large experiment at Rosewarne two bulb sizes (double-nosed and offset) were planted at four spacings (54, 108, 162, 216 bulbs m^{-2}) in ridges or beds and allowed to stay in the ground for 1, 2 or 3 years. Flower and bulb yield were recorded (Wallis, 1968).

In the two-year crop of offset bulbs, beds out-yielded ridges by 26–29% except at the lowest density where the difference was 15%. In the first year leaf area was a function of planting density and bulb size, reaching a peak

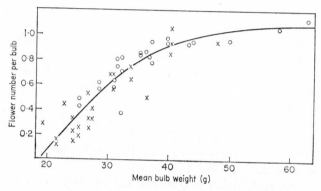

Fig. 3.14 Effect of mean bulb weight present in a plot on flower number per bulb in *Narcissus* 'Fortune' grown at Rosewarne. Crosses, double-nosed bulbs; circles, offset bulbs.

leaf area index between 6 and 7 for offset bulbs and between 10 and 11 for double-nosed bulbs at the highest planting density, irrespective of planting system. In the second year the density/leaf area index relation was less clear, and was generally lower in ridges than beds, presumably because of the different efficiencies of the two systems in producing new active growing points. Leaf area indexes were recorded for the original offset bulbs of 6 in ridges and nearly 8 in beds, whilst the corresponding values for the larger planted bulbs were 11 and 15–16 respectively. There is a tendency for the leaf area index of offset bulbs to reach a value between 6 and 7 after three years, irrespective of planting density, whilst double-nosed bulbs increased to about 10 after three years but there were wide variations from this figure.

The numbers of flowers produced increased regularly each year at low densities and less regularly at higher densities. When the number of flowers produced was plotted against the mean bulb weight present in that plot (estimated from similar plots sampled for bulb production) flower number was found to be a function of mean bulb weight and bulb number per unit area (Fig. 3.14). No effects of planting density on flower number were observed other than those acting directly on bulb number and bulb weight.

When the optimum planting density for maximum bulb weight increase was plotted against mean planted bulb weight, three curves were obtained, one for each crop-growing period. Conversion to mean planting weights per unit area gave the following values for three periods:

1 year	4·65 kg m^{-2}
2 years	3·29 kg m^{-2}
3 years	2·33 kg m^{-2}

Only in the one-year grown bulbs were the differences large between ridges and beds. The actual weight increases obtained ranged from below 1 to above 5 kg m^{-2}, the lowest increase occurring in general after one year and the highest after three years. Within any duration treatment, highest planting densities gave highest yields.

Maximum numbers of forcing bulbs (larger than 12 cm) per unit area were obtained at densities of 170–240 bulbs m^{-2} for two-year grown and 130–170 bulbs m^{-2} for three-year grown 15 g bulbs, but these values fell to 110 and 90 bulbs m^{-2} for 45 g bulbs. When considered as planting weights per unit area, higher weights per unit area were more effective for larger bulbs. Between 45 and 120 bulbs larger than 12 cm were produced per square metre, at the optimum density for the treatment, with a mean value of 69 bulbs m^{-2}. High yields of large bulbs were obtained in a number of treatment combinations, mostly in the one- and two-year grown crops of offset bulbs, or double-nosed bulbs grown for one year. Beds were usually better than ridges.

Unfortunately no clear picture emerged in this experiment of optimum planting densities for highest increase in bulb values, but the optimum planting weights increased with mean planting bulb weight (20–58 g) from 1·5 to 2·0 kg m^{-2}. Highest increases in value were obtained from the bed planting system rather than ridges, from two- and three-year cropping systems and from smaller bulbs rather than large ones.

In a ridge layout, in another experiment, bulbs of *Narcissus* 'Fortune' of four grades (6/8, 8/10, 10/12 and 12/14 cm) were each planted at four different spacings and lifted after one year. The experiment was repeated in three consecutive seasons at Kirton.

A grade/price structure was calculated and used to prepare a curve of lifted-bulb value per unit area with planting density. A linear relationship exists between density and planting bulb value per unit area. From these two relationships the increase in value was determined for each bulb size in each of three seasons, and the optimum planting density estimated, as shown in Table 3.1.

No clear optimum was apparent in some cases, with a wide range of planting densities giving similar results. The 6/8 and 8/10 cm planting material is too small to have any commercial value, no planting-material costs can be subtracted and the optimum densities for these two grades were outside the experimental range. There were quite large seasonal differences in both optimum planting rates and in financial returns. The bulb grade nearest to that used for replanting commercially (large bulbs

Table 3.1

Effect of season and bulb size on the optimum planting density for bulbs of *Narcissus* 'Fortune' grown as a one-year crop (Kirton, 1967–70).

Season	Grade	Optimum planting density (bulbs m^{-2})	Optimum planting density (kg m^{-2})	Increase in value £ m^{-2}
1967/8	6/8	>150	>3·8	>0·70
	8/10	>130	>4·8	>0·55
	10/12	50	2·3	0·15
	12/14	22	1·5	0·05
1968/9	6/8	>150	>3·8	>0·46
	8/10	>130	>4·8	>0·66
	10/12	100	4·8	0·45
	12/14	65	4·3	0·24
1969/70	6/8	>150	>3·8	>0·27
	8/10	>130	>4·8	>0·52
	10/12	120	5·5	0·41
	12/14	35	2·3	0·14

for sale are removed from the lifted material and all offset and small bulbs, together with a few large bulbs, are replanted) is the 10/12 cm grade, and the mean of the optimum planting weight for the three years is 4·2 kg m^{-2}, a value considerably higher than that normally planted commercially.

Tulip

Work is still in progress on optimum planting densities for tulips grown in ridges 71 cm apart, using 8/9, 10/11 and 12/13 cm 'Apeldoorn' bulbs at five planting densities from 28 to 138 bulbs m^{-2}. Over this range of bulb grades there was a three-fold increase in bulb weight, but this was

F

accompanied by a leaf area increase of below two. As leaf area index for optimum production was independent of bulb grade (for profit, L was between 2·0 and 2·9 for all three grades in two seasons at optimum planting densities) higher weights of planting material are required when using larger grade bulbs. The optimum planting densities for maximum bulb weight increase, for maximum numbers of saleable bulbs and for maximum increase in bulb value are shown in Table 3.2.

Table 3.2

Effect of season and bulb size on optimum planting densities (bulbs m^{-2}) for tulip 'Apeldoorn' (Kirton 1968–70).

Optimum density for	*Season*	*Bulb grade (cm)*		
		8/9	10/11	12/13
Max. weight increase	1968–9	78	45	46
	1969–70	105	58	65
No. bulbs >11 cm	1968–9	94	96	77
	1969–70	100	101	94
Increase in bulb value	1968–9	90	55	55
	1969–70	110	75	65

These figures are similar to corresponding ones quoted earlier for tulips grown in beds; the observed seasonal differences make detailed comparisons impossible.

Commercially tulips are planted at about 43–49 bulbs m^{-2} compared with the highest profit obtained with 8–9 cm bulbs (the nearest in this experiment to commercial practice) at 100 bulbs m^{-2}. As in *Narcissus* experiments, optimal planting rates are considerably higher than those used commercially, in the U.K. at least.

VI. Natural communities

Effects of picking flowers on natural communities of bulbous plants have not been widely studied, but some observations were made on bluebells (*Endymion nonscriptus*) in England (Peace and Gilmour, 1949). There were no ill effects of either cutting the inflorescences at ground level or of "pulling" the flowers, removing the stem down to its attachment to the base plate, but damage due to trampling on the leaves, if heavy, eventually leads to extermination of the community.

Dispersal of bulbs has been studied extensively in Israel (Galil, 1961).

In the case of *Allium ampeloprasum* two distinct forms of the species have been observed, growing on different soil types. In one, numerous small bulblets are produced annually in the foliage leaf axils whilst the other produces long stolons of axil-foliar origin bearing bulblets at their ends (similar to tulip "droppers"). The rate of vegetative reproduction and stolon length is affected by the depth of planting and stolons can grow in all directions away from the parent plant so effecting dispersal of the daughter plants (Galil, 1965).

Poor dispersal, lack of seed dormancy and of conditions suitable for germination are considered to be factors restricting *Endymion nonscriptus* in England to woodland habitats; as it appears impossible for the species to cross open country to colonize new woods, its present distribution is thought to be due to successful survival from times before continuous forest was fragmented. Vegetative reproduction is very infrequent but seedlings are found abundantly in all habitats (Knight, 1964).

Much work remains to be done on aspects of crop growth and productivity of bulb crops, although the broad picture of the life cycle has been known qualitatively for a long time and is now being understood quantitatively. In particular the short growing season is of over-riding importance in determining productivity, but little is known about the factors which cause the senescence of leaves and the termination of the active above-ground period. The seasonal differences observed in the length of the growing season and in yield suggest, however, that it is capable of modification.

Spacing is of special importance in the *Narcissus* and tulip crops because of the plants' morphology. Leaf area index can be modified to a certain extent by using different sized bulbs or, in *Narcissus*, by leaving the crop unlifted for more than one year, but in general the only agronomically useful method of changing leaf area index is by changing planting densities. The results of present experiments indicate that in current commercial practice, bulbs are planted too thinly, and that greater profits would result from densities up to twice those currently used. Some difficulties must be resolved before these high densities are adopted; fertilizer practice and irrigation could be affected, disease problems could be accentuated and mechanical problems of planting and lifting would have to be overcome.

Chapter 4

The initiation and growth of bulbs

"The biological significance of storage organs is to be understood first in ecological terms—specifically, in relation to adaptation to climate and particular types of biota."

J. Heslop-Harrison, 1970

I. Daughter bulb initiation and early growth

Some aspects of daughter bulb initiation and growth have already been discussed in Chapter 2, when dealing with bulb structure. A few bulbs e.g. hyacinth, only very rarely produce daughter bulbs under natural conditions and artificial methods of wounding, which result in daughter bulbs being initiated on the resultant callus tissue, are normally resorted to for propagation. Other bulbous plants produce daughter bulbs very freely, in the axils of every scale, with frequently more than one in each axil in the tulip. They may also be produced in the axils of aerial leaves, a usual occurrence in some lilies and exceptionally in tulip. In *Narcissus* each terminal daughter bulb in the branching system is replaced by two daughter bulbs, leading to a slow increase in apex number, whilst in *Hippeastrum* and some other bulbs, it appears that daughter bulbs are initiated only in the axils of senescing bulb scales in the outer parts of the bulb. The decay of these outer scales releases the daughter bulbs which appear as a ring of satellite bulbs around the parent. No systematic study of types of daughter bulb initiation has been made, the above examples are quoted to give an indication of the variation encountered.

There is also some variation in the exact location at which daughter bulbs are initiated. In the tulip the most common situation is in the middle point of the insertion of the subtending scale, but this is not invariable, and where more than one daughter bulb occurs in the axil of one scale, these are frequently clustered together, but may be in diametric opposition in the axil of the same scale. In *Iris* 'Wedgwood' the scales are not completely sheathing, but the edges leave a small gap which is the mid-line of the next outermost scale. In this gap is found, very regularly, a daughter bulb.

A. *Narcissus*

Terminal bulb units are initiated alongside the newly-initiated flower, and may be regarded as having an initiation date close to, or very shortly after, that of flower initiation, which usually occurs in May in south-east England. Lateral bulb units may be clearly seen by April in the year following initiation, but there is evidence that they are formed as early as December but grow very slowly. The lateral bulb units are usually initiated in the axil of the third leaf from the bulb centre, whilst in the non-flowering bulb unit the original apex remains active for a further season. Supernumerary daughter bulb units can also be initiated in the same year as the normal laterals, but also a year later, as judged by their small size. These may be in the axils of outer leaves in the axil of a bulb scale (usually the innermost) or may accompany the normal lateral bulb unit. In a study with cv. 'Fortune', of 19 supernumerary lateral daughter bulb units, seven were in the same leaf axil as the normal lateral (Rees, 1969c).

The life span of a bulb unit extends over about four years. There is some doubt about the end of the period because the time of death is not very clear; the scales and leaf bases gradually become brown, papery and die and there is a loss of identity before this. The lateral bulb units live for a shorter time than the main ones which are initiated earlier.

Bulb units grow continuously at different rates at different times of the year. Leaves and flowers become aerial when the bulb units are 9–18 months old, depending whether they are lateral or terminal, but the bulb units remain alive and functioning for many months after they have borne leaves. Figure 4.1 shows for two well-known cultivars the pattern of growth of daughter bulbs observed by successive sampling over a growing season. By assuming a correspondence between the end of one year's growth and the start of the previous year's growth in the generation one year older, a long-term record was built up. In 'Fortune', terminal bulb units (see

Chapter 2 for terminology) grow rapidly for only about 3–4 months after initiation, then the growth rate falls to a lower rate from September to February (relative growth rate (R) of $0.005 - 0.001$ g g^{-1} day^{-1}). In February growth increases to a rapid rate (R of $0.04 - 0.06$ g g^{-1} day^{-1}) which in turn slows to a period of slow growth in the autumn and winter

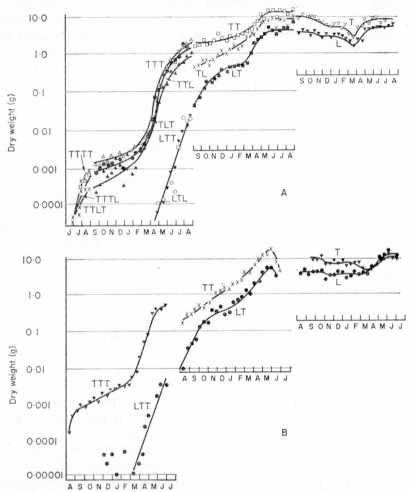

Fig. 4.1 Growth of bulb units of (A) 'Fortune' and (B) 'King Alfred' *Narcissus*, showing alternations of periods of slow and rapid growth. Data were collected over a single season, 1966–7 for A and 1965–6 for B, but by assuming a correspondence between the end of one year's growth and the start of the previous year's growth and the start of the previous year's growth a longer record can be built up. The discontinuities in August–September (A) and in July–August (B) show the failure of exact agreement (Rees, 1969c).

(R of 0·003 — 0·006 g g^{-1} day^{-1}). In February, growth again speeds up (R of 0·01 — 0·02 g g^{-1} day^{-1}) to reach a peak dry weight in May. There is some dry weight loss in the following February and March corresponding with the rapid growth-rates of the succeeding generations, but this loss is regained by May, and weight is maintained until August. Later this weight must fall as the scales, leaf bases and peduncle base become senescent and die, but because of difficulties of identification no quantitative information is available. The data for 'King Alfred' were very similar, although they were obtained in a different season; there was some loss in weight following leaf loss in 'King Alfred' which was not observed in 'Fortune', the loss and then gain in weight in the third year was not as clear as in 'Fortune' and there was more evidence for the early formation of lateral daughter bulb units than in 'Fortune'.

The lateral bulb units of both cultivars show the same alternation of rapid and slow growth, although the first two periods in 'Fortune' are apparently lost because of the late initiation of the later bulb units in this cultivar. The periods of rapid growth of the lateral bulb units correspond in time with those of the terminal ones, suggesting external control of the growth patterns.

The development of the full complement of scales and leaves in the young growing bulb unit occurs during the first period of rapid growth in both terminal and lateral bulb units; those of the terminal bulb units are, however, initiated at a lower bulb unit weight. After the formation of the scales and leaves, the apex is apparently inactive until the flower is initiated at the end of the second period of rapid growth of the terminal bulb unit about a year after the terminal bulb unit's initiation. In cases where flower initiation failed, there was some evidence of renewed leaf formation by the apex at the time of normal flower initiation, leading to unusually high numbers of leaves in non-flowering apices. Lateral bulb units do initiate flowers (but not very frequently, and this depends on cultivar and season) but no information is available on how their behaviour differs from that of the terminal bulb units.

Much of the difference in size, component part (scale and leaf) number and flowering potential can be traced back to the initiation of lateral bulb units some time after the terminal ones. In 'Fortune', this difference results in lateral bulb units composed of fewer parts, being lighter in weight and showing a considerably reduced tendency to flower, and an almost complete suppression of the development of their own lateral units in the next generation. It may be speculated that the lateral bulb units are affected by apical dominance exerted by the terminal bulb units, which are themselves only developed when the terminal apex becomes floral, and apical dominance is lost.

Abnormal growth patterns occur when apices are damaged by a pest or disease, or following inefficient hot-water treatment for eelworm control. Large numbers of daughter bulbs are formed under these conditions, suggesting that the capacity for regeneration exists along the base of leaf and scales within an old bulb, but that this capacity is not normally exerted because of the dominating influence of the main apices within the bulb.

After the loss of the aerial parts of the leaf scales, the basal parts, together with the bulb scales, perform a storage function, as evidenced by the loss in the dry weight of the parts at the time of rapid enlargement of younger bulb units.

B. Tulip

Unlike the *Narcissus* bulb, tulip daughter bulbs are initiated from about February, the outermost daughter bulb being initiated first and the innermost last of all. All the daughter bulbs are present early in July, so that about four weeks elapses between the initiation of successive daughter

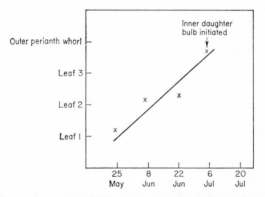

Fig. 4.2 Time course of daughter bulb activity in tulip 'Rose Copland' and the change from leaf production to flower initiation which is closely related to the initiation of the innermost second-generation daughter bulb (Rees, 1968).

bulbs. The life span of a bulb depends on its position and hence its date of initiation, but may be as much as 2·5 years. From the end of May when the first observations were made during a study of daughter bulb initiation and growth (Rees, 1968a), the outermost, first-initiated daughter bulbs were consistently larger than the inner ones, which formed a decreasing size gradient inwards. Bulbs in the innermost position were seen only on the last four sampling occasions, early in July, when the bulbs in other positions were up to three times their weight, and when its mother bulb apex was changing from the vegetative to the reproductive condition, as shown by the appearance of the outer perianth whorl (Fig. 4.2).

From their initiation until the beginning of August, the growth of daughter bulbs is considerably affected by their position within the parent bulb. The outermost, first initiated, daughter bulb had a low growth rate, but the innermost bulbs which were initiated later rapidly grew to become larger than the outer daughter bulbs (Fig. 4.3). It is well established that at lifting time the inner bulbs are the largest, so that during the growth of

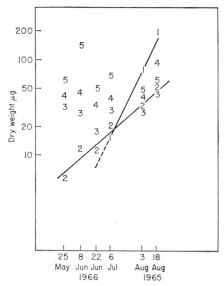

Fig. 4.3 Initiation and early growth of 'Rose Copland' tulip bulbs, within the daughter bulbs. Bulbs are numbered from the outside (No. 5) inwards. Two sets of data combined to show the difference in size between daughter bulbs until the initiation of the innermost bulb (No. 1) early in July. Thereafter growth of bulbs Nos. 1 and 2 is rapid and they soon weigh more than the slower-growing, older, outer bulbs (Rees, 1968).

the bulbs the relative magnitudes of bulb weights with position must be reversed, as shown in Fig. 4.3.

For each mother bulb scale, the rates of daughter bulb growth shown in Fig. 4.4 fall into three phases with rapid growth in autumn and spring, separated by slower growth in the winter. The data indicate that bulbs in outer positions are more variable than those in inner positions, so that delimitation of the various growth periods is more difficult.

The autumn rapid growth period was shorter for the inner daughter bulbs than the outer ones, the relative growth rates for the fitted lines of

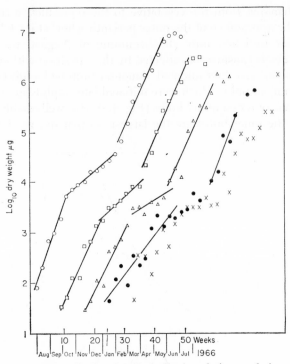

Fig. 4.4 Growth of 'Rose Copland' tulip bulbs in relation to their position in the mother bulb. Successive lines have been displaced eight weeks to the right, so the time scale applies only to the innermost bulb (open circles). Fitted lines are drawn only through the points to which they refer. Circles, squares, triangles, filled circles and crosses refer to bulbs of the first, second . . . fifth mother bulb scale, respectively (Rees, 1968).

Table 4.1

Relative growth rates (g g^{-1} day^{-1}) and standard errors for daughter bulbs in axils of different scales in the parent 'Rose Copland' tulip bulb for three periods of growth (1 = innermost position) (Rees, 1968a).

	Scale number			
	1	2	3	4
Autumn	0·057	0·044	0·040	0·025
	±0·0033	±0·0029	±0·0031	±0·0029
Winter	0·017	0·018	0·013	
	±0·0006	±0·0016	±0·0040	
Spring	0·045	0·047	0·045	0·052
	±0·0029	±0·0023	±0·0017	±0·0091

Fig. 4.4 are shown in Table 4.1, which shows that the relative growth rates of the innermost daughter bulbs were significantly higher than the others in autumn. No significant differences were detected between the winter relative growth rates of bulbs of different positions, to which lines could reasonably be fitted. The bulbs of all positions started rapid growth together in February, and no differences were found between the relative growth rates of bulbs in the axils of different scales.

The daughter bulbs tend to reach their maximum weights asymptotically, implying that any attempt to increase final bulb weight would influence the number of bulbs reaching a certain weight category, rather than increase the individual bulb size of the largest bulbs. There is also an apparently different upper limit to bulb weight in different positions. This effect persists later, because, as we have seen, bulb size has an important effect on bulb behaviour.

C. Iris

Examination of 8-cm bulbs of Iris 'Wedgwood' showed many points of similarity with tulip. There are, however, major differences in the different behaviour patterns of flowering and non-flowering bulbs. A non-flowering bulb typically produces three leaves, and more leaves are produced only if the apex is later going to initiate a flower. In the absence of a flower, the vegetative apex produces a large round bulb; if a flower is produced the daughter bulb alongside the peduncle is flattened and relatively small. Flowers are produced only by large bulbs, although storage techniques can increase the number of small bulbs which flower. There is a clear tendency (although this is by no means absolute) for biennial flowering; the large bulb produced by a vegetative plant will flower the next season by virtue of its size, but the small terminal bulb of the following season may not. Such a biennial flowering tendency has also been recorded for other bulbous plants e.g. *Allium ampeloprasum* (Jones and Mann, 1963).

In an analysis of daughter bulb growth it is therefore necessary to separate the innermost daughter bulbs of flowering plants from non-flowering ones, although the behaviour of daughter bulbs in other positions is sufficiently similar for them to be grouped together (Fig. 4.5). Early in the season (early October) the innermost daughter bulbs are the smallest, as was found in the tulip, but their growth rate is higher than that of the outer daughter bulbs and they soon become larger. There is also a significant difference between the relative growth rates of innermost daughter bulbs from vegetative and flowering mother bulbs. From the slopes of the fitted lines the relative growth rates (g g^{-1} day^{-1}) are 0·0104 ($\pm$0·00233) and 0·0219 ($\pm$0·00193) for the daughter bulbs from vegetative and flowering mother bulbs respectively, considerably lower than those for the autumn phase of tulip daughter bulb growth, but near the winter values. The difference between the vegetative and flowering samples adds weight to the conclusion drawn earlier from the tulip work that the coincidence of the initiation of the innermost daughter bulb and the transformation of the mother bulb apex to the reproductive state affects the daughter bulb growth rate. In *Iris*, flower initiation occurs at the end of the year and the benefits to daughter bulb growth are apparent from then onwards.

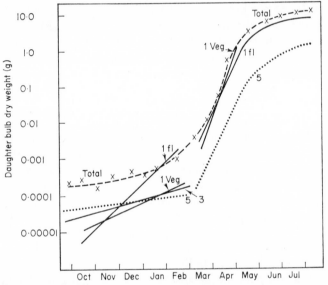

Fig. 4.5 Growth of daughter bulbs of *Iris* 'Wedgwood'. Fitted lines are shown for daughter bulbs in different positions (1, 3 and 5) within the mother bulb (1 = innermost). The innermost are differentiated into those from flowering and those from non-flowering mother bulbs. Note the change-over in the relative sizes of daughter bulbs with position, and the constant relative growth rates later.

The relative growth rates of daughter bulbs in the axil of the third and fifth scale from the centre show that there is a significant difference with position, that of the third being $0·00594$ ($\pm0·00071$) and the fifth $0·00279$ ($\pm0·00069$) g g^{-1} day^{-1}. These values are considerably smaller than those of the innermost daughter bulbs whether from vegetative or floral mother bulbs.

Total bulb weight increases rapidly from about mid-February—coinciding closely with the rapid growth periods in both tulip and *Narcissus*. The relative growth rates of daughter bulbs of vegetative and flowering mother bulbs are very similar in this period, although the former are larger because of their larger size at the start of this period. The mean value was 0.044 g g^{-1} day^{-1}, and although the lines in Fig. 4.5 show that the daughter bulbs from vegetative mother bulbs overtake those from the flowering mother bulbs, the slopes of the two lines are not significantly different (vegetative $= 0.05497$ (± 0.00576), flowering 0.04387 (± 0.00350 g g^{-1} day^{-1}).

The net outcome of the various changes in growth rates of daughter bulbs with position is a sigmoid curve showing relatively abrupt changes in relative growth rate about mid-February and mid-May.

II. Later growth of bulbs

Some consideration has been given to daughter bulb growth as it was considered worth investigating directly the growth of the plant parts of

Table 4.2

Relative growth rates (R, g^{-1} g^{-1} day^{-1}) of daughter bulbs of tulip 'Rose Copland' in the U.K. in a number of seasons in the spring phase of exponential growth (Rees, 1969b; 1971).

Site	Season		Mean R and SE		Bulb size (cm)
Kirton, Lincs	1964–5	inner	0·047	0·0016	
		↓	0·042	0·0035	
			0·038	0·0033	11
		outer	0·037	0·0035	
		total	0·045	0·0019	
G.C.R.I. Sussex	1965–6	inner	0·045	0·0029	
		↓	0·047	0·0023	
			0·045	0·0017	12
		outer	0·042	0·0091	
		total	0·045	0·0026	
G.C.R.I.	1966–7		0·043	0·0033	6, 8, 10, 12
G.C.R.I.	1968–9		0·052	0·0021	10
G.C.R.I.	1968–9		0·045	0·0018	11/12
G.C.R.I.	1968–9		0·053	0·0045	9/10

economic value to the grower—in this case the bulbs—in addition to a more formal investigation of rates of energy fixation and total dry matter gain as considered in Chapter 3. For an investigation of relative growth rates it is convenient to plot dry weights obtained at regular sampling

82   THE GROWTH OF BULBS

intervals on a log scale against time when the relative growth rates are the
slopes of the fitted regression lines.

Most of the growth of the daughter bulbs in tulip, which has been used
for nearly all this work, occurs during the latter part of the life of the
daughter bulb, i.e. during the "spring-phase" of growth. Four years' data
for 'Rose Copland' are shown in Table 4.2; although there was an effect of
position within the mother bulb in one season (1964–5) this was very small
and was not observed in 1965–6. The absence of large differences in
relative growth rate suggested that the relative growth rate is controlled by
internal factors such as rates of cell division or translocation.

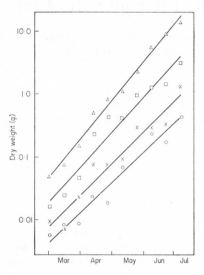

Fig. 4.6. Growth of daughter bulbs of tulip 'Rose Copland' in different positions
within the mother bulb. Triangles, squares, crosses and circles represent data
from the innermost to the outer positions, respectively. Bulbs grown at Kirton,
1964–5 season.

Figures 4.6 and 4.7 show that the logarithmic rates of growth persist
about 14 weeks. Mother bulb size has no effect on daughter bulb relative
growth rates although there are differences in final daughter bulb weight
attributable to the differences in daughter bulb weight at the start of the
observations—large mother bulbs contain larger daughter bulbs (Fig. 4.7).
Varietal differences do, however, exist, and significantly higher rates were
observed in 'Apeldoorn' than with two other cultivars 'Weber' and 'Golden
Harvest' (Fig. 4.8). The different relative growth rates are not the whole
reason for the eventual differences in final bulb weight because again
there is an effect of initial bulb size on final bulb weight, and although the

final daughter bulb weights were in the order expected; these were attained in different ways. With 'Apeldoorn', initial bulb weight was low but relative growth rate was high; in 'Boule de Neige' on the other hand, a low relative growth rate combined with a low initial daughter bulb weight to give the lowest final bulb weight. Both the other cultivars had high initial bulb weights but moderate relative growth rates (Rees, 1971).

In general terms, the final weight of an organ depends on its relative growth rate and initial size of the organ; the importance of these two factors

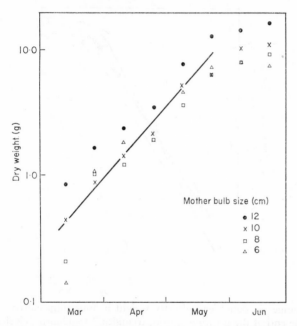

Fig. 4.7 Growth of daughter bulbs of tulip 'Rose Copland' from mother bulbs of four sizes (Rees, 1969b).

was established as long ago as 1919 by Blackman. Two other factors recognized by Ashby (1932) were the duration of the period of constant relative growth and the shape of the curve thereafter. These four factors completely define the system.

Considering the general form of the sigmoid growth pattern of daughter bulbs from the horticultural point of view, i.e. in order to increase the weight of daughter bulbs produced, our ignorance of some of these aspects becomes obvious, although some deductions can be made about others. The terminal part of the curve is probably the least important because it contributes only a small amount to relative growth, it persists only a short time and it occurs at approximately the same time in bulbs of different sizes and even of different cultivars. This suggests external control within a single season.

The relative growth rates of 'Rose Copland' are remarkably constant for about 14 weeks irrespective of season and site. Even in the faster growing 'Apeldoorn' daughter bulbs (with relative growth rates of 0.075 g g^{-1} day^{-1} compared with those of 'Rose Copland' at 0.047 g g^{-1} day^{-1}) the rate is low compared with a number of estimates available for similar organs such as

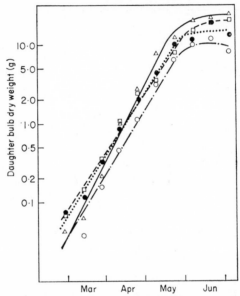

Fig. 4.8 Changes in daughter bulb dry weight in four tulip cultivars from early March to the end of the growing season, triangles, 'Apeldoorn'; circles, 'Boule de Neige'; squares, 'Golden Harvest'; solid circles, 'Weber' (Rees, 1971).

plant apices, buds and young leaves. These show a range of 0.14–1.4 g g^{-1} day^{-1}, whilst potato tubers have a relative growth rate of 0.12 g g^{-1} day^{-1} (Milthorpe, 1963). No information is available on the factors controlling the constancy of the relative growth rate, but it may be speculated that these operate at a fundamental level such as on the rate of cell division or enlargement, rather than on translocation rates, which could hardly be expected to remain constant for so long unless the flow of carbohydrates to the daughter bulbs was controlled by a feed-back mechanism operated by the bulbs. For the greater part of the period of growth, the rate is independent of total carbohydrate production by the leaves. The proximity of daughter bulbs to large quantities of food materials in the bulb scales ensures that food reserves do not limit growth in the early stages, and, as the daughter bulb contains very little non-growing tissue a logarithmic growth rate can be maintained. Later in the season, as the mother bulb reserves are depleted, there is a transition in the carbohydrate supply from the mother bulb to current photosynthesis, but this is not accompanied by any change in growth rate. Because of the exponential form of growth in the daughter bulbs, there are some implications on the demands made upon the photosynthetic system. The peak of photosynthetic production, controlled by leaf area and incoming radiation, coincides with the maximum absolute growth rate demands by the daughter bulbs.

Because of the coincidence in time of the slowing down of the relative growth of daughter bulbs and of leaf ageing and death, it is assumed that the latter is causative, although the available information is too scant to be definite. There is some further growth of daughter bulbs after leaf senescence has started and it is assumed that this is partly due to the transfer of materials to the bulbs from the senescing stem.

Attempts to delay leaf senescence by surgically removing daughter bulbs at the time of peak leaf area were ineffective. In some other plants the removal of major sinks (stem apices, or flowers in annuals) has prolonged leaf viability. It would appear that in the tulip leaf senescence is not a *result* of falling daughter bulb growth rates.

The time at which the constant relative growth rate ends varies considerably from season to season, depending on weather conditions, especially temperature, and probably also on water stress. It is probable that senescence is an irreversible process "triggered" by high temperature. Season-to-season differences in the start of senescence are important determinants of the large season-to-season differences in bulb yield. Similarly, there are site differences in productivity, as demonstrated by Waister and Joy (1968) who showed a 15% increase in dry bulb yield in 'Rose Copland' grown in the east of Scotland compared with growth in the English midlands in an identical medium with soil moisture controlled by tensiometers. This difference was attributed to cooler summer conditions further north, resulting in a longer growing season.

Daughter bulbs have a maximum size, characteristic for the cultivar, but the factors controlling this are not known. Presumably cell number and a limiting cell size are important and these may be determined some time before final bulb weight is reached, especially if cell division is more important early in the life of the daughter bulbs. It was shown earlier (Fig. 4.4) that the larger, innermost, daughter bulbs reached their final weight sooner than smaller bulbs within the same mother bulb, implying that available materials were translocated to the larger bulbs at an exponential rate until they neared their full potential size, after which time more

G

materials were available for the continued growth of the other bulbs. There appear to be differences in the potential size which can be attained by individual daughter bulbs, depending on their position within the mother bulb, the size of the mother bulb and the cultivar. Growth studies, as a tool for investigating yield, are then concerned with how closely the potential weight is approached under the growing conditions employed.

At the lower end of the phase of constant relative growth rate (early in March) two factors have an important bearing on final bulb weight. Firstly there is the time at which the linear growth rate starts and secondly there is the "initial" weight of the daughter bulbs and how this was determined. Only one set of data exists on early growth of tulip daughter bulbs (Fig. 4.4) and this shows that 'Rose Copland' daughter bulbs start rapid growth in mid-February, somewhat before the maximum total dry weight point of Fig. 3.1, and that all daughter bulbs start growing at the same time, irrespective of size (equivalent to position within mother bulb). This point in time is clearly demarcated; previous growth rates, although logarithmic, are slower. This curious time for the start of rapid growth in the field, when soil temperatures are low, suggests that the phenomenon may be a "bulbing" effect induced by the day length increasing beyond the critical value. A similar phenomenon has been demonstrated in onion (Jones and Mann, 1963) where it is more easily observed in plants grown from seed. This relative growth rate burst in early February has also been observed in *Narcissus* and in *Iris* (see Figs 4.1 and 4.5). In *Narcissus*, older parts lose weight at this time and materials are translocated to younger ones. No new parts are produced, so this is a true bulbing effect, whatever is the causal factor. Attempts to demonstrate a photoperiodic cause of the bulbing have not been successful however, perhaps because the temperatures used were too high. Heath and Holdsworth (1948) demonstrated strong temperature/photoperiod interactions in onion; similar phenomena may occur in other bulbous plants.

The early growth of daughter bulbs has been described previously; the "initial" bulb weight at the start of the period of rapid, spring, exponential growth is the result of a complex of circumstances including position within the mother bulb, the size of the mother bulb (which affects the time of initiation) the rate of early growth and also the duration of the various growth periods.

Apical dominance is a cause of some varietal differences in behaviour. This may affect the number of daughter bulbs surviving, especially under adverse conditions, e.g. high planting densities which result in large numbers of small bulbs or a few large bulbs being produced. Daughter bulb size at the start of the spring growth period may also be affected by apical dominance. In 'Apeldoorn', which shows strong apical dominance, daughter bulbs at the start of spring growth were smaller than in some other cultivars (Fig. 4.8).

Further work has shown that partial defoliation of tulip plants (removal of half the basal leaf or half every leaf, so that 76% and 52%, respectively of the original leaf area remained) reduced relative growth rate of daughter bulbs approximately in proportion to the area of leaf removed. An interesting result was that obtained when bulbs were heat-treated to kill flowers (*blindstoken*), a treatment frequently used commercially to increase bulb yield. This increased the daughter bulb weight at the start of the spring period of exponential growth, and led to higher bulb yields at the end of the season although plant leaf area and its duration were unaffected, and daughter bulb relative growth rates were not different in treated and untreated plants.

III. Yield improvement

Our knowledge of daughter bulb growth, and hence the process of yield determination, is very imperfect; but there are some features which could perhaps be modified in a search for higher yield. On theoretical grounds it would be advantageous to start the period of rapid spring growth with larger daughter bulbs and to maintain as high a rate of relative growth as possible, for as long as possible. This might be an idealized picture because some of these factors could be inversely correlated, e.g. rapid growth and large daughter bulb weight initially. Further, there could be limits to individual bulb size, so that growth could be considered only as falling short of potential maximum due to seasonal, competition or biotic factors. Little information exists on this point, apart from individual plant yields under "no-competition" conditions, which gave values for 'Rose Copland' and 'Apeldoorn' of 62 and 92 g fresh weight of bulbs per planted bulb. Clearly hybridization and selection for some of these factors are important; the great success of the Darwin hybrid cultivars (including the most popular tulip 'Apeldoorn') must be largely due to its high bulb productivity.

Although there is ample evidence that the constancy of relative growth rates of daughter bulbs is maintained through much of the growing season irrespective of site or season for one variety, it is surprising that it is constant for such a long period in a changing environment. From mid-February until nearly the end of May radiation and soil temperature both increase considerably. Data were available for the growth of daughter bulbs in a controlled-environment cabinet at $10°C$ and from bulbs grown in a glasshouse at $18°C$. From the estimates of the relative growth rates of the daughter bulbs a Q_{10} for daughter bulb growth of 2.2 was obtained. This value was used to derive fortnightly estimates of relative growth rate from the record of soil temperature at 10 cm and the resultant line was compared with the observed values, starting at a common point (Fig. 4.9).

The agreement between this theoretical line and that obtained from the linear regression is close and shows that the increase in daughter bulb relative growth rate due to higher temperatures as the season progresses is

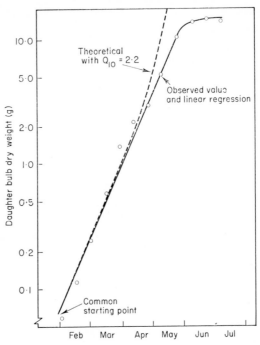

Fig. 4.9 Observed values of daughter bulb dry weights of tulip 'Rose Copland' compared with a curve constructed from a common starting point and a Q_{10} of 2·2, using weekly mean 10 cm soil temperatures (Rees, 1971).

almost exactly balanced by the falling off of the relative growth rate as the bulbs become larger. In the last few weeks of exponential rate, however, when the theoretical curve predicts an increase in growth rate above the previous exponential rate there is a divergence with the actual relative growth rate continuing at the same rate as earlier. This is evidence then, that the abrupt end of the exponential rate is an artefact, and that the upper end of the curve would fall off sooner in a more constant environment; the otherwise falling rate is compensated by the rising temperature during the spring. Similar comparisons with the other two sets of data of Table 4.1

showed close agreement between the theoretical curves and those actually obtained.

One obvious point of attack in the quest for higher yield is the built-in dormancy which results in early leaf senescence, and the ending of the exponential rate of daughter bulb growth. One extra week at the end of the exponential rate period would increase the daughter bulb weight of 'Rose Copland' from 18 to 23 g dry weight plant^{-1} and of 'Apeldoorn' from 26 to 36 g dry weight plant^{-1}. Some success has been achieved with other crop plants from spraying foilage to prevent senescence. Kinetin is an obvious possibility which is unlikely to be commercially useful because of expense. Wangerman (1965) concludes that competition for nitrogen is an essential factor in ageing, but Richards and Templeman (1936) stated that although senescence was accompanied by loss of nitrogen some other factor was involved. Little is known about root senescence and it was at least possible that nitrogen uptake was restricted at this time, leading to possible value of foliar nitrogenous sprays. Another possibility was the use of fungicidal sprays in an attempt to control leaf microflora (largely yeasts) associated with the breakdown of plant cuticle in senescing leaves (Last and Price, 1969).

Both possibilities were tested in the two seasons, 1966 and 1968. Sprays of ammonium nitrate (0·75 M) and fungicide (zineb at 1·8 g litre^{-1} in 1966 and a manganese, zinc, iron, dithiocarbamate complex at 10 g litre^{-1} in 1968) were applied fortnightly (or less frequently if adequate deposits remained on the leaves) to *Narcissus* and tulip plots in the field. The sprayed foliage remained green longer than those of the control plants, but the effect was small. However, a yield increase of 14·5% was obtained with nitrogenous sprays on *Narcissus* (but not tulip) in the first year and an increase of 10% with tulip (but not *Narcissus*) following both treatments in the second year. Clearly the method has some promise but further work is necessary on a large scale to confirm these gains and also to resolve some of the failures. On a field scale these benefits are probably already being achieved because of routine sprays to control leaf diseases. It is important that these are continued until the end of senescence for maximum benefit.

IV. Selection on the basis of daughter bulb growth

A method for selecting élite stocks of tulips has been developed by Hekstra (1968). This is based on the size distribution of daughter bulbs, which are described by their positions within the mother bulb. The innermost daughter bulb is called the A bulb, and the bulbs in the axils of the other scales are called the B, C, D and E bulbs, in order centrifugally. The bulb in the tunic axil is the H bulb.

In normal practice when a cultivar is being multiplied before it is commercially available, all daughter bulbs are replanted; when sufficient have been obtained the largest bulbs (above 11 cm, nearly all A bulbs) are removed from the stock for sale. Continuation of this process over a number of seasons is said to lead to a decrease in the production of large bulbs and an increased production of small bulbs. Hekstra's intention was to counteract the tendency to remove large bulbs from the stock by selection of planting material.

A number of experiments were done over three years where the bulb types A to D and H were graded into the following categories: 3–4 cm, 4–5 cm . . . 15–16 cm, and the characteristics of the resultant spectrum of bulbs were examined for three cultivars with different daughter bulb production characteristics. These were:

'Edith Eddy' (Triumph) which produces many daughter bulbs
'Apeldoorn' (Darwin hybrid) which has a "normal" daughter bulb
    production
'Pandion' (Darwin) which produces few daughter bulbs

The following main results were obtained:

1. Bulb weight decreases from A to D within a grade (E bulbs, which are rare in mother bulbs below 11 cm are included with D bulbs). H bulbs are as heavy as B bulbs. Only from large mother bulbs are B bulbs as heavy as A bulbs. Weight differences are largely attributable to the flatter shape of the outer bulbs.
2. Scale number within the daughter bulb decreases from A to D within a grade, but nearly disappear when the comparison is made on a weight basis.
3. There is little effect of the parent bulb size on daughter bulb production, and no effect of mother bulb type.
4. Positive linear relations exist between bulb weight and
   (a) scale number up to the maximum scale number for that cultivar in that season
   (b) the number of daughter bulbs, and
   (c) absolute weight increase.
5. The weight of the planted bulb shows a parabolic relation with the weight of the main daughter bulb produced from it, so that for large planted bulbs the weight of the main daughter bulb falls beyond a peak main daughter bulb weight.

Because the differences between planting bulb types lead to differences in the proportions of large saleable bulbs and smaller replanting stock, the combination of different bulb types in a bulb stock is important, especially in cultivars with a high number of daughter bulbs. The maximum production with a good balance of bulb types is achieved with a large proportion of A bulbs in the stock, and this can be achieved only by planting the very small bulbs (even as small as four cm) which are normally discarded. A scheme was described for the separation of bulbs, and this is shown in Fig.

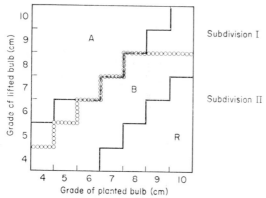

Fig. 4.10 Schema for separating lifted bulb types from different planting grades. In the sectors separated by solid lines, A contains more than 90% A bulbs and a few B bulbs; B contains more than 50% B bulbs, some R and some A bulbs; R contains mostly C, D and H bulbs and some B bulbs (see text) (Hekstra, 1968).

4.10. All grades are planted, harvested and graded separately. The bulbs are then divided into two stocks, shown by the dotted line of Fig. 4.10. Stock I comprises all bulbs that are larger than the planted bulb size (90% of these are A bulbs) and also includes 9 and 10 cm bulbs from the planting sizes 9 and 10 cm. Stock II comprises bulbs of the same grade as the planting material (except 9 and 10 cm) and, in addition, two or three grades below the planting size. In the second growing season Stock I is again split into two; from Stock II only Stock I is replanted and Stock II/II is discarded. These separations can be made mechanically.

This method is essentially a means for selecting bulbs on the basis of vigour; any bulbs which grow more slowly than the selected standard are discarded. Plants exhibiting the unfavourable characters of rapid multiplication and small daughter bulbs, which are commonly referred to as "wild" forms or "thieves", multiply at about three times the normal rate within the stock. This rate can be reduced considerably by the proposed selection methods.

Cultivars which produce few daughter bulbs, like 'Pandion', present different problems, and planting very large bulbs to produce many planting sized bulbs is to be recommended. Main bulbs in very small planted bulbs grow very rapidly and few small daughter bulbs are produced, so that planting bulbs as small as three cm is necessary and very useful for high production.

V. Temperature and bulb production

Effects of temperature on bulbing in the tulip were studied by Le Nard and Cohat (1968) using a complex series of temperature treatments involving transfers between 18–20°C, 10°C and 2–3°C, in an attempt to show whether the restricted elongation of shoots caused by some treatments was related to bulbing. These workers distinguished two processes in the bulb production of the tulip, the first an inductive process and the second the manifestation of bulbing. The first process requires low temperatures, with 2–3°C more effective than 10°C whilst 20°C was completely ineffective. At 20°C the daughter bulbs bore aerial parts in lieu of mother bulbs scales. After induction, bulb formation is more rapid at higher temperatures (at least from 2 to 16°C), so that bulbing occurs faster at 10°C than at 2–3°C for bulbs kept constantly at these temperatures.

The relationship between bulbing and elongation in the tulip depends on the degree of differentiation of the daughter bulbs. If the parts are well differentiated before the start of low temperature, and if the low-temperature treatment does not exceed 20 weeks at 10°C or 30 weeks at 2–3°C, elongation after planting is stimulated. Extending the low-temperature period beyond these limits results in flower abortion. In extreme cases new bulbs may form during low-temperature storage so that no elongation of the shoot occurs after planting.

If the organs are insufficiently differentiated when the cold period starts, or at planting, they cannot respond. Bulbing can, however, and the start of this process inhibits subsequent elongation either partially or completely. Thus cold storage started too early can reduce or prevent elongation in the same way as too long a period of low temperature. No flowers result in either case.

A period at low temperature stimulates an induction of bulbing and shoot elongation, and 30°C (provided the low-temperature period was not too long) can nullify both processes, suggesting that there may be a common mechanism for initial stages of both bulbing and shoot elongation.

VI. The appearance of tulip bulbs

Saleability of bulbs is often affected by the appearance of the tunics; if cracked or missing the bulbs are unattractive. Soil structure affects bulb skin appearance with open sandy soils and good constant water supply both promoting good quality skins. Very rapid drying of bulbs can cause split skins, and time of lifting the bulbs also determines the toughness of the tunic.

Some commercial systems are widely used for producing tough attractive skins; these vary somewhat in detail but basically involve lifting the bulbs whilst the skin is still white, washing the bulbs, then drying them for up to 48 h at 34°C. By this time the outer bulb scale has turned brown. This treatment can restrict rooting and is not recommended for bulbs to be used for rapid growing or forcing where poor root development produces blind flowers. Treated bulbs are less prone to storage troubles, and cleaning costs are reduced by up to a third.

VII. Artificial induction of daughter bulbs

In a number of commercially important bulbous ornamentals, especially those which normally produce very few daughter bulbs, artificial means are used to increase the number of bulbs produced. Hyacinths are normally propagated in this way, but similar techniques are used at times for lilies, *Narcissus* and *Hippeastrum*.

Scooping and cross-cutting are horticultural terms for techniques used for hyacinth propagation where the bases of the bulbs are wounded by removing a sector of the base plate or incising it by deep cuts which kill the shoot, Fig. 4.11. This removal of apical dominance results in the formation of numerous daughter bulbs along the cut edges of the scales (about 25 from cross-cutting and 25–50 from scooping). Originally, hyacinths were grown until the bulbs became large and showed some tendency to lose apical dominance naturally and form clusters of daughter bulbs. This method of propagation was not reliable, however, so by the end of the nineteenth century scooping of hyacinths had become an established procedure, starting from a simple removal of part of the base plate and developing into an accurate technique where the whole of the base plate was removed. Cross-cutting was a later development which was first used about 1935.

Because of the numbers of daughter bulbs which result from one mother bulb, it is important to segregate the mother bulbs a year in advance and to remove any plants exhibiting abnormal behaviour, especially those with virus symptoms. After lifting, hyacinth bulbs are dried for not more than two days in a shaded spot, then stored at 25°C for at least one week before cross-cutting (two weeks before scooping); a mercurial dip followed by drying ensures surface sterility.

Cross-cutting is more usually employed for large old bulbs of 19–20 cm grade, from which only a few young bulbs develop, but these grow to maturity in one year less than the bulbs formed after scooping. There are also varietal differences which determine whether it is better to use one technique rather than the other; cultivars which produce small bulbs are best treated by cross-cutting to reduce bulb number.

Bulbs are scooped using a special knife or spoon and a curved section is removed from the base of the bulb; in cross-cutting three incisions (four exceptionally) are made through the bottom of the bulb. In both cases the

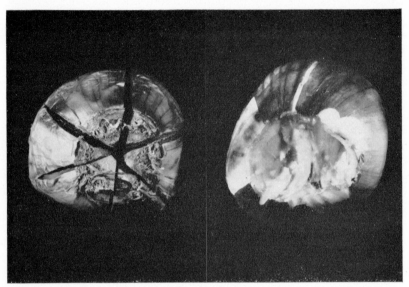

Fig. 4.11 *Narcissus* bulbs treated by cross-cutting (left) and by scooping (right) to induce the formation of daughter bulbs along the cut edges of the scales, viewed from below. (Photo. courtesy G.C.R.I.)

aim is to destroy the growing point and encourage the development and growth of the lateral bulbs. The operation requires skill because the lowest cells of the scales have the capacity to form new meristems; too deep a cut removes these cells. Too shallow a scooping leaves parts of the base plate attached to the scales; these prevent bulblet formation.

After scooping the cut surfaces are sterilized with hypochlorite solution and placed on wire-mesh trays in layers in a propagating chamber at 21°C and low humidity to encourage callusing. The temperature is gradually raised to 30°C and a relative humidity of 85% as the scale bases swell. Cross-cut bulbs are buried for two weeks in an inverted position under clean dry sand for callusing to occur. The bulbs are then transferred to a propagating chamber at 21°C and the temperature is raised gradually to

30°C with 85% relative humidity. After three months the bulbs are hardened off for a few days before planting, usually near the end of November.

A. Propagation from scales

Many bulbs when cut into constituent scales or scale parts, produce new bulblets, usually near the base of the scale. Essentially the method is therefore similar to those of cross-cutting and scooping where the removal of apical dominance results in the initiation and growth of new daughter bulbs. Propagation from scales is most frequently used with lilies (Figs 4.12 and 4.13).

The outer scales are normally removed after flowering from a well-established parent plant, which is then replanted to recover. The scales

Fig. 4.12 Production of daughter bulbs on scales of lily cv. 'Enchantment' that were removed from the mother bulb and kept in moist vermiculite at 23°C for four weeks. (Photo. courtesy G.C.R.I.)

are planted in soil 2 cm apart and 6 cm deep in open beds or frames or in rows 15 cm apart. Alternatively, scales can be removed in September and kept warm and moist in boxes of sand or sphagnum peat in alternate layers of scales and sand to a depth of 30 cm. The small bulbs which form can be transferred to the open ground in the spring.

Work in the Netherlands has defined more closely the optimum conditions for lily scale propagation (Schenk and Boontjes, 1970). Scales were stored in moist vermiculite in polythene-lined boxes and the best temperature regime was found to be 23°C (6 weeks) then 17°C (4 weeks) followed by 5°C (12 weeks).

For *Lilium speciosum* and *L. longiflorum* it was found that rapid and good bulblet production was obtained only from the outer and middle scales of parent bulbs. Earlier harvest and scaling resulted in much larger

Fig. 4.13 Daughter bulb production from "twin-scales" of *Narcissus* cut from whole bulbs and kept at 23°C in moist vermiculite for two months. (Photo. courtesy G.C.R.I.)

bulblets. Large effects of rooting media were also obtained, soil and sand being superior to vermiculite and sawdust, and temperatures of 15–25°C and 30–60% moisture in the medium were recommended. In an attempt to increase the numbers of bulbs produced from each scale, these were cut longitudinally or horizontally but this had little effect. Gibberellins at 50 and 100 ppm inhibited root and bulblet formation (Hosaka and Yokoi, 1959).

Robb (1967) investigated the growth of excised tissue from bulb scales of *Lilium speciosum*. Explants regenerated bulblets in 15–16 weeks from mesophyll tissue; buds being formed from cells in superficial layers, and roots from deeper layers. The regenerative capacity was found to be strongly seasonal, with 77% regeneration in spring, 52 in autumn, only 2 in summer and none in winter. Only basal explants regenerated freely, while those from scale tips never did so.

In lilies, the bulblet originates by the simultaneous division of epidermal and sub-epidermal cells following periderm and callus formation on the wound surface (Godden and Watson, 1962).

Hyacinths can be propagated from leaf cuttings and flower stems as well as from scales of the old bulb; here too the adventitious bulbs develop from epidermal and sub-epidermal cells and not from pre-formed meristematic tissue (Naylor, 1940).

Propagation from scales can also be used for *Narcissus*, *Amaryllis* and other genera if necessary (e.g. the propagation of valuable new cultivars or of virus-free stock) but the natural rate of multiplication is usually sufficiently rapid to make such techniques unnecessary.

Chapter 5 ⸺

Flower initiation and differentiation

"... the force that through the green fuse drives the flower."   Dylan Thomas

Flowering in bulbous plants was first studied intensively in the early 1920s by Blaauw in the Netherlands. This work, which started with a morphological investigation of the hyacinth, was later extended to other bulbous plants and to more physiological aspects of bulb behaviour, by Blaauw's school at Wageningen and by van Slogteren at the Laboratorium voor Bloembollenonderzoek at Lisse. Because of the commercial importance of bulb growing in the Netherlands, much of the work was directed towards commercial ends, and it has been criticized because it was almost completely descriptive. More recently, attempts have been made to explain the observed behaviour patterns and to investigate some of the biochemical changes associated with the observed effects of temperature treatments.

I. Time of flower initiation

Bulb plants differ in the time at which floral initiation occurs. *Narcissus* bulbs have usually initiated flowers by lifting time in June or July, and flower formation starts in early May in both southern England (Preece and Morrison, 1963) and in the Netherlands, where Gerritsen and van der Kloot (1936) observed that 40% of bulbs had initiated flowers by the first week in May. Tulip and hyacinth apices are in the vegetative state at lifting time in July and flower initiation occurs when the bulbs are in storage. Bulbous *Iris* (with the exception of *I. reticulata*) form their flowers some considerable time after replanting in the autumn; under Dutch conditions usually in March, but in some years as early as January. In *Iris* 'Imperator' grown at 9°C, floral initiation occurs when the sprouts are 6 cm long. In *Iris* 'Wedgwood' flower formation starts in mid-November or earlier, depending on previous temperature, with a greater requirement for a high temperature pre-treatment after harvesting following a cool summer (Hartsema and Luyten, 1940). Floral differentiation in 'Creole' Easter lily does not occur until the main axis is at least 25 cm long, which is about a month after planting (Emsweller and Pryor, 1943).

Because of the obvious relevance of bulb lifting date to any programme of storage, Hartsema (1961) has classified the initiation and subsequent growth of flowers into seven response groups, of which only five are of relevance to true bulbs:

1. Flowers initiated during the spring or early summer of the year preceding that in which they reach anthesis and before the bulbs are lifted, e.g. *Narcissus, Galanthus, Leucojum.*
2. Flowers initiated following the previous growing period, so that the bulbs have initiated flowers by replanting time in the autumn, e.g. *Tulipa, Hyacinthus, Iris reticulata.*
3. Flowers initiated after replanting, at the low temperatures of winter or early spring, e.g. bulbous *Iris* but not *I. reticulata.*
4. Flowers initiated more than a year before anthesis, e.g. *Nerine.*
5. Flower initiation alternates with leaf formation through the whole growing period e.g. *Hippeastrum, Zephyranthes*, both tropical species where young developing buds and large flower buds nearing anthesis are present in the same bulb.

II. Stages of flower differentiation

The developmental stages of flower differentiation have been described using general symbols by Beijer (1942) as follows:

Stage I apex vegetative, flat
Stage II apex dome-shaped
Sp spathe initiated (in *Narcissus*)
P1 3 outer perianth primordia distinguishable
P2 3 inner   ,,   ,,   ,,
A1 3 outer anther   ,,   ,,

A2 3 inner   ,,   ,,   ,,
G   3 carpel   ,,   ,,   ,,
Pc paracorolla apparent (in *Narcissus*)

This schema is not directly applicable to all bulbous plants; for instance there is only a single anther whorl in *Iris* and this is formed before the perianth parts. It is a very useful shorthand means of describing the

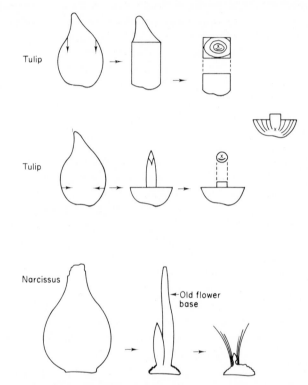

Tulip

Tulip

Narcissus

←Old flower base

Fig. 5.1 Diagrams illustrating methods of dissecting tulip and *Narcissus* bulbs. The position of the apex is shown by "x".

stages of apex development and is widely used. A number of descriptions exist of methods of dissecting *Narcissus* and tulip bulbs for determining the stage of apical development. This is done to see whether flower differentiation is completed, or whether it has started; because of the different amounts of shoot growth the techniques will differ somewhat. If the sole purpose is to find whether or not a flower is present, usually at a late stage, then a longitudinal splitting of the bulb is sufficient.

For tulips, where the apex is in the centre of the concentric scales and leaves, it is easiest to remove part of the four sides of the bulb to leave a cube standing on the base plate. The cube can then be cut away serially towards the base plate. The height of the shoot will depend on the time of year; before flower initiation has started, the apex is very near the base plate, and can be located under the split present in the basal part of the columnar innermost scale, see Fig. 5.1. At this stage the apex and associated leaves are very small and easily missed. Later, when flower formation is complete and some extension of the axis has occurred, the apex is larger and more easily found, in the centre of the bulb. An alternative method for tulips is to make an equatorial cut and remove the outer scales to leave only the central cylindrical scale. This can then be sliced transversely until a crescent-shaped slit is visible. Extending the ends of the slit and cutting downwards to the base plate opens the cavity in which the pale green apex is visible.

For *Narcissus*, it is most convenient to remove outer bulb tissues in three segments isolated by longitudinal cuts from the tip of the bulb to the base plate. When the innermost bulb unit (bud) is located next to the base of the previous flower (identified by its non-concentric base) this can be dissected by two longitudinal cuts along the wings of the bulb unit which will then separate the leaf primordia to expose the flower enclosed in its spathe. For information on developmental stages the spathe must be split open and the perianth parts removed. The final stage of development, that of the paracorolla, is very difficult to discern, partly because the cut edges of the perianth resemble the young paracorolla.

Einert *et al.* (1970) have recently described a technique for preparing intact apices of lily for determining floral initiation using scanning electron microscopy. The apices, after removing leaves under running water, were frozen in liquid nitrogen, freeze-dried on carbon discs and coated with carbon before viewing. The whole process takes less than 9 h, and can also be adapted for light microscopy.

III. Factors affecting initiation and differentiation

A. Bulb size

It is well known that bulbs below a certain size do not flower. Each species and cultivar has a minimum bulb size at which flowering will occur, although this is not the only internal factor determining flowering. A very small tulip bulb attached to a large bulb frequently flowers although the flower is small and usually valueless commercially. This indicates the

H

possible transfer of a flowering stimulus to the smaller bulb which overrides the normal size limitations. The critical size for the flowering of tulip bulbs is between 6 and 9 cm, with some varietal differences, whilst that for hyacinth is between 6 and 8 cm. Bulbs are measured by the circumference of circular holes used to sieve the bulbs and separate them into grades. For *Iris* 'Imperator', 'Wedgwood' and 'H. C. van Vliet' the critical sizes are, respectively, 5–6 cm, 7–8 cm and 5–6 cm, (Blaauw, 1934; Kamerbeek, 1965). Blaauw (1941) stressed, however, that critical size in *Iris* was unrelated to bulb age. After a cool summer, heat treatment of the bulbs after lifting is necessary to ensure a higher percentage of flowering, especially in bulbs near the critical size for flowering, but little is known about the mechanism whereby an otherwise non-flowering bulb is stimulated to flower.

Rodrigues Pereira (1964) has demonstrated the presence of gibberellin-like substances in *Iris* bulbs which are translocated to the apex during the cold treatment which normally precedes flower initiation. There is evidence suggesting that the failure of flowering in small bulbs may be due to an insufficient total amount of gibberellin-like substances in the bulb scales. The concentration of gibberellin in the bulb scales is relatively constant, but a larger bulb will contain a larger total amount; it is therefore more likely to flower than a smaller bulb. If these substances are shown to be implicated in floral initiation in bulbs, then the theory is an attractive one as it explains the dependence of flowering on bulb size.

Little is known of any factors controlling the timing of floral initiation. It appears that photoperiod is not involved, as flowers can be initiated at abnormal times of the year in tulip, *Narcissus* and *Iris* without recourse to photoperiodic treatments. Hartsema (1961) stated that flower formation in bulbous plants "is not affected by light, nor by daylength". In the non-periodic bulbs, e.g. *Hippeastrum*, flower initiation occurs regularly throughout the year irrespective of seasonal effects.

B. Stage of apex development

The stage of development of the apex is important in determining flower initiation times. To produce a normal tulip plant, for instance, the apex must clearly produce a number of scales, a number of leaves and finally a terminal flower, a sequence that takes over a year to complete. It is perhaps naïve to suggest that a minimum leaf number is necessary for flower initiation! It is a more realistic concept that flower initiation in the tulip plant *can* only occur at a certain stage in the life cycle, although the control mechanism is far from clear. In *Narcissus*, Hartsema (1961) suggested that the presence of assimilating leaves is essential for flower initiation; this was based on results of experiments where leaves were removed before flower initiation had begun. Continued removal of leaf bases was necessary to prevent flower initiation completely. Bulb size was reduced by the defoliation treatments, but bulb size was not a complicating factor, because flowers were completed in all cases where a spathe had been initiated. In hyacinth the change-over to the flowering state can be induced at any time by high-temperature treatment within the range 20–28°C.

C. Temperature

Temperature is the most important factor affecting initiation and subsequent flower development. It has been the subject of a large volume of work, and a number of reviews, the most important of which is that by Hartsema (1961). The temperatures for most rapid floral initiation are shown in Table 5.1. All these estimates were made some years ago in the Netherlands, and with the exception of *Iris*, all have high optima. Although the

Table 5.1

Floral initiation in relation to temperature

Genus	Optimum Temperature °C	Temperature Range °C	Authority
Narcissus	17–20	13–25	Gerritsen and van der Kloot 1936
Tulipa	17–20	9–28	Luyten *et al.*, 1926
Hyacinthus	25·5	20–28	Blaauw 1924, Waterschoot 1927
Iris	13	5–20	Blaauw 1941, Hartsema and Luyten 1955
Lilium	20–23	13–23	Hartsema, 1961

optimum temperatures are often well-defined, the range over which flower initiation will eventually occur is very wide. *Iris* is an exception because flower initiation occurs after planting in the autumn and has an optimum near 13°C. A high storage temperature (such as 25·5°C) strongly inhibits flower initiation and the bulbs remain vegetative. This temperature has long been accepted as the most favourable for the storage of bulbs both experimentally and commercially (Beijer, 1952). Between 20 and 25·5°C flower primordia are formed but these are short-lived and soon abort. Storage at temperatures between 2 and 20°C may result in floral initiation; the rate of the process is closely dependent on storage temperatures.

More flowers are initiated in *Iris* bulbs if they are stored at high temperatures before transfer to 13°C. After 1–5 weeks above 20°C all the bulbs in the experiment of Hartsema and Luyten (1955) initiated flowers, and higher temperatures, up to 33°C for one week, accelerated the process. In contrast, low temperatures (2–9°C) for 5–10 weeks decreased the number of bulbs flowering, and the lower the temperature the more marked the decrease. Only in *Iris* has evidence been obtained for effects of temperature on flower initiation as a qualitative process.

The effect of temperature on flower initiation in tulip 'Pride of Haarlem' was investigated in detail by Luyten, Joustra and Blaauw (1926), who stored uniform large bulbs at a range of 11 temperatures from 1·5 to 35°C and dissected 10 bulbs from each treatment every fortnight. After two weeks, flower initiation had begun between 13 and 23°C. After four weeks of storage the optimum temperature for rapid development dropped slightly from 17–20°C. Eventually flower initiation started over the whole range except for 35°C.

A study of the effects of temperature on flower initiation in *Narcissus* is more difficult because flower initiation has begun or may even be completed before lifting, but from early lifted 'King Alfred', Gerritsen and van der Kloot (1936) concluded that the optimum temperature was 20°C at first, but that the optimum gradually fell to 13°C.

D. Seasonal effects

Although it is known that growing season differences do affect flower initiation and differentiation, few sets of comparable data exist to indicate

Table 5.2

Dates of completion of flower differentiation in *Narcissus* and tulip cultivars in different seasons at Kirton, after storage in an unheated building following lifting (*Narcissus*) and at 20°C (tulip) (Turquand, unpublished).

Cultivar	1965	1966	1967	1968	1969
Narcissus					
'Golden Harvest'	20 July	26 July	4 Aug.	26 July	—
'Fortune'	20 July	26 July	26 July	26 July	—
'Carlton'	26 July	30 July	4 Aug.	26 July	—
Tulip					
'Apeldoorn'	9 Aug.	9 Aug.	9 Aug.	6 Aug.	25 Aug.
'Paul Richter'	12 Aug.	9 Aug.	17 Aug.	12 Aug.	18 Aug.
'Rose Copland'	9 Aug.	9 Aug.	9 Aug.	12 Aug.	22 Aug.
'Merry Widow'	18 Aug.	9 Aug.	22 Aug.	14 Aug.	27 Aug.

the range of variation likely to be encountered, or the reasons why seasonal differences occur. Such data as are available for one site in the U.K. are shown in Table 5.2; considerable variation occurs which may be expected to have an effect on other aspects of growth, such as forcing date and the timing of temperature-treatments leading to forcing.

E. Effects of light intensity and photoperiod on initiation in lilies

When plants of 'Georgia' Easter lilies (*Lilium longiflorum*) were grown under glass in central Mississippi with 50, 75 and 100% natural sunlight, the numbers of flowers initiated per stem was significantly reduced at the lowest light. The magnitude of the effect was, however, small, as flower number per stem in high light was 13·3, compared with 11·9 in half light (Einert and Box, 1967).

Long days are effective in flower initiation in Easter lilies as well as vernalization, although separate physiological mechanisms are apparently involved. Vernalization is, however, slightly more effective than long days and both treatments together are not more effective than either alone provided that the stimulus is adequate (Bahadur and Blaney, 1968). These authors classify the Easter lily as a quantitative long-day plant. Long days, like vernalization, reduce the number of flower initials.

F. Vernalization

For flower initiation to occur in *Lilium longiflorum*, it is necessary that a minimum temperature requirement must be satisfied *before* flower initiation. According to Weiler and Langhans (1968a), this was first suggested by the Bermuda Agricultural Experiment Station (Anon., 1935) because flower buds were visible on shoots of cooled bulbs earlier than on those of uncooled bulbs, and anatomical work showed that flower buds were initiated after cool storage (Pfeifer, 1935; MacArthur, 1941). This was confirmed by the observations of Emsweller and Pryor (1943) that flower buds were initiated after growth began in the glasshouse.

Weiler and Langhans (1968a) concluded that, as non-stored Easter lilies cv. 'Ace' did not flower when grown in a glasshouse kept above 21°C, this cultivar has a qualitative vernalization requirement. The highest temperature effective in vernalizing 'Ace' was found to be near 21°C, and 15·6°C caused flowering only after an extended growing period of 233 days. They concluded that 15·6°C *was* a vernalizing temperature but 21°C was not. Temperatures below 21°C vernalize. All plants flowered when the bulbs were cold stored (7·2°C) for six weeks before planting at 21°C in the glasshouse, but not all the plants flowered after fewer than six weeks at 17°C. The numbers of days to flower and the numbers of leaves produced were lowest after twelve weeks' storage, so that there is a *quantitative* as well as a *qualitative* vernalization requirement. The vegetative plants which had been growing in the 21°C glasshouse for about 300 days all flowered at 21°C after four weeks at 7·2°C indicating that the plants as well as the bulbs are receptive to vernalization treatment. Hill and Durkin (1968) compared storage of planted and dry bulbs at 10°C, and found that the planted bulbs were the first to flower (after 109 days compared with 143 days) after four weeks at 10°C, and a smaller (but still significant) difference was observed after six weeks at 10°C. Response to vernalization is more rapid in the growing bulb, a feature that can explain the variable performance of the lily, due to field conditions varying considerably from year to year.

In a further paper Weiler and Langhans (1968b) describe how the vernalization requirement of 'Ace' Easter lilies is affected by photoperiod. It appears that daylength affects the qualitative vernalization requirement. Bulbs cool-stored from 0 to 6 weeks and subsequently grown in a glasshouse kept above 21°C under long or short daylengths required less cooling to flower when under the long daylength. This replacement by long days of part of the low-temperature requirement is a common feature of plants with a vernalization requirement. The generally accepted "rule of thumb" that the Easter lily requires six weeks of cool storage to flower in 120 days (Miller and Kiplinger, 1966a) is misleading because in long days the cold requirement is considerably less than six weeks. Miller and Kiplinger (1966a) also showed that for 120-day flowering bulbs given 21°C for three weeks before vernalization required a week longer at 4·4°C than bulbs not stored at 21°C. This was interpreted as a de-vernalization by the treatment at higher temperature.

In a comparison of lily 'Enchantment' with Easter lily, Miller and Kiplinger (1967) found no evidence of de-vernalization by 21°C in the former cultivar, and exposure of plants of 'Enchantment' to temperatures which led to most rapid flowering also gave most flowers, in contrast with previous results with Easter lilies.

The major difference in flower initiation behaviour between Easter lilies and *Narcissus*, tulip and hyacinth is that the last three have flowers fully initiated and differentiated by planting time. When the flowers are initiated in summer there is very much less opportunity for mechanisms to develop relating flower initiation to daylength or low-temperature requirement. The work done by the various American schools has, however demonstrated unequivocally that the cold treatment has an inductive effect on flower initiation, and is therefore a vernalization.

The position of the *Iris* is less clear, depending upon which definition of vernalization is adopted. Chouard (1960) defined the process as the substitution of chilling of a plant for the natural exposure to winter in order to permit the initiation of flower primordia later, whilst Lang (1952) uses a wider definition: the induction of flowering by the use of cool temperatures, or cold induction. As the optimum temperature for *Iris* flower initiation is 13°C, and as flower initiation occurs when the plant is at this temperature, it *is* vernalization according to Lang's definition, but not Chouard's.

If, however, the low temperature is regarded as a *requirement* for development to *anthesis* (rather than flower initiation), then all the commonly grown bulb plants, *Narcissus*, tulip, hyacinth, *Iris* and lily have a cold requirement but others do not, e.g. *Hippeastrum, Zephyranthes*. The trouble experienced with definitions of vernalization then disappears: in *Narcissus*, tulip and hyacinth, flower induction, initiation and some differentiation takes place in warm temperatures, but flower maturation and anthesis are more rapid if the plants are exposed to low temperatures after or during flower differentiation.

IV. Rates of differentiation

Although in their native habitat many bulbs are subjected to very high soil temperatures in the summer, in an average summer in Lincolnshire it is unusual for soil temperatures to rise above about 24°C and soil temperatures between 24 and 27°C occur only for very short periods during July or after normal bulb lifting time. The high temperatures of bulb storage result in more rapid flower initiation and differentiation.

Luyten *et al.* (1926) showed that at the optimum temperatures for flower differentiation in tulip (17–20°C), apices in the vegetative state on 20 July were on average at Stage A1 by 4 August (Fig. 5.2). Similar bulbs stored at either 5°C and below or 28°C and above, were still at the vegetative stage, or were just showing early stages of becoming floral by 18 August. At the optimum temperature, from flower initiation to completion takes about 30 days. Within an apparently uniform bulb population, there is, however, considerable variation from bulb to bulb. Of the ten bulbs examined on 4 August which had been stored at 17°C, one was at P1, four were at P2, one was at A1, two were at A2 and two had completed differentiation. For an accurate assessment of stage of flower differentiation, it is essential that a sufficiently large sample is dissected; because of the volume of work, this is seldom done, especially in large experiments with large numbers of treatments. The source of this variability is at least partly due to different temperatures in the soil; different sides of ridges experience different

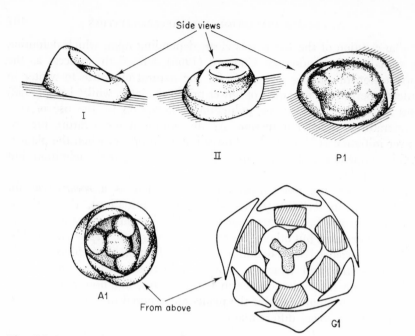

Fig. 5.2 Flower initiation and differentiation in the tulip. The symbols refer to stage of development, see text.

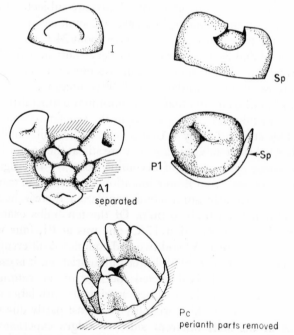

Fig. 5.3 Flower initiation and differentiation in the *Narcissus*. The symbols refer to stages of development, see text.

temperatures, especially in ridges running E–W. Similarly soil temperatures within small beds of bulbs can be considerably lower than at the edges of plots; this can affect flower differentiation by a week or more, especially in *Narcissus* where flower differentiation is well under way by lifting time.

For *Narcissus*, the time scale is somewhat longer because flower differentiation occurs at the lower temperatures in the soil and also because there are two more parts to be differentiated—the spathe and paracorolla (Fig. 5.3). The whole process takes about eight weeks in *Narcissus* 'Fortune' and no evidence was found of any difference between flowers in terminal and lateral daughter bulb units. Because of variations in the stage of development in the individual bulbs of a population, and of difficulties in identifying some stages e.g. for some time after its initiation, the paracorolla is very small and difficult to distinguish, any estimate of the duration of process of flower differentiation cannot be very accurate.

V. Floral abnormalities

Flower abnormalities occur occasionally in all bulb flowers; most frequently these consist of extra members in the flower-part whorls, often resulting in cruciform flowers. These are of little commercial importance and can be considered as morphological "accidents". Other abnormalities are associated with temperature-treatment, especially if extreme.

Narcissus flowers can be severely damaged by the hot-water treatment applied for eelworm control if the bulbs are treated early. Typical damage is corolla splitting, and, as this is the last part of the flower to be formed, it is reasonable to expect this part to suffer from the high-temperature treatment of, commonly, 43°C for 3 h. Methods of avoiding this flower damage are described later.

Blaauw and Versluys (1925) showed that although leaf number was little affected by extremes of temperature during storage, floral abnormalities frequently result from these treatments in tulip. Increased number of floral parts (commonly four members in each whorl instead of three, although other combinations were found) results from low-temperature treatment, and normal flowers were rarely found by them below 20°C. The increased number of parts does not occur at the expense of leaves, indicating that the abnormality occurs after the onset of initiation and is not a change in the timing of initiation. Much of the work on floral abnormalities was done some years ago on varieties which are not so popular now; there are, however, varietal differences with 'Pride of Haarlem' producing the normal 15 floral parts at 28°C whilst 'William Copland' does so only at 9°C. Both cultivars, however, produced more parts than normal at lower temperatures. This behaviour was explained by Blaauw as due to the larger plant apex developed at lower temperatures which could, on the basis of current thinking on morphogenic fields at the apex, allow the formation of extra primordia in the whorls of floral parts developed. It frequently occurs that if extra perianth parts are formed, extra anther and gynoecium parts are also produced.

Another condition which affects floral appearance and saleability in the tulip is that called "tied-leaf" where the demarcation between the last leaf and the perianth is unclear so that the last leaf is petalloid or partly so in texture and colour and may be partly fused to the perianth. This prevents the elongation of the stem just below the flower on one side so the flower frequently is bent to an angle with the pedicel. Little is known about the cause of the condition, although it can obviously be interpreted as a "switching on" of flower initiation before the last leaf is finally formed. Significantly less "tied-leaf" occurred in an experiment on 'Rose Copland' after 17°C storage than 20°C.

Kamerbeek and de Munk (unpublished) have elegantly demonstrated for *Iris* how extra parts can be produced by temperature-treatments at or near flower initiation. Hartsema and Luyten (1961) had earlier shown that high temperatures produced a greater number of abnormal *Iris* flowers. At the optimum temperature of 13°C a normal *Iris* flower is formed which consists of two whorls of three perianth parts, three anthers, which are concealed between the perianth parts and the pistil lobes, and a tricarpellate ovary. If the temperature is below zero during flower formation, aberrant flowers result, most of which have increased numbers of floral parts which may be completely regular to give quaternate, quinate or biternate flowers.

Fasciated hyacinth stems are preferred commercially as a denser, more attractive inflorescence results. More fasciated stems follow a storage period at 20°C after lifting and similar soil temperatures just before lifting. This improvement only occurs, however, at the expense of the number of flowers in each inflorescence. Beijer (1936) advocated a compromise with 20°C for ten days followed by 25°C or 30°C.

Fasciated stems occur in *Narcissus* and tulip, sometimes quite frequently in a single cultivar at a single site. In one case a few per cent of all the flowers of *Narcissus* 'Barrett Browning' in a field showed fasciation symptoms to a greater or lesser degree. Fasciation can occur in most vascular plants, sometimes being a regular feature of some cultivars, while other occurrences are associated with a range of external factors such as temperature extremes, insect mutilation, infestation by nematodes or bacteria or high levels of fertilizers (White, 1948).

VI. Temperature and morphogenesis in *Iris*

Kamerbeek (1965a) has analysed, for *Iris*, the effects of temperature on flower initiation and other changes at the apex (Fig. 5.4). He distinguished four developmental phases:

vegetative   1. formation of bulb scales
               2. formation of leaves
flowering   3. formation of more leaves (potentially generative)
                 stem and flower (actually generative)
              4. elongation growth

Treatments applied during the second phase can induce the third phase and treatments during the third phase and early in the fourth phase can affect final elongation.

Temperature determines whether or not a flower will be formed and

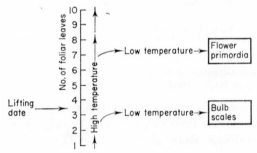

Fig. 5.4 Schema of morphological differentiation in the *Iris* growing point (after Kamerbeek, 1962a).

also the time at which the flower is formed. If a bulb is kept at a high temperature after lifting (by which time three leaf primordia have been produced), leaf production continues until as many as ten leaves are formed within the bulb, giving a "retarded" bulb. Transfer to low temperature at the three-leaf stage results in bulb scale formation and the prevention of flower initiation. The mature plant formed from this bulb will then have three leaves only, and will be identifiable from an early stage as a non-flowering plant. If high-temperature treatment is continued after lifting so that further leaf primordia are initiated then the plant is potentially generative, and reduced temperature (optimum 13°C) then leads to flower initiation, as shown in Fig. 5.4. Transfer of retarded bulbs stored at 30°C to 13°C results in flower initiation. The timing of flower initiation can thereby be closely regulated. The normal sequence of growth and flowering is then as in Fig. 5.5.

Bulbs of *Iris* intended for flowering are normally stored at a temperature higher than ambient to induce the highest percentage to flower. In a test of a number of temperatures (20, 25, 30, 35°C) for 1, 2 and 4 weeks on bulbs of *Iris* 'Wedgwood' grown in Cornwall and lifted in early August, all three bulb grades (7/8, 8/9 and 9/10 cm) produced more flowers with higher temperatures and longer durations of storage, the increase being

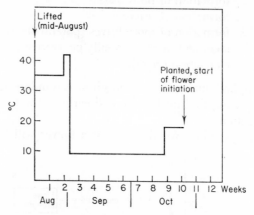

Fig. 5.5 Temperature-treatment leading to rapid flowering of *Iris* 'Wedgwood' (after Kamerbeek and Beijer, 1964).

similar for all three bulb grades. Other benefits of warm storage were earlier flowering; earliest flowering followed 2 weeks' storage at 30°C or above, and warm storage also slightly increased flower size (Wallis, 1969).

A. *Iris:* flower initiation in isolated apices

Rodrigues Pereira (1962) studied flower initiation in isolated *Iris* buds (young shoots not extended) to resolve the importance of the mother bulb scales and other organs in flower initiation. The sterile apices were grown on a sucrose-agar medium. Floral induction was promoted by primordial leaves and also by a factor in the scales which can diffuse from the cut surface of the scale along an agar bridge to the excised dwarf shoot. Growth of young leaves was apparently in competition with the flower primordium for some growth-promoting substances; in the presence of leaves the flower primordium developed more slowly and when gibberellin was added, flower induction occurred only when leaves were removed from the dwarf shoot.

Further studies revealed the importance of several gibberellin-like substances which were successively transported from the scales to the dwarf shoot, depending on the duration of the cold treatment and the developmental stage of the primordium. It seems likely that these growth-promoting substances are not formed during, or as a result of, low-temperature treatment, but in the summer during the growth of the bulb, so that the effect of cold treatment is on the transport of the promoters to the apex which then forms a flower (Rodrigues Pereira, 1964). High-temperature inhibition of flower initiation (at 25·5°C) in *Iris* acts by preventing the formation of a thermo-stable flower-inducing compound which is synthesized in isolated bulb scales at 13°C. The compound has not yet been identified, neither have two other active compounds which apparently play a lesser role in flower initiation (Rodrigues Pereira, 1965). These two compounds have a function similar to that of gibberellic acid, because they are most active after flower initiation, as Halevy and Shoub (1964b) found with gibberellic acid applied to bulbs after the start of flower initiation but before the end of differentiation.

Flower formation has also been induced in excised apices separated from bulb scales, so that an increase in flower-inducing substances in the dwarf shoot may not be entirely dependent on transport from bulb scales. The role of inhibitors of flower formation such as 2-thiouracil has also been investigated. This substance inhibits nucleic acid metabolism, and its inhibition can be overcome by gibberellin. The peak in respiration rate of the dwarf shoot at the transition to the reproductive condition was eliminated by 2-thiouracil, and was not restored on a medium containing 2-thiouracil and gibberellic acid. It was concluded that a specific RNA is active in the early stages of flower formation in *Iris* 'Wedgwood'. (Rodrigues Pereira, 1966).

VII. Temperature treatment after initiation

After flower initiation the parts which will eventually appear above ground develop. A great deal of empirical work has been done on post-initiation storage temperatures for changing the dates of flowering and also flower quality, but nearly all this work has been assessed in terms of the flower at anthesis. Because of this, knowledge of the immediate effects of various temperature-treatments are not known, and almost nothing is known about the biochemical aspects of the period from flower initiation to anthesis. The determination of an optimal temperature for early flowering is complicated by the fact that the different stages leading to flowering (such as organ initiation and extension growth) have different temperature requirements. Further, a temperature-treatment may have one effect at the time of its application, but a different one later. There is method, therefore, in empirical work which produces a régime which gives a sensible commercial end-product.

Because the bulbs, after the senescence of the above-ground parts, are "complete" organisms comprising storage tissues and developing parts, it is not surprising that they have been widely used since the early 1920s as experimental material for the elucidation of effects of temperature on development. Temperature has been accurately controllable for a much longer period than the other environmental variables which affect plant growth and which have necessitated the development of complex controlled-environment installations for comparable studies on other crops which require carbon dioxide, water and light for adequate growth.

Early studies of the optimum temperature for flower development after initiation showed a general downwards temperature shift, although this is not always very marked. Luyten *et al.* (1926) indicated that development at Stage A1 is most rapid between 14 and 20°C, and the temperature at which flower length increases fastest showed only slight evidence of a shift from 17°C to below 15°C over a period of eight weeks, which is similar to that shown by the main axis of the flower. In hyacinth, Blaauw (1924) presented somewhat better evidence for a shift in the optimum for extension growth of the apex over 9·5 weeks from 25·5–28°C down to 17°C.

The use of high storage temperatures immediately after lifting has been shown to be beneficial for subsequent flowering in *Narcissus*, tulip, hyacinth and *Iris*. These temperatures have different effects in the various species, thus in *Narcissus*, protection from hot-water treatment damage of flowers results, tulip and *Narcissus* flower earlier, hyacinth shows improved extension growth and in *Iris*, the flowering of smaller bulbs may be induced. Little is known, however, about the mechanism(s) involved in producing the benefits following high-temperature treatment. In *Iris*, high temperature encourages leaf formation which leads to the potentially generative condition. In *Narcissus*, although flower initiation has already begun at lifting time, four days at 34°C are recommended because early lifting and immediate transfer to 9°C inhibit root growth after planting (Beijer, 1955). Early treatment at 34°C for four days avoids this, and the associated adverse effect on flower quality is overcome by an interpolated 17°C for two weeks between the 34 and 9°C treatments. Although these observations are very valuable, they are only of limited usefulness in the full interpretation of the underlying physiology of beneficial effects of high-temperature treatments.

In an investigation of warm storage of bulbs of 'Paul Richter' and 'Rose Copland' tulips, three lifting dates (1, 8, 15 July 1964) and three storage temperatures (26, 30, 34°C) and a control of 17°C were used (Rees and Turquand, 1967b). The bulbs were kept at the high temperatures for a week before transfer to 17°C with the controls, and the bulbs were then forced early, or late or were planted in the field. Warm storage after early lifting resulted in 'Paul Richter' flowering up to eight days earlier than the controls, with increased earliness following higher temperatures, without affecting flower quality. Late-forced and field-grown crops were also earlier but the effect was very small and of no commercial significance. Early lifting of 'Rose Copland' was not beneficial and warm storage was not worthwhile because the effect on early flowering was very small, even for the early-forced bulbs.

It would be reasonable to expect an interaction between lifting date and the effectiveness of warm storage, and Kamerbeek has indicated that warm storage treatments are effective in tulip only if the bulbs are lifted early. It has been commonly observed that warm storage is effective in a cool season, i.e. when soil temperatures are low. This suggests that warm storage is a substitute for the high soil temperatures which occur in the Mediterranean climate origin of the bulbous plants when the summer drought and high temperatures supply a "curing" treatment for bulbs.

Chapter 6 ——————

The storage of bulbs

"Tulip bulbs . . . are in reality natural cuttings since they
represent detached buds. . ." E. J. Salisbury, 1942

Storage treatments to promote early flowering of bulb plants date from
the turn of the century, when the Dutch bulb grower Nicolaas Dames
experimented successfully with hyacinths by adopting a system of early
lifting and storage under artificial conditions. His treatments extended the
period of hyacinth flowering and made these plants a favourite Christmas
flower. A monument to commemorate this pioneer of flower bulb culture
stands before the Laboratorium voor Bloembollenonderzoek at Lisse,
Netherlands.

In *Narcissus* and tulip there is a low-temperature requirement after the
completion of flower differentiation which must be satisfied before normal
extension growth can occur at the higher temperatures in spring or in the
glasshouse in the case of forced flowers. This low-temperature treatment
(at 9°C or lower) of *Narcissus* and tulip bulbs is given to a complex structure
containing a flower, whereas other bulb plants have a low-temperature

116

requirement before flower initiation (*Iris*, lily) or have an optimum higher than that of *Narcissus* and tulip (e.g. hyacinth, 13°C). It is therefore difficult to make generalizations about different genera which are at different stages of development during the post-lifting storage period. It is more convenient to consider the various genera separately, within the context of normal commercial practice which has been evolved over nearly half a century.

I. Warm storage of *Narcissus* and tulip

Earlier flowering of *Narcissus* and tulip can be obtained by storage of just-lifted bulbs at fairly high temperatures. The actual temperatures appear not to be very critical, and the duration of this storage period is not well-defined, but the following combinations have been found effective:

34°C (7 days); 35°C (2 days); 30°C (7 days); 35°C (5 days).

This treatment is more effective when the bulbs are lifted earlier than normal, and it has been considered that the treatment is a replacement of the high temperatures which the bulbs receive in their native environment, although there is little evidence on this point.

For *Narcissus* to flower before Christmas, it is recommended to lift early and to store at 35°C for five days. Work at Kirton has indicated that anthesis is earlier by 12 days for 'Golden Harvest', 14 days for 'Fortune', 13 days for 'Carlton' and 7 days for 'Actaea' when compared with storage at 17°C from lifting until the start of pre-cooling. It is not very convenient commercially to lift bulbs and transfer them directly to a warm store before cleaning, and experiments under British conditions have shown that although a delay between lifting and warm storage is important for 'Golden Harvest', for 'Fortune' and 'Carlton' a nine-day period between lifting and warm storage has no retarding effect provided warm storage starts by 12 July. This treatment has no effect on the date of completion of flower differentiation in 'Golden Harvest', 'Fortune' or 'Carlton' when the high temperature was followed by 17°C.

Similar work on tulips has shown that storage at 34°C for seven days after lifting results in anthesis 7–9 days earlier than from bulbs stored at 20°C but that flowers are smaller and stems shorter. For maximum benefit the bulbs should be lifted before they are brown; 'Paul Richter' shows no benefit from the warm storage if not lifted before the beginning of July. In tulip, flower differentiation is completed several days earlier after warm storage than after 20°C storage, so that cool storage can be started earlier.

Kamerbeek and Hoogeterp (1968) described briefly how work done at Lisse in the last few years has shown that the time between Stage G and

I

anthesis in tulip is almost constant given constant conditions, i.e. the season during which the bulb was developing has very little, if any effect on the rate of development after the end of flower differentiation. The time taken to reach Stage G, however, does vary with season and is to some extent dependent on lifting date. It is obviously advantageous for early flowering that flower initiation and development are completed as soon as possible. How can this be achieved?

Lifting a week earlier than normal and storage at 34°C for a week before 20°C results in Stage G being reached earlier, but the optimum time for starting high-temperature storage is not known. If too late, flowering will be delayed, not accelerated. Kamerbeek and Hoogeterp (1968) suggest that high-temperature treatment stimulates leaf development so the apex reaches the point of transition (initiation time) earlier than in the absence of high-temperature treatment.

More recent results indicate that in an early season with soil temperatures 3°C above normal, flower differentiation is completed 7–10 days earlier than in a normal season, and warm storage at 34°C for 7 days speeds the process by a further 7–10 days. Warm storage is effective only if started before Stage II (beginning of flower initiation), if given later than this Stage G is delayed about 5 days later than in bulbs not given 34°C, and stored at 20°C (Hoogeterp, 1970).

Investigations on cv. 'Apeldoorn' showed that different storage temperatures after the completion of flower differentiation, and before starting low-temperature treatment (5°C for 9 weeks), interacted with the duration of this storage treatment. Stems were satisfactorily long after 17°C for up to 30 days, after 20°C for up to 48 days, after 23°C for up to 71 days and at 25°C for at least 105 days. Beyond these limits stem length fell rapidly, and unsaleable flowers were produced (Hoogeterp, 1969b). When long durations of storage were used, which would lead to short stems, this effect could be reversed, and commercially acceptable long stems produced, by lengthening the period at 5°C to 12 or 15 weeks. Alternatively, responses to even lower temperatures (2°C) can overcome the induced tendency to short stems, as can a lower glasshouse temperature in the final stages of forcing.

Experiments on warm storage at 38°C have recently been undertaken at Lisse (Hoogeterp, 1969b). This temperature is near the limit for tulip bulb storage (40°C), and must be used with care. It is not recommended for use by growers at present, although there is a possibility that forcing might be shortened by about 8 days because flower development after Stage G is faster after 38°C than after 34°C.

Following the high-temperature treatment, storage at 17–20°C results in the most rapid development to the stage of completion of flower differentiation. There is an effect of a lower temperature (13°C), however, which is valuable in growth after flower differentiation, about 10 days' earliness results compared with the effects of 17, 20 and 23°C (Hoogeterp, 1969b). It is too soon yet to evaluate these observations or to explain their physiological basis.

Rasmussen (1965) found that early lifting combined with a warm-storage treatment at 30°C for a week had very little effect on the forcing behaviour of the bulbs but that the lifting of the bulbs ten days before the senescence of the above-ground parts reduced bulb yield considerably. He therefore recommends against the practice of early lifting of tulips, a conclusion which is difficult to reconcile with other work in Europe which shows definite benefits of early lifting and warm storage in early forcing.

It is a common practice on the Isles of Scilly to burn straw on fields of bulbs not due for lifting ("burning-over"). The benefits of early flowering which result outweigh the high cost of the treatment. Beneficial effects have been observed with *Iris* 'Wedgwood' and *Narcissus* 'Grand Soleil d'Or', but it is difficult to explain the effects in terms of increased soil temperature because only very small increases of temperature have been observed which do not persist long. All other explanations for the earlier flowering and for the production of *more Iris* flowers than in un-treated plots are, however, less likely than an explanation based on soil heating.

II. Low-temperature requirement of *Narcissus* and tulip

Bulbs grown in the field in temperate climates normally have their low-temperature requirements satisfied by the low temperatures of winter, irrespective of whether the bulb passes through the winter cold before or after flower initiation. Much physiological work has been directed towards resolving this cold requirement and using the requirement to control date of anthesis. Traditionally *Narcissus* and tulip bulbs are stored at 9°C for six weeks before planting in soil in boxes; the bulbs are then called "pre-cooled". After planting the boxes are placed outside, and attempts are made to keep temperatures at 9°C or below by covering the boxes with soil, straw or peat ("plunging") and keeping the covering moist if necessary by watering, Fig. 6.1. A large bulb-forcing industry is based mainly on the replacement of the natural cold of winter by artificial cold. The timing of this operation has been dictated by the outdoor temperatures; too early a start to cooling would have resulted in the bulbs being ready to be taken outside when the outdoor temperatures were too high. In areas of very severe winters (parts of Canada, Scandinavia) outdoor temperatures are too low although autumn temperatures may fall earlier than in other parts. This has led to the use of cellars or controlled-temperature rooms where some heat is applied. In still other areas further south, winter temperatures may be too high or the cool period too short for effectively satisfying the low-temperature requirements. For these areas nearly all the low-temperature requirement can be given to the dry bulb before planting in

Fig. 6.1 Appearance of a bulb standing ground in winter. The bulbs are planted in boxes which are laid in rows and covered with straw. Glasshouses used for forcing are seen in the background of the picture. (Photo. courtesy D. Price.)

the warm soil. This has led to the development of the five-degree method of forcing which will be discussed later.

Effects of long durations of low temperature on the initiation and growth of daughter bulbs in the tulip have already been described (Chapter 4).

III. Storage of *Narcissus* bulbs for forcing

Narcissus are normally pre-cooled for 6–8 weeks starting from early to mid-August in south-west England (Anon., 1970a) after the completion of the flower differentiation phase, defined by the appearance of the paracorolla. Bulbs are then removed from store in late September or early October for planting in boxes and plunged out of doors.

The optimum temperature of the pre-cooling period has long been accepted as 9°C, although very close control of temperature is not essential and reasonable results follow pre-cooling at 7–11°C (Anon., 1970a). Outside these limits, however, quality and earliness of flowering are affected. In general, lower temperatures accelerate flowering but at the expense of quality.

According to Beijer (1955), 9°C was first used following early experiments on tulips. Later work on *Narcissus* (Hartsema and Luyten, 1938) showed that 11, 13 and 15°C retarded flowering, and that although 7°C accelerated flowering, it had an adverse effect on flower quality and was undesirable commercially. A critical assessment of the temperature and duration of low-temperature treatment has not been published for a

Table 6.1

Effect of various low-temperature treatments on the flowering of *Narcissus* 'Golden Harvest' (Turquand, 1967).

Date of start of pre-cooling (*July*)	Stage	Duration at 9°C (weeks)	Flowering date (Dec.)	% Grade 1 flowers
10	G	4	20	45
		6	21	41
		8	21	38
17	Pc	4	24	57
		6	25	55
		8	22	43
31	Pc + 2 weeks	4	28	71
		6	28	73
		8	26	68

number of varieties of *Narcissus*, despite the suggestion that earlier flowering follows temperatures below 9°C and that excessively low temperatures cause dwarfing (Griffiths, 1936).

An experiment was carried out in Lincolnshire to study the effects of cool storage for 4, 6 and 8 weeks at 9°C, starting on 10 July, 17 July and 31 July, at Stage G, Pc and Pc + 2 weeks. After planting the bulbs were kept at 11°C until housed. Flower quality, and especially flower size certainly improved with later cool storage, but flowering was also later. The different durations of cool storage had no effect on quality or flowering date (Table 6.1).

Experiments were also done in Lincolnshire on three *Narcissus* cultivars ('Fortune', 'Golden Harvest' and 'Carlton') to establish whether different low temperatures (4·4, 6·7 and 8·9°C) for different storage periods (4, 6 and

Table 6.2

Treatments to produce *Narcissus* flowers before Christmas (Turquand, unpublished).

Cultivar	Lifting date	Storage at 35°C for 5 days, start	Storage at 17°C to P_c stage	Storage at 9°C for 6 weeks	Planting date	Housing date	Flowering date
'Fortune'	1–4 July	before 7 July	to 29 July	29 July–9 Sept.	9 Sept.	15 Nov. ± 8 days	28 Nov. ± 8 days
'Golden Harvest'	20–28 June	before 28 June	to 29 July	29 July–9 Sept.	9 Sept.	15 Nov. ± 8 days	6 Dec. ± 8 days
'Carlton'	2–6 July	before 10 July	to 30 July	30 July–10 Sept.	10 Sept.	1 Dec. ± 5 days	20 Dec. ± 6 days

Note: Early planting is essential for early flowering, and standing ground temperatures must be kept low by watering, burying under a thick layer of straw and irrigation to encourage evaporative cooling in a warm autumn. Storage at 7°C instead of 9°C will give slightly smaller flowers 2–3 days earlier in most seasons.

8 weeks) affected subsequent flowering. The bulbs all received preliminary storage at 35°C for five days after lifting. No clear benefits of modifying the low-temperature treatment were apparent; the lowest temperature did not affect early flowering but flower quality was impaired. Extra earliness followed 6·7°C, but quality was better after 8·9°C. Longer storage periods gave earlier flowers but quality suffered. The differences between the cultivars were larger than those resulting from the different storage treatments, so that earlier flowering can more easily be achieved by selecting the most appropriate cultivar rather than by attempting to modify the behaviour of an unsuitable one.

Despite this unpromising result, methods have been developed for treating of *Narcissus* bulbs to flower before Christmas. Early lifting, storage at 35°C for 5 days followed by 17°C to Stage Pc (usually reached by the end of July), then 9°C for 6 weeks and planting in early September, achieves a housing date which varies with season, because of variations in the post-planting outside temperature, but which can be as early as mid-November (Table 6.2). There is some reluctance among growers to adopt this scheme, partly because of fears that adverse effects of warm temperatures will nullify the pre-cooling in a warm autumn. There is little doubt that this does occur, but there are still residual effects, so that all the benefits of pre-cooling are not lost and some earliness is retained. If controlled-temperature growing-rooms are available, then flowering will be even earlier because the optimum temperature can be maintained until the plants are ready for transfer to the glasshouse.

This method results in considerably earlier flowering than those recommended until recently, with a planting date in October to avoid high temperatures outdoors after planting. With the present market structure early November is probably as early as *Narcissus* flowers will be required.

IV. Low-temperature and field flowering of *Narcissus*

In south-west England some *Narcissus* bulbs are pre-cooled before planting in the field to produce an early flower crop. Completion of flower differentiation (Stage Pc) is reached early, about mid-July, a few weeks earlier than in eastern England (Anon, 1970a).

End of flower differentiation (Stage Pc) means for 1964–6:

'Actaea' 4 July	'Golden Harvest' 14 July
'Carlton' 10 July	'King Alfred' 24 July
'Fortune' 12 July	'Magnificence' 24 July

'Cheerfulness' and 'Grand Soleil d'Or' are at a comparable stage from September.

The aim of pre-cooling before field planting is not solely for earlier flowering, but because a longer flower-cropping season is desirable for labour and marketing considerations. Some bulbs are given short periods of pre-cooling at different times so that the numbers of bulbs passing through the store can be increased. The benefits of earliness derived from the pre-cooling treatment are augmented by the benefits from early planting *per se*. Soil temperatures in south-west England are frequently low enough to permit the planting of pre-cooled bulbs in late August or

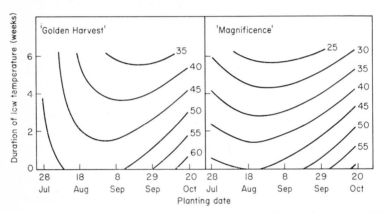

Fig. 6.2 Response-surface analysis of effects of planting date and duration of low-temperature treatment (9°C) on the date of flowering of two *Narcissus* cultivars. The numbers next to the contour lines are dates, 1 = 1 January (Rees and Wallis, 1970). Reproduced with permission of the Controller of Her Majesty's Stationery Office.

early September. Pre-cooled bulbs flower up to six weeks earlier in the field than normally treated ones, the flowers grow more quickly but they are brittle and more susceptible to wind and frost damage.

Rees and Wallis (1970) described three years' experimentation at Rosewarne on pre-cooling 'Golden Harvest' and 'Magnificence' bulbs for 0, 2, 4 and 6 weeks at 9°C before planting in the field. Five planting dates, three weeks apart, were used in each season starting in late July. The results showed that early flowering could be achieved without loss of flower quality, on a number of treatment dates (Fig. 6.2). Flowering dates were up to 22 days earlier than the experimental means with 'Golden Harvest' and up to 28 days earlier with 'Magnificence', although there were considerable seasonal variations in earliness. Longer durations at 9°C resulted in earlier flowering, and there were some adverse effects of late treatment on flower quality. The numbers of flowers produced were little affected by the treatments, but late treatments were least satisfactory. Bulb yields in the following season were reduced by treatments leading to early flowering, but no lifted bulb weights were lower than those planted.

V. Storage of tulip bulbs for forcing

Experiments in Lincolnshire have been directed towards a re-investigation of general recommendations for forcing based upon work done in the Netherlands. There were fears that these recommendations were not necessarily the best for bulbs grown under British conditions, although it was realized that for tulips, at least, growing conditions were similar to those in the Netherlands. This was not meant as a criticism of the Dutch recommendations; indeed with the spread of the Dutch bulb industry into heavier polder soils, differences due to these different soils are also being investigated in Holland.

The treatments applied to 12 cm bulbs of 'Paul Richter', 'Rose Copland', 'Apeldoorn' and 'Merry Widow', were 4·4, 6·7 and 8·9°C, for 4, 6 or 8 weeks after the completion of flower differentiation (Rees and Turquand, 1969a). Some benefits were obtained from temperatures lower than the traditional 9°C, earlier flowering was obtained in two of the cultivars ('Rose Copland' and 'Apeldoorn') and longer stems in three (not 'Paul Richter'), (Table 6.3). Adverse effects of lower temperatures were also observed; the numbers of marketable flowers and first grade flowers were reduced in two cultivars ('Paul Richter' and 'Rose Copland') and 'Merry Widow' had more small flowers. Despite the adverse effects of lower temperatures on flower quality, especially reduced flower size, the advantages of earlier flowering and longer stems could be of value if these factors outweighed those of loss of quality. Only with 'Apeldoorn' was there a very slight benefit from pre-cooling for longer than four weeks.

The varietal differences in response were large, emphasizing the difficulties of a general recommendation. Four weeks' pre-cooling were superior to six, however, and if the forcing industry reaches the sophisticated heights of special treatments for individual cultivars, then lower temperatures could be adopted for the sake of the longer stems and earlier flowering for those cultivars which, like 'Rose Copland', respond.

Another experiment in Lincolnshire was designed to show any beneficial effects of low-temperature treatment of bulbs intended for late forcing. Bulbs of the three cultivars—'Paul Richter', 'Apeldoorn' and 'Rose Copland'—were lifted on 4, 12 and 18 July, respectively, stored at 20°C until the end of flower development, and thereafter at 17°C. The cooled bulbs were removed to 9°C for 6 weeks starting on 7 September, whilst the

Table 6.3

Effects of temperature and the duration of low-temperature treatment on flowering date and flower quality in four tulip cultivars (Rees and Turquand, 1969a). Reproduced with permission of the Controller of Her Majesty's Stationery Office.

Temperature (°C)	Duration (Weeks)	Flowering date (1 = 1 Dec.)			
		'Paul Richter'	'Rose Copland'	'Merry Widow'	'Apeldoorn'
4·4	4	23·5	37·0	41·0	57·5
	6	25·0	38·0	42·0	53·5
	8	23·0	39·5	42·5	55·0
6·7	4	23·5	38·5	41·0	58·5
	6	22·5	37·5	41·5	57·0
	8	25·5	40·0	41·5	53·5
8·9	4	23·0	39·5	41·0	58·0
	6	24·5	42·5	42·5	62·0
	8	25·5	42·5	41·5	58·0
	SE	0·53	0·41	0·37	0·38

Percentage marketable flowers

Temperature (°C)	Duration (Weeks)	'Paul Richter'	'Rose Copland'	'Merry Widow'	'Apeldoorn'
4·4	4	95·0	87·5	100·0	97·5
	6	30·0	82·5	97·5	97·5
	8	52·5	25·0	97·5	80·0
6·7	4	92·5	82·5	97·5	100·0
	6	80·0	95·0	97·5	95·0
	8	87·5	72·5	90·0	92·5
8·9	4	100·0	100·0	100·0	95·0
	6	97·5	90·0	97·5	100·0
	8	95·0	92·5	100·0	70·0
	SE	8·0	10·0	2·2	2·2

Perianth length (cm)

Temperature (°C)	Duration (Weeks)	'Paul Richter'	'Rose Copland'	'Merry Widow'	'Apeldoorn'
4·4	4	4·80	5·00	4·75	6·55
	6	4·90	5·05	4·75	6·40
	8	4·10	4·70	4·75	6·35
6·7	4	4·95	5·05	5·05	6·40
	6	4·90	4·75	4·95	6·10
	8	4·60	4·75	4·80	6·45
8·9	4	5·05	5·15	5·30	6·30
	6	5·05	4·95	5·45	6·35
	8	4·70	4·85	5·10	5·90
	SE	0·087	0·105	0·085	0·094

uncooled bulbs remained at 17°C. Both lots were planted on 26 October, remained outside until 26 January and were then housed at 18°C. The results are shown in Table 6.4. All the cooled bulbs flowered slightly, but

Table 6.4

Effects of six weeks' treatment at 9°C on flowering date and flower quality of three tulip cultivars. The uncooled control bulbs were stored at 17°C. Both sets of bulbs were planted on 26 October, and housed on 26 January at 18°C (Turquand, 1970).

	'Paul Richter'		'Rose Copland'		'Apeldoorn'	
	cooled	uncooled	cooled	uncooled	cooled	uncooled
Median flowering date						
(1 = 1 Feb.)	10	13	14	16	14	16
% marketable flowers	92	88	90	88	96	98
Stem length (cm)	39	31	39	28	40	33

significantly, earlier than the uncooled although the differences were small, but stems were longer after cooling in all three cultivars. There were no significant differences with treatment in the percentage of marketable flowers.

Some cultivars cannot be pre-cooled in the usual way without damage. The cultivar 'Elmus' shows "feathered" perianth parts and aborted

Table 6.5

Effect of different durations of low temperature and different dates of starting low-temperature treatment on flower quality (% marketable flowers) in tulip 'Elmus' (Turquand, 1967).

Duration period at 9°C (weeks)	Date and stage of apex when bulbs transferred to 9°C			
	20 Aug. A1 +	27 Aug. G	3 Sept. G + 1 week	12 Sept. G + 2 weeks
5	34	69	49	32
7	38	87	79	33

anthers following 9°C at Stage G. An investigation of delaying the cool storage for a week and for two weeks after this stage, and of using low-temperature periods of 5 and 7 weeks gave the results shown in Table 6.5

(Turquand, 1967). Lengthening the pre-cooled period results in more marketable flowers, and there was no improvement in the percentage of marketable flowers if cooling was delayed until two weeks after Stage G. Although later cool treatment affected more flowers, the degree of damage was less. The general conclusion, however, is that 'Elmus', and presumably other cultivars which have not been tested, cannot be successfully cool stored.

Another experiment compared effects of pre-cooling 'Golden Harvest' tulip bulbs at 4·4 and 6·7°C with a control at 9°C for six weeks. Although the lower temperatures led to 4 days' earlier flowering, quality was poor, with small flowers on long stems, especially after 4·4°C (Turquand, 1967).

A. "Five-degree forcing"

This method, also called "direct forcing", was developed to provide tulip bulbs with all their cold requirement before planting. Although the whole of the low-temperature treatment can be given to the dry bulb at 9°C, flower quality is poor and 5°C was found more suitable (Slootweg, 1968); this resulted in the term "five-degree forcing". The prepared bulbs are then planted in a warm rooting medium so that growth starts immediately.

Five-degree forcing has its origins in work done on treating bulbs with low temperature for planting outdoors in areas where winters are insufficiently cold to prevent the production of dwarf plants, with flowers opening within the leaves. Because interest in five-degree bulbs was greatest in areas where bulbs were normally not grown, investigations were also concerned with effects of transporting bulbs from the producing areas to the consumer, and the effects of transporting bulbs on previous low-temperature treatment.

Dickey (1954) described work in Florida on the low-temperature treatment of tulip bulbs for planting outdoors. Storage at 4–10°C for 60 to 120 days resulted in satisfactory flowering in northern Florida, but 30 days' treatment was unsatisfactory. If the bulbs were stored for only 60 days at low temperature, then 4°C was better than 10°C. In later work a range of cultivars was grown outdoors after storage for 50 to 120 days at 4–10°C, and also at 2°C (Dickey, 1957). This very low temperature also resulted in good quality flowers when the duration of the treatment was 50, 60 or 75 days, but not 90 days.

These observations were confirmed by Gill et al., (1957) in southern Georgia, a co-operative venture between American and Dutch bulb interests which led to further studies, especially in Holland, on the development of five-degree forcing, as opposed to a pre-treatment for garden planting. Slootweg and Hoogeterp (1965) described the principles of five-degree forcing, and some of the early observations. During experiments on treating bulbs for outdoor planting in warm areas, it was found that these bulbs would grow well in glasshouse soil at 10–13°C, and the possibility was realized that tulips pre-treated in this way could be grown as a winter crop under glass. Anthesis was relatively late, however, so that if the bulbs were planted late in November, flowers could not be cut before mid-February.

Attempts to speed up flower maturation led to failures. Bulbs which have received five-degree treatment cannot be transported easily because they must be planted within 10 days, and not be subjected to temperatures above 9°C. Gill et al. (1957) also reported that delayed planting after pre-cooling can reduce flower production in some cultivars.

Slootweg and Hoogeterp (1957) described the unfavourable effect of five-degree treatment on flower quality, and how important are temperature treatments of the bulbs before the start of the low-temperature period. They recognized two treatment periods before the start of cooling, the first being until the end of flower development when the temperature requirement is fairly high, followed by a second (intermediate) period when the optimum temperature is lower. Two typical examples quoted are:

1. 23°C to 1 September; 20°C until 1 October; 9 weeks at 5°C
2. 20°C to Stage G; 2 weeks at 17°C; 12 weeks at 5°C

The first is suitable for good early and late forcing cultivars, provided the glasshouse air temperature is below 13°C. Treatment with the second régime allows the bulbs to be grown at 18°C, but only a few of the very best early cultivars give good results. Early experience also suggested that a number of precautions are essential for success, these include using only bulbs of 12 cm grade or above, the adoption of light, open soil mixes, abundant watering and close control of growing temperatures. The major drawback of the five-degree method, as first used, was that the growing period was 6–8 weeks. It was not possible to obtain flowers by this method for the profitable Christmas market unless the bulbs had been specially grown in France or Italy or in heated soil in Holland, and lifted very early.

Further work has shown that a period of warm storage (at 34°C) associated with early lifting has enabled the flowering of some cultivars grown in northern Europe in time for Christmas. This warm storage is then followed by 20°C to Stage G, and then, to prevent floral abortion, storage at 17°C for 1–3 weeks before cooling at 5°C for 9 weeks (Slootweg, 1968). The bulbs can be planted after cooling at the end of October in a glasshouse at a soil temperature of 16°C and an air temperature of 18°C, and anthesis is reached before Christmas.

Hoogeterp (1966) states that if lower soil temperatures are adopted, flowering is delayed about 5 days for each degree below 16°C. This temperature sequence is ideal for a large number of cultivars, but not all; the widely grown 'Apeldoorn' does best when kept at 20°C up to the end of flower differentiation, followed immediately by 12 weeks at 5°C. Hoogeterp (1967) showed how storage at 17°C decreased the flower size of 'Apeldoorn' from 6·3 cm after one week to 5·0 cm after 5 weeks. Flower size was reduced in 'Paul Richter' by five-degree storage for longer than nine weeks from 5·3 cm (at nine weeks) to 4·9 cm at 12 weeks. 'Apeldoorn' is the only Darwin hybrid suitable for forcing into flower by Christmas.

Hoogeterp (1966) interprets the earliness derived from the warm storage treatment after lifting for five-degree tulips as follows:

The growing season has no direct effect on the early forcing properties of the tulip, but only on the time at which flower differentiation is completed. Early lifting and storage at 34°C for one week before transfer to 20°C is best, but there is some evidence that after a warm season the 34°C-treatment should be followed by 20°C and after a cold season by 17°C, because the lower temperature apparently accelerates leaf formation which will still be in progress in a cool season. There is still some uncertainty about the interaction of the 34°C-treatment with season; it is beneficial after some seasons, but no information is available on how to determine whether, in any one season, it will be beneficial. It has, however, been established that flower initiation in early-lifted bulbs is completed earlier than in bulbs not given this treatment. Earlier flowering is therefore achieved, whether or not the 34°C-treatment has any after-effect.

Current recommendations are, therefore:

1. Lift the bulbs slightly unripe
2. Immediately after lifting: 1 week at 34°C, 20°C until Stage G, 2 weeks at 17°C, 9 weeks at 5°C, (For 'Apeldoorn' omit the 17°C-treatment and store for 12 weeks at 5°C)
3a. Early flowering – grow in glasshouse at 18°C and a soil temperature of 16°C.
3b. Later flowering – grow at lower temperature (below 13°C)

The following cultivars have given successful results (Hoogeterp, 1967).

'Apeldoorn'	'Apricot Beauty'	'Charles'	'Christmas Marvel'
'Emmy Peeck'	'Karel Doorman'	'Madam Curie'	'Mirjoram'
'Paul Richter'	'Pink Trophy'	'Preludium'	'Snowstar'
'Sulphur Cloud'	'Tommy'		

Clearly five-degree forcing is a promising alternative to more traditional methods, although the growing conditions are more critical, better temperature control is required and many cultivars cannot be grown successfully. For later forcing, the lower temperature allows the use of a wider range of cultivars and gives excellent flower quality, but growth is slow. The method is attractive for some growers already equipped with, for instance, mobile glasshouses.

Work in Lincolnshire on the more practical aspects of five-degree forcing has confirmed the results obtained at Lisse. As used in Lincolnshire the method was found to be fairly reliable for certain cultivars and to have advantages over traditional methods of boxing and transfer to outside conditions, where troubles can occur due to a variety of causes and a difficult decision has to be taken on readiness to transfer into the glasshouse. Drawbacks were encountered, however; soil for planting can be cold and wet in November, the process takes about two weeks longer than traditional forcing, and flower size and quality are less good.

Work in Lincolnshire has also been directed towards a study of *Narcissus* flowering after five-degree treatment. The conclusions reached were that there were no advantages to be gained from this method, and that there were a number of disadvantages such as poor quality and prolonged flowering. It is unlikely, then, that five-degree forcing of *Narcissus* will be adopted commercially. In the Netherlands, however, some more promising results have been obtained and the following are suggested as treatments for different flowering dates:

> December: 34°C (1 week); 17°C (2 weeks); 5°C (9–12 weeks)
> January, February: 17°C then 5°C (9–12 weeks)

For December flowering, treatment should be started between 15 and 20 July; for January flowering bulbs should be planted between mid-November and early December, depending on the duration of cold treatment, and for February flowering bulbs should be planted between mid-December and early January, again depending on the duration of cold treatment (Hoogeterp, 1969a).

Outdoor forcing of five-degree tulips

For very early flowers, the bulbs must be stored at 20°C until Stage G followed by 17°C for 1–3 weeks before starting low-temperature treatment. Low-temperature treatment is extended until 12 weeks, but the forcing of treated bulbs after early January is difficult; it can be resolved by selecting suitable cultivars and by slow forcing. Mobile glasshouses are particularly well suited to this form of forcing and four series of five-degree tulips can be flowered in a single season (Slootweg, 1968).

Recent Japanese work tested the forcing behaviour of 21 tulip cultivars by changing storage temperatures and durations (Kosugi *et al.*, 1968). The best treatment for Christmas forcing of most of the cultivars was 14°C for 14 days followed by 2°C for 55 days, but two other groups behaved differently. One flowered poorly after these conditions (e.g. 'Red Matador') whilst another flowered well in a wide range of cold-storage treatments (e.g. 'Emmy Peeck'). It would appear that there is scope for further modifying temperature-treatments for some cultivars to accelerate anthesis but still maintain quality.

VI. Hot-water treatment and warm storage

The immediate practical importance of warm-storage treatments to prevent hot-water treatment damage to flowers of *Narcissus* has led to a great deal of work on this aspect of storage. It has been known for many years that warm storage before hot-water treatment both prevents flower damage (Wood, 1940, 1944; Slootweg, 1962) and promotes earlier flowering. The warm-storage treatment apparently originated from the recommended storage for two weeks at 30°C for early forcing; the hot-water treatment was introduced after one week of warm storage for pest control. The similarity of the behaviour of a number of bulb species in response to warm storage probably means that the same process is being affected in *Narcissus*, tulips, *Iris* and lily, although there is very little information available.

Table 6.6 shows the effect on leaf damage, flower production and flower damage of a series of temperatures between 7·2°C and 18·3°C on five *Narcissus* cultivars (Turquand and Rees, 1968). The leaf damage was typical of what had previously been observed and was attributed to late hot-water treatment. In the 1965 season the symptom did not appear after the bulbs had been hot-water treated during the warm July/August of 1964, so that it appeared that if the bulbs were too cold at the time of hot-water treatment, then damage would result. At 15·6°C before hot-water treatment, little leaf damage was observed although some cultivars (e.g. 'Carlton') are more sensitive and are completely damage-free only at 18·3°C. Temperatures below 15·6°C killed all the flowers of 'Actaea' and 'Cheerfulness' and caused severe flower damage in other cultivars, especially 'Golden Harvest'. These temperatures define the lower limits of warm-storage treatments. The optimum values are, however, considerably higher.

Rees and Turquand (1967a) investigated various durations and temperatures of warm storage on the *Narcissus* cultivars 'Fortune', 'Golden Harvest', 'Carlton' and 'Actaea'. The benefits of warm storage were amply confirmed, and produced over 90% marketable flowers compared with almost total loss of the flower crop in the absence of warm storage. In one

Effect of different warm-storage temperatures for three weeks before hot-water treatment at 44·4°C for three hours on leaf and flower damage, flower number and bulb yield in the following season in five *Narcissus* cultivars (Turquand and Rees, 1968).

Cultivar	Pre-h.w.t. storage temp. °C	Leaf damage score[1] (1966)	% flowers damaged	Flowers per 100 bulbs	Bulb yields, kg per 100 bulbs
'Actaea'	7·2	6	—	0	3·6
	10·0	6	—	0	3·6
	12·8	6	—	0	3·6
	15·6	4	—	54	4·3
	18·3	0	—	93	4·6
'Cheerfulness'	7·2	8	—	0	3·8
	10·0	8	—	0	3·8
	12·8	8	—	0	3·8
	15·6	6	—	14	4·1
	18·3	4	—	85	4·3
'Carlton'	7·2	8	100	90	7·0
	10·0	8	100	65	6·6
	12·8	6	40	90	7·7
	15·6	4	0	96	8·3
	18·3	0	0	99	9·8
'Fortune'	7·2	6	100	90	5·0
	10·0	6	90	94	5·2
	12·8	4	80	100	5·7
	15·6	2	30	102	6·2
	18·3	0	10	98	7·0
'Golden Harvest'	7·2	6	100	94	6·6
	10·0	6	100	90	6·4
	12·8	4	100	91	7·0
	15·6	2	50	92	7·5
	18·3	0	10	93	8·4

[1] 0 = healthy, 8 = severe damage.

K

experiment there was very little difference between 34°C for 3 days and 30°C for 7 days, with the latter giving slightly better results. In another experiment, best results followed 32·5°C for 8 days or 35°C for 5 days. These combinations were superior to most at 30°C and to all of 2 days' duration.

Iris bulbs can also be subjected to hot-water treatment at 43·5°C for 4 h to eliminate *Sclerotium rolfsii* (Gould, 1957) or 57°C for 30 min to eliminate *Fusarium oxysporum* f. *iridis* (Vigodsky, 1970). In an investigation of storage treatments to harden *Iris* 'Wedgwood' bulbs to enable them to withstand the hot-water treatment, it was found that 30 or 35°C were suitable temperatures (Vigodsky, 1970). Hot-water treatment after storage at 25°C killed all the bulbs. Warm storage at 30 or 35°C of two weeks was as effective as longer storage periods.

No investigations have been made with either *Narcissus* or *Iris* on how warm-storage treatment allows the bulb to be successfully hot-water treated. Bulb respiration rates and apical activity have been considered in this context, and Vigodsky (1970) concluded that the reduced apical activity (rate of growth of leaf primordia) at higher temperatures was associated with induced hardiness. Respiration of *Iris* is lowest at 25–30°C but increases at 35°C, whilst hardiness is maximal after 30°C-treatment.

VII. Hyacinth preparation and storage

Most of the hyacinths grown in the Netherlands are sold for flowering indoors, and most of the large numbers of bulbs sold are "prepared". Very few hyacinth bulbs for sale are grown outside the Netherlands: it is there that we look for information on preparation. The current recommendations are:

Extra early (3rd week November to 2nd week December)
lift: 14–21 June
pre-treatment: { 2 weeks 30°C + 3 weeks 25·5°C; or
1 week 30°C, 1 week 29°C, 1 week 28°C, 1 week 27°C and 1 week 25·5°C.
interim treatment: 20°C to A1 of top florets
after-treatment: 13°C to planting
planting: from 20 September

Very early (2nd week December to early January)
lift: 14–21 June, and air dry the bulbs
pre-treatment: { 30°C for 2 weeks, 25·5°C for 3 weeks; or
1 week 30°C, 1 week 29°C, 1 week 28°C + 1 week 27°C, and 1 week 25·5°C.

interim treatments: 23°C to A1 of top florets
                    20°C to A1 of top florets
after-treatment: 17 or 13°C to planting
planting: between 20 and 30 September

For extra-early flowering a treatment producing a flat stem (7 to 10 days at 23°C at the start of pre-treatment before Stage II) cannot be used because of the time involved, but this is frequently included in the very early treatment. Treatments inducing a flat stem are not always desirable because they sometimes cause curved inflorescences, rotting tips and the failure of floret development in some cultivars.

A great deal of varietal difference of response has been recognized and storage treatments for individual cultivars developed. For instance 'Jan Bos' and 'L'Innocence' tend to form green buds, but this is prevented by continuing the interim treatment at 23°C for a week after the top florets have reached Stage A1. Herein lies much of the art of the bulb preparer.

Bulbs required for early flowering (January to early February) are no longer prepared. The following schedule is followed:

Lift: end of June to early July, and air-dry the bulbs
pre-treatment: 25·5°C to about 10 September (Stage G)
after-treatment: 17°C to planting
planting: between 1 and 15 October

For later flowering (February to early March) the same schedule is followed as for early flowering, but the pre-treatment is continued until 1 October and the bulbs are planted a month later. Late and very-late flowering may be achieved by continuing the pre-treatment at 25·5°C until 1 November and planting between 1 and 15 December. Cultivars are classified into four groups, depending on their flowering date, described as "very early", "early", "later" and "late".

The largest bulbs produce the heaviest blooms, but small bulbs will force equally successfully with a small inflorescence. For early forcing 17–18 cm bulbs are best, but 15–16 cm are usual in yellow cultivars. A top size 18–19 cm bulb should not be older than 5 years since propagation, and considerable care and attention to nutrition, storage and general culture is needed to achieve this. Quality can be judged by the relation between the root ring diameter and bulb diameter, the former should not be more than a third of the latter except in yellow cultivars where the ratio may be a half.

VIII. Storage of *Iris* bulbs for forcing

Kamerbeek (1965b) stressed that although the temperature-treatment of the *Iris* bulb for rapid flowering in the glasshouse consists of an initial heat treatment, followed by a period at 9°C, as in the tulip, the processes being affected by the temperature-treatments are very different. High temperatures in the tulip after lifting ensure good flower development, but the corresponding treatment in *Iris* prevents the formation of a new bulb which would preclude flower formation. Further, in the tulip the low-temperature treatment is essential for the subsequent rapid elongation of the shoot, in *Iris* it is necessary for flower initiation, and a period at 9°C has little or no effect on the subsequent growth of the initiated flower.

Iris plants are normally grown in glasshouses at low temperatures of about 15–16°C. Higher temperatures hasten flowering but increase the risk of flower failure. Further work at Lisse has shown, however, that temperature is critical only in the day, and that night temperature can be increased to 23°C without ill effect with the possibility of accelerating development (Kamerbeek and Beijer, 1964).

Planting *Iris* bulbs at 9°C immediately after warm treatment prevented flower initiation until the shoots were 8–10 cm long, whereas those stored dry at 9°C after warm treatment showed flower initiation at planting time. Storage at 9°C for longer than 9 weeks is not, however, recommended because of excessive sprout elongation and retarded flowering (Hartsema and Luyten, 1962).

Work at Lisse has indicated how *Iris* flowers may be obtained throughout the year. Flowers can be produced as early as January ("very early"); those flowering in February to April are termed "early". The normal flowering season is May–June, and retarding the bulbs produces flowers in July–August (late season) and September–November (very late), (Durieux and de Pagter, 1967).

For the different flowering dates of 'Wedgwood' the following schedules are recommended following lifting in August:

very early: 35°C (2 weeks); 40°C (3 days); 17°C (2 weeks); 9°C (6 weeks)
early: 30°C (4 weeks); 40°C (3 days); 17°C (2 weeks); 9°C (6 weeks)
normal ⎫
late   ⎬ 17°C (4–6 weeks)
very late ⎭

Beijer (1952) demonstrated that the development of *Iris* bulbs could be retarded by temperatures above 20°C, later work showed that 25°C was more suitable for long-term storage of several months, but the current recommendations are for 30°C, as above. Still higher temperatures are not suitable because of excessive losses of water and dry matter by respiration (Kamerbeek, 1962). The blue and white Dutch *Iris* cultivars are more suitable than the yellow ones for long retardation periods. Four to six weeks at 17°C give the best results after storage at 30°C and about 3 months elapse between planting and anthesis of the retarded bulbs (2·5 months for 'Wedgwood').

A considerable amount of experimentation in the U.S.A. has emphasized the importance of early lifting, and the use of degree-days during the growing season as an indication of the amount of heat treatment (curing) necessary to ensure good flowering. Heat-curing is best given to the bulbs within 5 days of lifting and the bulbs performed well after 32°C for 10 days or 34–37°C for 5 days. Temperatures of 27–29°C tended to maintain dormancy. Pre-cooling at 10°C for 6 weeks increased earliness, and was better than either 18 or 4°C. It was also found that more small bulbs fail to flower as the pre-cooling temperature is lowered, but this was prevented by curing the bulbs at 24 or 29°C (Stuart and Gould, 1954, 1967; Stuart et al., 1949; Stuart et al., 1963).

These results complement those obtained in Europe; they can be explained in terms of ideas developed in the Netherlands on effects of temperature on flower differentiation.

IX. Storage of lily bulbs

Most of the work on the storage of lily bulbs has been done in the U.S.A., where lilies are a widely grown crop traditionally prepared for Easter. The centres of research include Beltsville, California, Cornell, Georgia, Minnesota, Ohio, Purdue and Washington, and a considerable volume of information is now available on the response of lilies to temperature-treatment especially during storage.

Thirty years ago it had been established that low-temperature storage accelerated flowering, with 10°C more effective than 4 or 0°C up to 10 weeks' storage (Brierley, 1941), and this was confirmed by Stuart (1943) and Emsweller and Pryor (1943), who found that storage at 10°C for 6 weeks resulted in flower bud appearance 35 days after planting, and anthesis in 86 days. Stuart (1946) found that flowers were obtained as early as November or December if bulbs were stored in moist peat as soon as mature for about six weeks at 7°C, but that for later flowering the bulbs stored best if kept sufficiently moist and at 0°C or slightly below. These findings have been widely adopted commercially although it is generally recognized that the optimum storage temperature for longer than six weeks is lower, and 4°C is commonly used experimentally. Difficulties in defining optimum temperatures arise because all temperatures below 21°C can vernalize, although the optimum is about 4°C. For long-term storage, temperatures near zero are best, but for short-term storage there are advantages from using 2–10°C.

It has already been indicated that Easter lilies have a vernalization requirement for flower initiation (Chapter 5). If bulbs are not exposed to cold before transfer to a glasshouse at 16°C, the plants grow very slowly, and take much longer than the normal 110–120 days to anthesis (Miller and Kiplinger, 1966a). Low temperature can be given to the dry bulb (pre-cooling) or to the planted bulb (natural cooling) (Carlson and De Hertogh, 1967). Temperatures near 4°C are most effective, but commercially, bulbs are stored at −1° to +2°C for four to six weeks because stores at these temperatures are available.

Stuart (1946) found that 'Ace' Easter lilies flowered after 140 days with a mean of 8·4 flowers per plant after exposure to 18·3°C for 4 weeks followed by 1·7°C for 4 weeks. Extending the period at 1·7°C to 8 weeks produced flowers in 116 days with a mean of 5·9 flowers per plant, and longer periods of cold accelerated flowering and reduced flower numbers even further.

Prolonged storage of lily bulbs at low temperatures results in a poor quality product with reduced flower number, leaf number and leaf length in the lower leaves, and accelerated development to anthesis, and this led Miller and Kiplinger (1964) to study effects of high temperatures (21, 27, 32°C) prior to cold treatment. They found that anthesis was delayed by about 11 days, but mean flower number per plant was increased by 2·5. They suggested that temperatures of 21°C prevent vernalization and might even erase previous vernalization. When the latter hypothesis was tested (Miller and Kiplinger, 1966) by subjecting bulbs to 4°C or 21°C for continuous periods or alternated at 6-weekly intervals, it was found that the time to flower was controlled by the last temperature to which the bulbs had been subjected, indicating a reversal of vernalization. Devernalized bulbs could be revernalized when exposed to 4°C for 6 weeks, so the system is clearly reversible.

Durkin and Hill (1966), however, studied the effect of various durations of low (10°C) and high (21°C) temperatures and found the greatest effect of 21°C on leaf and flower number and time to flowering when the high temperature was interpolated between two low-temperature periods and concluded that devernalization was not the main effect of the warm treatment. Weiler and Langhans (1968c) also are of the opinion that devernalization has not been clearly demonstrated by experiments where heat treatments are given before and after cold ones.

Many of the problems of storage of lily bulbs arise because of the need to produce flowers at anthesis by Easter, whose movable date precludes the development of rigid forcing schedules. Weather is also important when the bulbs are maturing in the field. Unusually cool summers increase the amount of cold to which the bulbs are subjected and this affects their behaviour later when they are forced. The greater control of vernalization now possible by the initial storage of bulbs at devernalization temperatures followed by a closely controlled duration at a fixed temperature would appear promising as a basis for the more accurate timing of flowering dates.

A feature of the storage of Easter lily bulbs is that they readily lose water during storage, so that they are normally held in slightly-moistened peat or sawdust, or kept in polythene-lined boxes to restrict water loss. The adoption of these techniques, however, results in other complications; the bulbs are more susceptible to rots, and prolonged storage in these conditions leads to the growth of shoots and roots. About two-thirds of the fresh weight of lily bulbs is water (Stuart et al., 1955) and it is suggested that the packaging medium should contain a slightly lower moisture content than the bulb. Maximum storage life followed packing the bulbs in dry peat (20–30% moisture) in cases lined with 150 or 300 gauge (0·038–0·076 mm) polyethylene film and storing at −0·5°C. In experiments on the storage of *L. auratum* for export from Japan, Hosaka, Yokoi and Komat-suzaki (1962) obtained best results from medium and large (20–27 cm circumference) bulbs stored in vermiculite at 25–35% moisture content at 8°C. The lowest temperature used was 8°C, so this result does not conflict with that of Stuart et al. above.

X. Storage of *Nerine* bulbs

Storage temperatures for *Nerine* were investigated between 2 and 13°C (Sytsema, 1965), and the best treatments for *N. bowdennii* were 2°C followed by 4 weeks at 13°C and planting in early June. For 'Pink Triumph', however the best results were obtained after 5°C followed by 13°C for 4 weeks and planting after the third week in April.

XI. Storage of small *Iris* bulbs to prevent flowering

Very small *Iris* bulbs do not flower and can be stored at 20–23°C during the summer. After replanting a good crop results the following season. Storage of large flowering-size bulbs presents no problem, but bulbs below marketable size require special storage to prevent them flowering when they are replanted. Storage at low temperatures (5–9°C) prevents subsequent flowering but also has an unfavourable effect on the growth of new bulbs. Higher temperatures which have a beneficial effect on bulb growth induce flower formation. Hartsema (1953) attempted to compromise by adopting an intermediate treatment such as 6–7 weeks at 5°C to prevent flower initiation followed by 4–5 weeks at 20°C to induce good growth, but although some success was obtained the method has been abandoned because of its unreliability.

The following temperatures are now used:

1. 'Wedgwood' rounds below 6 cm ⎫
   flats   below 8 cm ⎬ at 20°C
   other cultivars   below 5 cm ⎭

2. 'Wedgwood' rounds above 7 cm ⎫
   flats   above 8 cm ⎬ at 10°C
   other cultivars   above 5 cm ⎭

XII. Storage of bulbs for export to the southern hemisphere

For decades bulbs have been exported from the Netherlands, and some of these bulbs are despatched to the southern hemisphere. Because the seasons are six months out-of-phase with those in Europe, these bulbs must receive special storage treatment so that they can be planted in the autumn in the country of arrival with a reasonable chance of survival.

For *Narcissus* a constant 28°C was recommended by Hartsema and Blaauw (1935) but Beijer (1958) preferred 30°C until mid-October, followed by −0·5°C until the end of December and 25·5°C thereafter (for long sea journeys, e.g. to New Zealand, 25·5°C may be used from the end of November). Bulbs treated in this way can be shipped from the end of February to March and be planted in April for flowering in July or August. This retardation of *Narcissus* for about six months led to the development of methods allowing all-year-round-flowering *Narcissus* by using either bulbs prepared for early flowering or retarded bulbs (Beijer, 1955). An identical temperature sequence is recommended for hyacinth but low temperatures must be applied before the flowers are initiated. If an inflorescence has already been initiated before cooling it will be damaged by the low temperature, but may be replaced by a new inflorescence formed in the lateral bud at the base of the one destroyed. High temperatures are not used for retarding tulips, but temperatures near zero (e.g. −1°C, −0·5°C) are recommended for 6–8 months followed by 25·5°C. At this higher temperature leaf formation and flower initiation are then resumed normally, but flowers already initiated are destroyed by the low-temperature treatment. *Iris* bulbs can be kept for many months at 25·5°C without adverse effects and flowers are initiated when the bulbs are transferred to lower temperatures.

These storage treatments are all effectively long-term storages which have been modified and extended to allow year-round planting of bulbs for forcing. Only with *Iris* and lily is extensive use made of retarded material to allow out-of-season flowering.

XIII. Storage of *Narcissus* and tulip bulbs for replanting

Little experimental evidence is available on storage temperatures for *Narcissus* bulbs intended for planting in the field. Bulbs are therefore commonly stored in unheated well-ventilated sheds where sufficient air movement allows the bulbs to dry, and prevents root formation before planting.

Because tulip bulbs initiate their flowers after lifting, there is evidence for improved performance of bulbs after carefully controlled storage. There are reasons for believing that the behaviour of different cultivars can be affected by different storage treatments. Cultivars can be divided into two extreme groups, one where the mother bulb is replaced by a large number of small bulbs and where a main bulb is not well formed, and the other where a good main bulb is produced but small bulbs are less numerous. An intermediate group represents the ideal, and storage treatments are aimed at the first two groups to make them behave like the intermediate one. The recommended storage treatments are:

Group I (produce many small bulbs), e.g. 'Merry Widow', 'Paris'.
Group II (produce normal daughter bulbs), e.g. 'Apeldoorn', 'Rose Copland', 'Elmus', 'Paul Richter'.
Group III (produce few large bulbs), e.g. 'William Pitt', 'Demeter'.
Recommended treatments (in °C):

	first 3–4 weeks after lifting	August	September	October	November
I	25	20–17	17	17–15	15
II	25	20	20	17	15
III	23	23	25–27	20–17	17

Some difficulty can be experienced in classifying the growth habits of cultivars on different soils, e.g. on the Lincolnshire silt soils, 'Elmus' and 'Apeldoorn' tend to produce few very large bulbs, whilst 'William Pitt' which produces a normal cluster in Lincolnshire is classed by the Dutch in Group III. The Dutch recommendations above are apparently based on growers' assessments of bulb behaviour, as it is most unlikely that the 445 cultivars quoted have all been subjected to three temperature régimes shown above, but no information on the basis of the recommendation is available (Papendracht, 1955).

These recommendations were tested using Lincolnshire-grown bulbs in the following experiment done in two halves.

A. Cultivars   = 'Apeldoorn', 'Rose Copland', 'Elmus', 'Paul Richter' (all Group II)

Treatments = 1. 17°C to planting
2. 20°C to planting
3. 25°C (July), 20°C (August and September), 17°C (to planting), II above
4. 20°C (July), 25°C (August and September), 20°C (to planting)

B. Cultivars   = 'Merry Widow' (I), 'Paris' (I), 'William Pitt' (III) and 'Demeter' (III)

Treatments = 1. 17°C to planting
2. 20°C to planting
3. 25°C (4 weeks), 20, 17°C (August), 17°C (September and October) I above
4. 23°C (July–6 September) 27°C (6–17 September), 20°C (17 September–10 October), 17°C (October) III above

Treatments 1 and 2 in each case were average temperatures to simulate a store with minimum heating and a better store, respectively. The combinations of cultivars and treatments resulted in cultivars of all three kinds receiving two simple treatments, treatments recommended for the cultivar types and, in the case of extreme ones (I and III) opposite treatments.

After treatment, the bulbs were planted in the normal way and the effects of the treatments were assessed after lifting the following summer. During the growing season, bulbs were dissected and the weights of daughter bulbs obtained in relation to their position within the mother bulb. The experiment was repeated in two successive seasons.

For the Group II cultivars it was concluded that there was no evidence that the third treatment (supposedly best for Group II cultivars) was any better than the simpler storage régimes of constant 17 or 20°C when the criterion employed was the number of bulbs produced of grades above 11 cm. The arbitrarily selected fourth treatment was inferior to the other three. All four cultivars responded similarly. For the second half of the experiment some agreement was found between recommendations and findings, although in most cases the effects were of small magnitude.

'Demeter' showed no effect of treatment. Even treatments opposed to the recommendations had very little effect.

It is therefore concluded that the best temperature for a store used for a wide selection of cultivars is 20°C.

This result is in agreement with that of Liemburg (1960) who found for nine tulip cultivars that the highest yield of saleable bulbs and the highest percentage of large bulbs were produced after 20°C throughout the period between lifting in June and planting in November. The next best yield, which was very close to the best treatment, was 20°C for 4 weeks followed by 13°C, whilst two other treatments were less successful.

In a comparison of storage treatments on 'Brilliant Star' (I), 'Bartigon' (II), 'Korneforos' (II), 'Peach Blossom' (I) and 'Rose Copland' (II) over five consecutive seasons (1955–60), Rasmussen (1963) used the following treatments for the comparatively short period between lifting and planting normal in Denmark.

1. 17°C from lifting to planting (all 5 cultivars)
2. 20°C from lifting to planting (all 5 cultivars)
3. 20°C (15 days) 23°C (30 days) 20°C (15 days) (first 3 cultivars)
4. 23°C (15 days) 26°C (30 days) 23°C (15 days) (first 3 cultivars)
5. 23°C (15 days) 20°C (until planting) ('Peach Blossom' only)
6. 23°C (15 days) 23°C (until planting) ('Peach Blossom' only)
7. 17°C (15 days) 20°C (30 days) 17°C (15 days) ('Rose Copland' only)
8. 23°C from lifting to planting ('Rose Copland' only)

Rasmussen concluded that forcing-bulb yield was highest after storing at 20°C with 'Brilliant Star', 'Bartigon' and 'Rose Copland' whilst 'Peach Blossom' was best after treatment 5. 'Korneforos' was equally successful after treatments 1, 2 and 3.

Grower observation in Japan suggests that the high summer temperatures in southern Japan cause excessive splitting in the widely grown 'William Pitt' (III) (J. Kawata, personal communication).

XIV. *Blindstoken* of tulip

There has been considerable interest among growers in methods of killing flowers in tulip bulbs by high temperatures applied before re-planting. This treatment, termed *blindstoken*, kills the flower and higher bulb yields are claimed following the treatment. It is not clear, however, whether the killing of the flower at an early stage is responsible for the extra bulb yield obtained or whether the death of the flower is coincidental. In terms of dry matter change, the weight of the fully-developed flower is small and cannot account *per se* for the increase in bulb weight, although it is possible that during the maturation of the flower there is considerable dry weight loss due to respiration. It seems more likely that the high-temperature treatment changes apical dominance, allowing the more rapid early growth of the daughter bulbs.

Effects of too high a temperature late during storage are illustrated by Hekstra (1968). Axillary buds form stems instead of bulbs and bulb-formation may be reduced or almost eliminated. Large numbers of well-developed offsets result from high-temperature treatment during September and October of the previous season. This effect is interpreted as a loss of apical dominance induced by the high temperature.

Although the practice is widespread in Holland and in the U.K., little published information is available; this may well be because a number of firms undertake to treat bulbs commercially without revealing the treatment details. Hartsema and Luyten (1950) tested a range of temperatures (28, 31, 33 and 35°C) each for one, two or three weeks at the end of the summer storage period. They concluded that as no important increases were obtained in lifted bulb weight after treatment, there was little to recommend the practice. The Japanese workers Toyoda and Nishii (1957, 1958) have indicated that yield increases may be obtained from these treatments, and the persistence of the practice commercially prompted a study of effects of treatment duration and date of treatment at 33°C (Rees, 1967). High temperature was continued for one, two or three weeks, on three dates four weeks apart, starting in mid-July (Table 6.7). Flower and leaf damage increased with duration of treatment and on later treatment dates. The optimum treatment was in mid-August for four weeks. About half the flowers were killed by this treatment, and the yield increase above that of the bulbs treated in mid-July (which showed no effect on flower damage) was 42%. Two and four weeks of high temperature in September produced severe leaf and flower damage; it is not surprising that the lifted bulb weight was reduced. It appeared in this experiment that bulb-to-bulb variation is sufficiently high to prevent the attainment of the ideal of complete flower kill without leaf-damage—which would be likely to give highest yields. Seasonal differences have also been observed; in good growing seasons little benefit results from *blindstoken*. Further examination of the growth of daughter bulbs in large and small mother bulbs given *blindstoken* treatment indicated that treated bulbs contain larger daughter bulbs but the relative growth rates of the daughter bulbs was unchanged (Rees, 1971). Treatment did not affect leaf area, so the improved bulb weight at the end of the season is due to an accelerated start of daughter bulb growth. During the growing season daughter bulbs within treated mother bulbs reach a given size earlier than those in untreated mother bulbs. In a poor growing season growth of daughter bulbs would

Table 6.7

Effect of high-temperature treatment (*blindstoken*) on bulbs of tulip 'Rose Copland' (Rees, 1967).

High temperature started	Duration of high temperature (weeks)	Dead flowers (%)	Plants with leaf damage	Bulb fresh wt lifted per 10 bulbs g	No. of bulbs > 12 cm lifted per 10 bulbs g
July 22	1	2	0	328	4·0
	2	2	0	359	4·8
	4	5	0	384	3·2
Aug. 19	1	0	0	354	4·2
	2	8	5	406	4·8
	4	42	0	504	8·0
Sept. 16	1	40	0	389	5·0
	2	95	92	351	3·2
	4	90	88	307	0·8
S.E.				25·8	0·84

stop before maximum weight was achieved, and the final yields would differ. In a good growing season the untreated daughter bulbs would continue to grow until their potential size was achieved and no difference would be apparent in the final weights of treated and untreated material.

Commercial descriptions exist for the method and the success achieved. In one account the numbers of saleable bulbs per hectare after different treatments were; flower-heads removed, 74,000; flowers cropped 30,000–50,000, heat-treated 200,000–250,000. The cost of treatment was estimated at £54 per hectare, and the gross increase due to heat treatment was about £810 per hectare. Cultivars treated successfully included the Copland group, 'Merry Widow', lily-flowered and some hybrids and Double and Single Early (Oldroyd, 1967).

Chapter 7

Post-storage development

"One of the outstanding results of the accumulation of
reserves in an abbreviated shoot is a capacity for the production of flowers at a time when no assimilating organs are
in active work."   A. Arber, 1925

The stage of development which a bulb has achieved at the end of the
storage period will depend on the use which will be made of the bulb later.
Forced bulbs of *Narcissus* and tulip will probably have received part of
their cold requirement as dry bulbs before planting, although late-forced
bulbs are usually stored at 17 or 20°C and start their low temperature at
planting. Five-degree tulips, on the other hand receive all their low-
temperature requirement as dry bulbs which are then planted into conditions warm enough to allow rapid growth to anthesis. Bulbs of *Narcissus*
and tulip intended for field planting usually receive no low-temperature
treatment before planting, but *Narcissus* sometimes do in order to induce
earlier flowering in the field.

I. Effects of temperatures after pre-cooling

Because the low-temperature period is split into two, it is common practice
to refer to the pre-planting period as pre-cooling and the post-planting
period as the rooting period, because the roots emerge very shortly after

planting. It is, of course, important that the emergence of roots does not occur during the pre-cooling period, as they would be damaged at planting, and flower quality and yield would suffer. Bulbs are usually pre-cooled in shallow layers 10–12 cm deep and store humidity is kept at about 75% with sufficient air circulation to prevent the formation of pockets of high-humidity air.

Normally the planted boxes of bulbs are kept in outdoor situations where care is taken that the autumn temperatures are not too high nor winter temperatures too low. Increasingly, however, use is being made of controlled temperature rooms for avoiding the uncertainties of autumn and winter temperatures, especially where these are severe.

Forcers of spring flowers in the United States and Canada originally used the traditional procedures developed in western Europe. In areas of severe winter temperatures growers had to move their material indoors to produce marketable flowers by a reasonable date. In the southern part of the U.S.A. the winter cold is insufficiently prolonged or not cold enough to satisfy the cold requirements. These considerations led to the development of rooting rooms where temperature and moisture can be maintained at predetermined levels irrespective of weather. De Hertogh *et al.* (1967) list the following advantages of growing rooms to a grower in Michigan:

1. The flowering period can be extended by about eight weeks, so that the tulip, hyacinth and *Narcissus* flowers are produced from mid-December to mid-May. Without a growing room no flowers are picked before February.
2. By suitable management two crops can be treated in the same growing room; a very early crop for Christmas followed by a late-season crop.
3. Bulb development can be supervised constantly.
4. Dangers of damage by frost or poor drainage are eliminated.
5. The boxes of planted bulbs can be transferred to the glasshouse when desired, irrespective of weather.
6. Bulbs intended for late flowering do not have to be treated very early and quickly to avoid early frosts.
7. Labour requirements are decreased and damage to the plants due to digging the boxes from frozen soil is minimized.

Programmes for the use of rooting rooms described by De Hertogh *et al.* (1967) are summarized in Tables 7.1, 7.2 and 7.3.

Root development is rapid after planting; normally the boxes of soil are completely filled with roots after 3 or 4 weeks. The shoot within the *Narcissus* and tulip bulb is also growing during this period, and eventually emerges from the tip of the bulb. Root growth in tulip is apparently most rapid at 9°C (Blaauw, 1926) but maximum root development follows storage at 13°C (Blaauw and Versluys, 1925).

Table 7.1

Rooting room programme for *Narcissus* (De Hertogh *et al.*, 1967).

Anthesis date	Pre-cooling	Planting date	Rooting room temperatures	Date of transfer to glasshouse at 16°C
Very early (15 Dec.–15 Jan.)	9°C (6–7 weeks) Start 3rd week August	1–7 Oct.	9°C	Weekly from 27 Nov.
Early (16 Jan.–4 Feb.)	9°C (5–6 weeks) Start last week August	1–7 Oct.	9°C (5 weeks) 5°C	Weekly from 27 Dec.
Mid-season (5 Feb.–12 Mar.)	None	15–20 Oct.	9°C (3–5 weeks) 5°C, then 2°C if necessary	Weekly from 15 Jan.
Late (13 Mar.–16 Apr.)	None	15 Nov.–1 Dec.	9°C (3 weeks) 5°C (4–5 weeks) 2°C	Weekly from 21 Feb.
Very late (17 Apr.–13 May)	None	1–7 Dec.	9°C (3 weeks) 5°C (4 weeks) 2°C	Weekly from 28 Mar.

Table 7.2

Rooting room programme for tulips as cut flowers (De Hertogh et al., 1967).

Anthesis date	Pre-cooling	Planting date	Rooting room Temperatures	Date of transfer to glasshouse
Very early (15 Dec.–15 Jan.)	5°C (6–7 weeks) Start 3rd week August	1–7 Oct.	9°C	Weekly from 27 Nov.
Early (16 Jan.–4 Feb.)	None (See Note 3)	15–20 Sept. (See Note 3)	9°C (3 weeks) 5°C	Weekly from 27 Dec.
Mid-season (5 Feb.–12 Mar.)	None (See Note 4)	1–7 Oct.	9°C (3 weeks) 5°C	Weekly from 15 Jan.
Late (13 Mar.–16 Apr.)	None	1–14 Nov.	9°C (3 weeks) 5°C (4 weeks) 2°C	Weekly from 21 Feb.
Very late (17 Apr.–13 May)	None	15 Nov.– 7 Dec.	9°C (3 weeks) 5°C (4 weeks) 2°C	Weekly from 28 Mar.

Notes

1. Minimum low temperature for all flowering dates except very early is 15–16 weeks.
2. Programme designed for glasshouse at 18–20°C.
3. Pre-cooling recommended only for Darwin Hybrids and Late Flowering cultivars. For this pre-cool 9°C (5–6 weeks) starting in last week of August, planting date then should be 1–7 Oct.
4. Pre-cooling recommended only for Darwin Hybrids and Late Flowering cultivars. Begin pre-cooling at 9°C first week in September. Planting date unchanged.

Table 7.3

Rooting room programme for pot hyacinths (De Hertogh *et al.*, 1967).

Anthesis date	Prepared bulbs	Planting dates	Rooting room temperatures	Date of transfer to glasshouse
Very early (15 Dec.–15 Jan.)	Yes	20 Sept.–1 Oct.	9°C	Weekly from 1 Dec.
Early (16 Jan.–4 Feb.)	Some cultivars	24–30 Sept.	9°C 5°C if necessary	Weekly from 27 Dec.
Mid-season (5 Feb.–12 Mar.)	No	20 Oct.–7 Nov.	9°C (4 weeks) 5°C	Weekly from 23 Jan.
Late (13 Mar.–16 Apr.)	No	15 Nov.–7 Dec.	9°C (3 weeks) 2°C	Weekly from 26 Feb.
Very late (17 Apr.–13 May)	No	1–7 Dec.	9°C (3 weeks) 2°C	Weekly from 3 Apr.

Notes

For very early and early flowering, glasshouse temperatures should be 24°C until florets begin to colour, then lowered to 18–20°C.
For other flowering dates forcing can be done at 18–20°C.

Spacing for forcing

Planting densities adopted for forced tulip and *Narcissus* are not critical; growers usually plant the bulbs very close together for economic considerations. A few workers have examined spacing under forcing conditions. In Japan, bulbs of tulip 'William Pitt' at 8, 10 and 12 cm square spacings behaved very similarly, the flowers being slightly taller under close spacing but no less luxuriant than those given more generous amounts of space (Yokoi, 1964). No qualitative differences were observed for three tulip cultivars by Stoffert (1965) who recommends that spacing should be very close in boxes 4 cm deep. Forcing-size bulbs not being grown at unduly high temperatures can be planted as densely as possible, i.e. bulbs touching one another, in boxes of convenient size for handling. As a guide it is usual to allow 200 tulip bulbs per m² of glasshouse space; this allows for the area taken up by paths, heating pipes etc. For *Narcissus*, which are usually sold by weight for forcing, an approximate figure is 1000 kg for every 100 m² of total glasshouse area. The number of flowers produced from 1000 kg varies considerably with cultivar, e.g. 'Edward Buxton' often produces 35,000 flowers whilst 'Magnificence' rarely produces more than 20,000. 'Golden Harvest' and 'Fortune' are intermediate.

For Easter lilies a maximum density of 32 plants per m² is recommended because closer spacing results in an undesirably high loss of lower leaves (Kiplinger *et al.*, 1969).

Iris require more space than *Narcissus* and tulip, especially in winter; figures recommended range from 100 (10 cm 'Wedgwood' flowering in January–April) to 150 (other cultivars March–May) bulbs per m².

A. Narcissus

Experiments on different rooting temperatures for *Narcissus* have been reported (Turquand, 1967). Temperatures above 9°C are no better than the traditional 9°C, despite the promotion of early root and shoot growth, because of the retarded flowering. After 9°C for six weeks starting in 13 September, bulbs of 'Carlton' were planted and kept at 8·9, 11·1, 13·3 and 15·6°C until transfer to a glasshouse on 18 December. The bulbs which received 8·9°C after planting flowered three weeks earlier than those at 15·6°C (Table 7.4).

In another experiment on 'Fortune' and 'Carlton', temperatures of 6·7, 8·9, 11·1 and 13·3°C were used for the post-planting period (Turquand, 1967). All the 'Carlton' bulbs were taken to the glasshouse on 12 December, and all the 'Fortune' on 25 November except those rooted at 6·7°C, which were so slow-growing that transfer was delayed for a week (Table 7·5). Better root growth followed higher temperatures, but retarded flowering.

Experiments on pre-cooled bulbs in south-west England were also carried out (Wallis, 1965). The same temperatures from 6·7 to 13·3°C were used, and the boxes were all transferred to the glasshouse when those stored at 9°C were judged to be ready. One series of bulbs was forced and the other was grown outdoors, for each of the two cultivars 'Fortune' and 'Magnificence' (Table 7·5). The earliest flowers were from bulbs rooted at 11·1°C, followed by those treated at 8·9, 13·3, 6·7 and 15·6°C. The duration of flowering was shorter after 6·7 and 8·8°C, while those given 15·6°C took longer to flower.

'Golden Harvest' and 'Carlton' were used to test the possibility of using

Table 7.4

Effects of different storage temperatures after planting on the flowering of *Narcissus* 'Carlton' (Turquand, 1967).

Temperature °C	Median flowering date 1 = 1 Feb.	Duration of flower harvesting days	% Grade 1 flowers	% Unmarketable flowers
8·9	5	12	74	1·2
11·1	9	15	75	0·5
13·3	29	19	77	1·3
15·6	36	16	75	2·7

two different temperatures in the rooting period. Temperatures of 4·4, 8·9 and 13·3°C were used throughout the period, compared with 4·4°C for six weeks followed by 13·3°C and 13·3°C for six weeks followed by 4·4°C, before transfer to a glasshouse at 15·6°C (Turquand, 1967). For 'Golden Harvest', the 4·4/13·3°C-treatment was first ready for transfer to the glasshouse, and were first to flower, but flower quality was poor because of the small numbers of flowers produced. Bulbs kept at 4·4°C throughout were retarded and this delayed flowering although flower maturation was shortened. Storage at 13·3°C delayed flowering, but not the time of the transfer to the glasshouse. Turquand concluded that some of the adverse effects of rooting at a high temperature could be counteracted by low temperature immediately prior to housing. 'Carlton' behaved similarly, except that 13·3°C had a greater retarding effect and that 4·4°C *after* 13·3°C did not reverse the retardation as much as in 'Golden Harvest'. The most successful temperature for good quality 'Carlton' flowers was

Table 7.5

Effects of different storage temperatures after planting on the development and flowering of forced *Narcissus* 'Fortune' and 'Carlton' (Turquand, 1967) and flowering dates of forced and outdoor-grown 'Fortune' and 'Magnificence' (Wallis, 1965).

	Temperature (°C)	Root[1] length (cm)	Shoot[1] length (cm)	Median flowering date 1 = 1 Dec.	Mean stem length of mature flower (cm)
'Fortune'	6·7	8·4	5·0	26	37
	8·9	10·6	5·1	22	38 ±0·30
	11·1	11·4	8·8	23	39
	13·3	15·0	7·8	27	39
'Carlton'	6·7	11·7	7·1	43	37
	8·9	13·2	7·6	46	39 ± 0·045
	11·1	15·5	8·9	57	42
	13·3	16·0	8·1	71	41

[1] Measured at date of transfer to glasshouse.

	Temperature (°C)	Median flowering date 1=1 Dec.	
		Outdoor	Forced
'Fortune'	6·7	80	26
	8·9	76	24
	11·1	72	23
	13·3	78	26
	15·6	110	24
'Magnificence'	6·7	71	27
	8·9	65	26
	11·1	67	24
	13·3	70	26
	15·6	81	40

9°C, but 4·4/13·3°C led to earlier flowering, but at the expense of smaller flowers (Table 7·6).

Went (1948) suggested that the optimum temperature during the rooting period was a smoothly-increasing curve through the experimentally-determined step-like pattern (Luyten *et al.*, 1932). To test this, a number of temperature régimes were investigated, using small steps and large

Table 7.6

Effects of different temperatures after planting on the forcing of two *Narcissus* cultivars (Turquand, 1967).

Temperature (°C)	Housing date (1 = 1 Nov.)	Shoot length at housing (cm)	Root length at housing (cm)	Median flowering date (1 = 1 Dec.)	Duration of anthesis (days)	Stem length (cm)	Flower diameter (cm)	% Grade 1 flowers	% Marketable flowers
'Golden Harvest'									
4·4 to housing	47	4·4	8·1	40	13	34	8·5	63	94
8·9 to housing	32	5·3	14·6	27	21	37	8·7	66	96
13·3 to housing	32	3·3	16·2	36	29	39	8·6	71	99
4·4 (6 wks.) 13·3 to housing	30	10·9	13·5	21	22	37	8·7	47	93
13·3 (6 wks.) 4·4 to housing	39	3·3	12·3	40	15	36	8·9	77	88
'Carlton'									
4·4 to housing	53	4·5	10·3	46	11	35	8·6	37	85
8·9 to housing	34	7·7	13·1	31	19	38	8·6	68	98
13·3 to housing	45	8·1	16·7	55	31	38	8·3	22	80
4·4 (6 wks.) 13·3 to housing	30	12·2	13·3	20	17	36	8·3	42	95
13·3 (6 wks.) 4·4 to housing	53	3·2	19·6	53	26	37	8·6	44	95

Table 7.7

Effect of a range of temperature régimes after planting on the development and flowering of two *Narcissus* cultivars (Turquand, 1968).

Treatment*		Housing date (1 = 1 Nov.)	Shoot length at housing (cm)	Root length at housing (cm)	Median flowering date (1 = 1 Dec.)	Duration of anthesis (days)	% Grade 1 flowers	Mean stem length (cm)
'Golden Harvest'	1	24	3·7	8·6	19	16	67	40
	2	18	4·6	6·8	13	17	60	36
	3	16	4·4	7·3	19	23	71	42
'Carlton'	1	26	3·0	9·2	25	18	50	41
	2	18	3·2	6·2	18	24	37	37
	3	16	3·1	7·7	33	33	31	42

*1 8·9°C from planting to housing.
2 4·4°C for 1 month after planting, then raised 2·8°C every 2 weeks until 15·6°C (glasshouse temperature) reached.
3 8·9°C for 1 month after planting, then 12·8°C for 1 month, then 15·6°C.

ones. Bulbs of 'Golden Harvest' and 'Carlton' were stored at 17°C until ready for cool storage at 9°C for 6 weeks before planting and transfer to the experimental temperatures. The three storage treatments were 9°C throughout; 4·4°C for a month, followed by a 2·8°C increase in temperature every two weeks until the glasshouse (forcing) temperature was reached; or 9°C for a month, then 12·8°C for a month, then 15·6°C. The glasshouse temperature was 15·6°C. The results are shown in Table 7·7 (Turquand, 1968). Similar results were obtained by Wallis (1967).

Increasing the temperature from 4·4°C in small frequent steps resulted in flowering 6–7 days earlier than with the standard 9°C, but the third treatment was less successful, retarding the flowering of 'Carlton' and prolonging the cropping period of both cultivars.

It will by now be apparent that temperature during the rooting period has two quite distinct effects on development. Firstly, there is the encouragement of root and shoot growth by the *higher* temperature of those tested, such as the 13°C-treatment, and secondly there is the satisfying of the low-temperature requirement for the later stages of flower maturation, which is most effective at the lower temperatures such as 4·4°C. Flower maturation occurs over a long period, the encouragement of shoot and root growth early in the period is at the expense of the satisfying of the low-temperature requirement and, conversely, early low temperatures delay root and shoot development, although the low-temperature requirement is satisfied more successfully. The general acceptance of 9°C as an optimum is a recognition of a compromise between the benefits of the more extreme temperatures. An indication of how well the low-temperature treatment has been satisfied can be obtained from Table 7·6. After 13·3°C, early development is rapid so that the bulbs appear ready for transfer to glasshouse temperatures, but 34 and 40 days respectively elapse for 'Golden Harvest' and 'Carlton' between transfer and mean anthesis date compared with 25 and 27 days for the bulbs treated at 9°C, and 23 days for both cultivars given 4·4°C. A practical consideration is that bulbs given relatively higher temperatures *appear* to be ready to transfer to the glasshouse sooner than the others, but in fact are not ready in the sense of having their low-temperature requirement satisfied.

B. Tulip

Hartsema (1961) summarized the early Dutch work on the temperature for 'William Copland', done by Hartsema *et al.* (1930). In those days transfer of tulips to 9°C from 20°C was thought to be best done at Stage P1, or the start of flower differentiation; subsequent work has indicated the benefits of delaying the transfer until the end of flower differentiation. The effect of an intermediate step between 20°C and 9°C was tested, but was found to delay flowering. Flowering was earlier if 8°C was used instead of 9°C for the first three weeks, and 5°C gave even greater acceleration but proved too low for good quality flowers.

In experiments in Lincolnshire, Turquand (1967, 1968) found that, as in *Narcissus*, the housing and flowering of tulips are retarded by low rooting temperatures, and this is accompanied by increased stem length and reduced flower size. A safe average temperature for early flowering and quality is 9°C. Rooting temperatures above 9°C retard flowering in spite of the apparently earlier attainment of "readiness to house" and give short-stemmed flowers, although the flowers are large.

Cultivar 'Elmus', stored at 9°C before planting on 11 October and

Table 7.8

Effect of temperatures after planting on the flowering of tulip 'Elmus' (Turquand, 1967).

Temperature (°C)	Median flowering date (1 = 1 Feb.)	Mean length of mature flower stem (cm)
6·7	14	48
8·9	16	49
11·1	20	42
13·0	22	38
15·6	26	36

transferred to the glasshouse on 19 December (all treatments) flowered as shown in Table 7.8. The higher the rooting temperature, the later the flowers reached anthesis, and the shorter the stems. In the bulbs of all the treatments the flower bud had grown above the neck of the bulb, the normal criterion of "readiness to house", but the long time taken to anthesis implies that the bulbs were housed too early.

In another experiment, effects of rooting temperatures on the flowering of 'Rose Copland' and 'Golden Harvest' were examined using continuously-maintained 4·4, 8·9 and 13·3°C and 4·4°C for six weeks followed by 13·3°C and, finally 13·3°C for six weeks followed by 4·4°C (Turquand, 1967). The bulbs were housed when judged to be ready, and the flowering dates and flower quality were as shown in Table 7.9. The two cultivars responded differently; 'Rose Copland' bulbs rooted at 8·9°C flowered earlier than those given 6·7°C and gave better quality flowers. 4·4°C retarded housing and flowering whilst 13·3°C gave an early housing date

Table 7.9

Effect of post-planting temperatures on the flowering of two tulip cultivars (Turquand, 1967).

Temperature (°C)	Housing date (1 = 1 Dec.)	Median flowering date (1 = 1 Jan.)	% Grade 1 flowers	Stem length (cm)	% Blind flowers
'Rose Copland'					
4·4 to housing	32	34	28	49	3
8·9 to housing	18	20	78	40	4
13·3 to housing	9	18	48	33	7
4·4 (6 weeks), 13·3 to housing)	2	8	45	38	38
1·3 (6 weeks), 4·4 to housing	32	35	58	40	0
'Golden Harvest'					
4·4 to housing	42	46	19	52	0
8·9 to housing	28	34	39	38	0
13·3 to housing	23	38	38	34	0
4·4 (6 weeks), 13·3 to housing	21	22	66	39	0
13·3 (6 weeks), 4·4 to housing	42	47	68	46	0

Table 7.10

Effect of a range of temperature régimes on the development and flowering of two tulip cultivars (Turquand, 1968).

Treatment*		Housing date (1 = 1 Nov.)	Shoot length at housing (cm)	Root length at housing (cm)	Median flowering date (1 = 1 Dec.)	Duration of anthesis (days)	% Grade 1 flowers	Mean stem length (cm)	% Blind flowers
'Paul Richter'	1	36	6·3	10·8	33	11	63	35	9
	2	50	25·4	13·6	32	10	45	36	25
	3	33	9·0	7·7	28	14	41	34	9
'Rose Copland'	1	40	9·1	11·4	39	10	66	42	13
	2	44	18·1	12·4	35	15	50	42	17
	3	30	10·2	6·6	34	19	71	40	13

*1 8·9°C from planting to housing.
2 4·4°C for 1 month after planting, then raised 2·8°C every 2 weeks until 18·3°C (glasshouse temperature) reached.
3 8·9°C for 1 month after planting, then 12·8°C for 1 month, then 15·6°C.

but slow flowering, poor quality and short stems. Transfer of bulbs from 4·4 to 13·3°C resulted in an earlier housing date than 4·4°C continuously but quality suffered drastically. Transfer from 13·3°C to 4·4°C retarded housing and flowering but quality and stem length were improved compared with continuous 13·3°C. The earliest and best quality 'Golden Harvest' flowers were produced after 4·4/13·3°C; 4·4°C continuously increased stem length but retarded flowering and reduced flower size; 13·3 throughout was ready to house early but flowered over a long period and produced low-quality flowers; 13·3/4·4°C reduced the duration of cropping and increased stem length but retarded flowering, compared with 13·3°C throughout.

In a similar experiment to that described for *Narcissus* (Table 7.7), tulips 'Paul Richter' and 'Rose Copland' were kept at 9°C for the whole rooting period, at 4·4°C for a month followed by a temperature increase of 2·8°C every two weeks or 9°C for a month followed by 12·8°C for a month then 15·6°C. (Table 7.10). The two step-wise treatments did give some extra earliness of flowering compared with the standard 9°C throughout but at the expense of a high percentage of blind flowers in 'Paul Richter' and fewer first-grade flowers in 'Rose Copland'. The third treatment of large steps gave early flowers with short stems.

The comments made in the previous section on the behaviour of *Narcissus* in response to temperatures in the rooting period are also relevant to tulip. Higher rooting temperatures favour early rooting and extension growth and apparently hasten the development to the "readiness to house" stage as judged visually, but the cold requirement is satisfied better by the lower temperature. A temperature of 9°C is then a good mean value for early flowering compatible with quality, a fact which has long been recognized, and which Blaauw called a "general optimum" which by compromise results in the best "all round" product compatible with earliness.

Temperatures of 25·5°C or above after the planting of tulip bulbs delay both root and shoot emergence, and the plants reach anthesis later. This check to development persists throughout the growing season and bulb lifting in the following summer is delayed. Leaf area is also reduced and stems are shorter (Timmer and Koster, 1969a).

II. Duration of cold treatment

Outdoor-grown bulbs of tulip and *Narcissus* will receive sufficient cold during the winter to satisfy their cold requirement in all except the most low-latitude temperate-region areas. Figure 7.1 shows mean soil temperatures for two sites in the U.K. and for Erzincan in Turkey, which is near

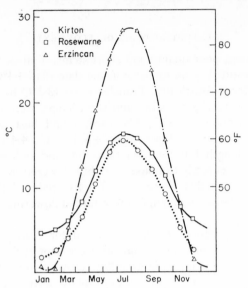

Fig. 7.1 Mean soil temperatures at 10 cm depth for two sites in the U.K. (1962–7) and for Erzincan in Turkey (1929–65).

Table 7.11

Tulip shoot height (10 plants) and tip of flower relative to bulb tip (2 plants) at the time of transfer to the glasshouse after different periods of low temperature outdoors (negative values obtained before emergence of shoot tip from bulb) (Rees, 1969).

Duration of outdoor cold	Mean shoot height (cm)		Mean height of flower tip (cm)	
weeks	'Apeldoorn'	'Paul Richter'	'Apeldoorn'	'Paul Richter'
0	0	0	−2·1	−2·4
1	0	0	—	—
2	0	0	−1·4	−1·9
3	0	0·06	−1·2	−1·4
4	0·11	0·42	−1·2	−1·8
5	0·64	1·20	−0·8	−0·8
6	1·43	2·64	−1·0	0
7	1·07	2·93	−0·6	0
8	1·80	3·07	−0·2	0·2
9	1·79	4·57	−0·2	0·9
10	3·05	5·34	1·0	1·8
11	2·81	6·94	0·4	3·0
12	3·46	7·38	1·5	3·8
13	4·26	9·39	3·0	4·9
14	4·90	10·47	1·3	7·4
15	4·51	10·42	1·8	5·8
16	6·47	13·65	4·3	7·4
17	9·40	17·36	5·2	10·3

the original habitat of the cultivated tulip. In western Europe and other areas where large-scale bulb growing is practised the cold requirement is more than satisfied but it is difficult to assess its duration from observations

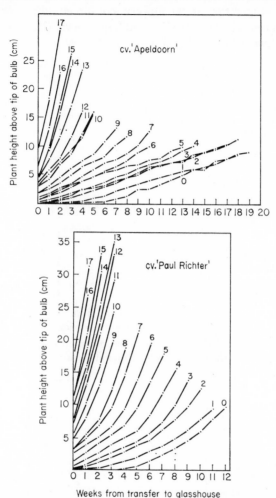

Fig. 7.2 Rates of extension growth of shoots of two tulip cultivars following different periods (0–17 weeks) of low temperature after planting (Rees, 1969).

in the field, and few estimates appear in print. De Hertogh *et al.* (1967) do however suggest a minimum duration for tulips of 13–16 weeks, depending somewhat on cultivar and the use to which the plants are put (plants in pots are more attractive with shorter stems than are cut flowers).

Experience over years of forcing has indicated that too short a period of post-planting low temperature (and, similarly, a sufficiently long period but at too high a temperature) results in stunted growth, irregular, late flowering or complete flower failure. The effect of the duration of post-planting low temperature on the flowering of forced tulips was investigated using 12 cm bulbs of 'Paul Richter' and 'Apeldoorn' (Rees, 1969a) and the *Narcissus* cultivars 'Fortune' and 'Golden Harvest'.

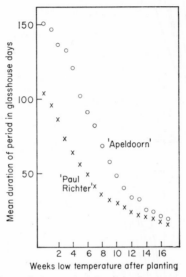

Fig. 7.3 Mean duration of the period in the glasshouse at 18°C until anthesis relative to the length of the previous low-temperature period outdoors (Rees, 1969).

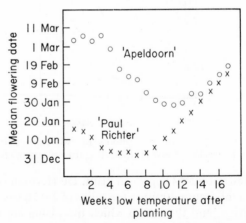

Fig. 7.4 Median flowering dates in a glasshouse at 18°C after different periods of low temperature outdoors after planting (Rees, 1969).

The tulip bulbs were pre-cooled at 9°C for six weeks and transferred to a standing ground at temperatures which followed ambient temperatures. The mild winter prevented the temperature in the bulb boxes from falling very low, but the temperatures were well above the optimum of 9°C for most of October. One box of 20 bulbs of each cultivar was then transferred to the glasshouse immediately after planting and at weekly intervals thereafter for seventeen weeks. Two representative bulbs of each cultivar were dissected at the time of transfer to the glasshouse and shoot heights were measured at weekly intervals after this transfer until anthesis. The shoots showed increases in height from planting until transferred to the glasshouse, slowly at first but more rapidly later (Table 7.11).

After transfer to the glasshouse, plants which had received short periods of low temperature grew more slowly than those given longer periods, giving a family of curves for each cultivar when shoot height after transfer was plotted against time (Fig. 7.2). The duration of the period in the glasshouse from transfer to anthesis was 151 and 104 days for 'Apeldoorn' and 'Paul Richter' respectively but decreased regularly to 19 and 15 days respectively after 17 weeks' low temperature (Fig. 7.3) and the median date of anthesis was successively earlier, then became later as the longer-cooled treatments were housed later and later in the year (Fig. 7.4).

Although the shoots which had received short cold treatments grew slowly, their anthesis was also delayed so that they grew for a longer period. Insufficient low temperature can also damage the perianth parts; perianth length was unaffected but 'Apeldoorn' showed white-tipped perianths and 'Paul Richter' showed green-tipped perianth parts if the post-planting low temperature was shorter than six weeks. Extreme forms of tulip produced from similar bulbs given different low-temperature treatment are shown in Fig. 7.5.

The results showed clearly that there is no readily-observable stage of "readiness to house". Following transfer to the glasshouse, growth was faster after longer periods of cold, with no indication of deleterious effects of very long cold periods. As a rule of thumb, however, a shoot length of 3 cm seems satisfactory provided temperatures are near 9°C—experiments discussed earlier show that at higher temperatures, misleadingly good growth of shoots occurs but this is not a satisfactory indication of readiness to transfer to the glasshouse.

Little is known about the mechanism which relates the cold requirement to the rapid extension growth which follows, but there are isolated pieces of evidence. In the work described above (Rees, 1969a) measurements were made at anthesis of epidermal cell lengths from stem and leaf. The cell lengths increased with duration of low temperature from about 0·15 mm to as much as 0·3 or 0·4 mm in the middle of the lowest leaf and

M

from 0·1 mm to over 0·4 mm in the mid-section of the stem and from 0·1 mm to about 0·3 mm in the basal and distal stem sections. A comparison of cell-size differences with organ-size differences allowed an

Fig. 7.5 Extremes of tulip stem length produced by different durations of low-temperature treatment. Left, 9°C for six weeks, right 9°C for 16 weeks. Bulbs 10 cm 'Apeldoorn'. (Photo. courtesy G.C.R.I.)

assessment of how completely the latter could be accounted for by cell growth. With 'Paul Richter' differences in plant height could be completely accounted for by cell growth although there was evidence for some cell division in the basal part of the stem, with 'Apeldoorn' some cell division occurred in both basal and mid-stem sections and in the leaf, although most of the differences could be explained by cell extension.

In the past few years there has been great interest in promoting early forcing of bulbs because the season can be extended and better use can be made of existing glasshouse facilities. Much of the relevant experimentation is, however, bedevilled by the need to assess by some morphological method when bulbs are ready to house, and appearance is often a poor measure of the satisfying of the cold requirement.

Recently an attempt has been made to collate the results of a number of experiments using a series of curves of the form shown in Fig. 7.3 for two

Table 7.12

The effect of duration of low-temperature storage on time to flower and flower number in Easter lily 'Croft' (after Smith, 1963).

Weeks of storage	No. of days to flower	Flower number
0	196	10·0
2	160	9·1
4	123	6·4
6	109	5·6
8	110	5·2
10	100	4·9
14	103	4·5

tulip cultivars, where the duration of the time in the glasshouse to anthesis is plotted against the duration of the low-temperature period. For any low-temperature duration there is an expected period in the glasshouse, and treatments such as warm storage after lifting or low-temperature treatments below the standard 9°C can be assessed in comparison with the controls more accurately than hitherto (Rees, in press).

For *Narcissus* cultivars 'Carlton', 'Fortune' and 'Golden Harvest', a period of 35°C for 5 days after lifting promoted earliness by 4–10 days and pre-cooling at 7°C for 8 weeks instead of the usual 9°C for 6 weeks promoted earlier development of 9–18 days. Both treatments together resulted in 15–24 days earlier flowering than using no 35°C treatment and pre-cooling at 9°C.

With seven tulip cultivars, response curves were quite consistent for one cultivar in a number of seasons but differed considerably between cultivars because of their different low-temperature requirements. The results of seven forcing experiments showed that warm storage resulted in 2–11 days' earliness and pre-cooling temperatures below 9°C gave 1–7 days' earliness compared with controls.

It was possible also to construct timetables for very early forcing and for forcing so that the time in the glasshouse could be cut to 21 days. These timetables are being tested at present. A further point revealed by this work was that the selection of cultivars with short low-temperature requirements should receive more consideration than at present.

Data obtained for the response of Easter lilies to different durations of low-temperature storage are shown in Table 7.12; increasing storage up to about six weeks hastens flowering but decreases flower number (Smith, 1963).

A. "Frozen" tulips

In recent years it has been found that tulips planted in boxes in the autumn and allowed to root normally can be stored at −2°C for many months. After careful thawing the bulbs can be flowered at any time and thereby given an all-year-round crop. The method is, however, very expensive and risky, and the present indications are that it is unlikely to have commercial value (Slootweg, 1968).

III. General aspects of forcing *Narcissus* and tulip

For the *Narcissus* and tulip we now have sufficient background information to understand bulb forcing as it is commercially practised. Basically, forcing systems are aimed at giving the bulbs the necessary cool period at a time when the outside temperatures are ineffective, and transferring the bulbs into warm conditions when the cold period has been satisfied. Timing is vitally important during forcing, and as anthesis is the last stage of a long chain of developmental events and storage treatments, which start at floral initiation, it is sometimes necessary, in the interests of early anthesis, to change the development of the shoot months earlier. A great deal of experimental work on bulb forcing has been done in an attempt to shorten the time interval from lifting to anthesis.

Flower initiation can be induced somewhat earlier than normal in the tulip by early lifting and storage at 34°C or a similarly high temperature for about a week. The optimum temperature for flower differentiation (20°C) is then given until the flower parts are fully formed, followed by low temperature. In traditional forcing, outdoor temperatures are generally too high at this time, so that the bulbs are pre-cooled, i.e. stored dry at 9°C for six weeks before planting and transferring to outdoor temperatures.

By this time autumn temperatures are sufficiently low to prevent the nullification of the cold storage effect, although this does depend on geographical location. After a sufficiently long time in cold the bulbs can be transferred to the glasshouse to complete their growth rapidly to anthesis.

There is commercial interest in the flowering of bulbs over a long period of the year, certainly from mid-November until the anthesis of outdoor-grown bulbs. The later flowering can be achieved by omitting the treatments leading to early flowering such as early lifting and storage at 34°C or so, and also by omitting the pre-cooling treatment at 9°C and storing the bulbs at 17°C. If a controlled-temperature rooting room is used, late flowering results from the use of low temperatures at the end of this period and thereby retarding flower maturation. De Hertogh *et al.* (1967) suggest the range of treatments for *Narcissus*, tulip and hyacinth reproduced as Tables 7.1, 7.2 and 7.3. These are based on two years' trials at Michigan State University, and are more comprehensive than the Dutch recommendations prepared for the use of outdoor standing grounds for the low-temperature period after planting.

It should perhaps be emphasized here that experimentation on temperature régimes involving a series of perhaps five temperatures is more complex than would appear at first sight. Temperature as an experimental variable can only be varied, not eliminated (there is no equivalent to dark-ness in experiments on light intensity!) so that bulbs must be at some temperature all the time. The times of transfer from one temperature to another can also be varied and it is useful to relate temperature-treatment to some morphological stage if this is biologically meaningful. The experimentation involving a number of temperature periods, each at a number of levels, and transfer from each temperature to the next on different dates combined with the effect of a few lifting dates, all on a few cultivars leads to impossibly large experiments! It is not surprising therefore that many of the bulb recommendations now available are based partly on experimentation of this kind and partly on trials where a successful treatment régime (as judged by flower quality and flowering date) forms the basis for the next series of trials. The experimenter is more concerned with selecting successful treatment combinations than main effects and inter-actions of his experimental variables.

Commercial considerations have prevented the temperature recommendations from becoming too complex. Growers are understandably reluctant to erect and run more bulb stores than are necessary, and each transfer of bulbs must be justified because of the costs involved.

IV. Forcing of hyacinth

Hyacinth forcing is similar to that used for tulips but the glasshouse temperatures can be much higher, and a shorter low-temperature period is adequate. The time of transfer of bulbs to the glasshouse is critical; for the first four days the glasshouse temperature must be kept between 10 and 13°C and the plants must not be watered. These precautions help to avoid the loss of the whole inflorescence which becomes detached from the base plate and can be carried up by the growth of the leaves (see Chapter 9). For very early flowering a temperature as high as 23°C can be used until the first signs of colour development when it is best to lower the temperature to 18–20°C. For later flowering 18–20°C can be used throughout the period in the glasshouse; it is best to avoid high day temperatures in bright, sunny weather. During the first 10–12 days in the glasshouse or other high-temperature room, darkened conditions are desirable to increase stem length and prevent the early separation of leaves. During this period the shoot will grow to about 7 cm when the shading can be removed.

V. Forcing of *Iris*

When *Iris* bulbs are planted they contain no initiated flower, and as flower initiation occurs at a low temperature in *Iris* (unlike most bulbous crops) the temperature after planting is kept low to allow rapid flower initiation and differentiation; growth is then accelerated so the plant reaches anthesis as quickly as possible. The optimum temperature for the glasshouse is about 15–16°C (Kamerbeek, 1965). Higher temperatures result in faster growth, but the risk of flower loss by "blasting" is increased. The recommended temperature régimes for *Iris* forcing have changed somewhat over the years. Planting the bulbs and maintaining them at 13°C was originally recommended, and flower differentiation was completed by the time the shoots had emerged 6 cm above the tip of the bulb, which takes about three weeks. Then it was advised that the temperature could be raised to 15°C at the 6 cm stage (Hartsema and Luyten, 1940). Later work showed that higher temperatures could be given before the end of flower formation.

More recently evidence has been accumulating on the interaction between temperature and light in *Iris* forcing. The optimum temperature of 15–16°C is only applicable during the day. Higher temperature can be given at night without adversely affecting growth and temperatures as high as 23°C have been successfully used to shorten the growing season by several weeks (Kamerbeek and Beijer, 1964). Figure 7.6 shows the combinations of temperature which lead to success. Best results, in terms of flower quality and earliness, follow day/night temperatures of 15/20 or 15/23°C. It is known that extension growth occurs mainly at night; this may have a bearing on the ability of the plant to grow more rapidly at high night temperatures.

Treatments of bulbs at 9°C can be beneficial too, but some earliness is lost, although the time from planting to anthesis can be shortened by

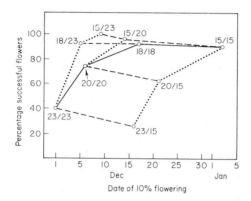

Fig. 7.6 Effects of different day/night combinations of temperature on the date of flowering and percentage successful flowers of *Iris* 'Wedgwood' after 40°C (3 days), 30°C (2 weeks), 9°C (6 weeks), 17°C (2 weeks). Full lines join points of the same day and night temperatures, dashes link points of constant day temperature and dots link points of constant night temperature (Kamerbeek and Beijer, 1964).

50 days. Hartsema and Luyten (1962) give the following example for *Iris* 'Imperator':

Warm storage (31°C)	23 August–6 September (2 weeks)
Cool storage (9°C)	6 September–8 November (9 weeks)
Light treatment	29 November onwards
Anthesis	15 February

The storage period at 9°C has no subsequent effect on the rate of growth of the young flower parts, and little or no effect on the sugar content of the bulb.

Light is important in the forcing of *Iris*. *Iris* plants can be flowered as early as December or January, and many failures which occur then are due to poor light. Hartsema and Luyten (1962) estimated that for *Iris* 'Imperator', about 30 cal cm^{-2} day^{-1} are needed to ensure flowering of near 100% (Fig. 7.7), a similar value to that described by Wassink and Wassink-van Lummel (1952) (a minimum of 2000 lux for 14 h per day). This figure is near to that achieved under the best glasshouse conditions in winter, emphasizing the risks in mid-winter *Iris* forcing. A further effect of light in *Iris* 'Wedgwood' and 'Imperator' is that spikes with more than two flowers are more frequent at light intensities above the minimum for 100% flowering. Preliminary investigations in controlled environment

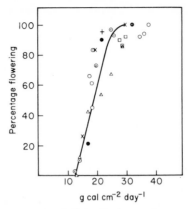

Fig. 7.7 Relation between mean daily radiation and percentage flowering in seven seasons. Radiation measured with a spherical radiation meter for the 40 days before anthesis (Hartsema and Luyten, 1962).

conditions have indicated considerable and important temperature/light interactions which are being actively pursued in the Netherlands at present.

In Finland difficulties experienced in mid-winter forcing of *Iris* 'Wedgwood' led to experiments where additional lighting was used at different

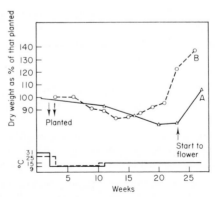

Fig. 7.8 Changes in plant dry weight of *Iris* 'Imperator' grown in a glasshouse at 15°C (A) and in artificial light (B). The percentages of plants flowering were (A) 7%, (B) 100% (Hartsema and Luyten, 1962).

temperatures. Bulbs planted on 30 November, 14 and 28 December gave no satisfactory results at any temperatures although 10°C was better than higher values. 5 February plantings were satisfactory at 10, 16 and 20°C (Kurki, 1962). The duration of the period of high-light requirement is at most 2–3 weeks (Kurki, 1964).

For 'Imperator', Hartsema and Luyten (1962) have followed changes in total plant dry weight at very similar temperatures in a glasshouse at 15°C or under artificial light (Fig. 7.8). The higher dry weight of the artificially-lit plants at anthesis was associated with higher percentage flowering (100% compared with only 7%). From this work and similar observations it seems likely that the growth of *Iris* to anthesis is partly dependent upon current photosynthesis. In poor light the carbohydrate status of the plant is too low to allow successful flowering. It is likely that temperature effects interacting with light also act on the carbohydrate status of the plant, either consuming carbohydrates very rapidly, or conserving them, depending on the temperature in relation to the corresponding respiration.

At planting up to six sheath leaves are present; these do not function as normal leaves but protect the foliage and flower buds during their early growth. The recommended storage temperatures (°C) for the forced flowering of *Iris* following lifting in mid-August are:

	Second half August	*September*	*October*
Early	35[1]	17/9	9 (9 for 6–7 weeks)
Normal	25–23	25–23/9	9
Late	25–23	25/23—17	17

[1] Improvements results from 3 days at 40°C at the end of the period at 35°C. This gives very early flowering in 'Wedgwood'.

Out-of-season flowering is achieved by storing the bulbs at 25·5°C immediately after cleaning and grading, and certainly before the end of August, until a month before planting in the following year. The bulbs are kept at 9°C for the month before planting. Planting in mid-June gives flowers in September, and flowers in October and November can be obtained by planting in early and mid-June, respectively.

Because active work on *Iris* forcing is still in progress, a number of recommendations are available in the literature which, although agreeing in general do show some discrepancies of detail. Such a case occurs if the data shown as Fig. 7.7 are compared with those described by Kamerbeek and Beijer (1964). They suggest that the standard treatment for early flowering (35°C (2 weeks), 40°C (3 days), 17°C (2 weeks), 9°C (6 weeks)) can be considerably improved by transposing the 9°C and 17°C treatments (i.e. 35°C (2 weeks), 40°C (3 days), 9°C (6 weeks), 17°C (2 weeks)). This treatment reduces the number of flower failures and accelerates anthesis by a week (Kamerbeek, 1963).

Much work on the forcing of *Iris* emphasizes the importance of carbo-hydrate in the flower failures. Thus small bulb size, poor light conditions (due to season or spacing or poor glasshouse light transmission) and effects of high temperature are all related through the carbohydrate status of the plant. Preliminary work at Lisse and Naaldwijk have indicated, however, that carbon dioxide enrichment does not affect the loss of flowers by drying out late in their development ("blasting"), neither does spraying the plants with sugar solutions. There is obvious scope for studying effects of temperature on translocation and respiration in the whole plant prior to anthesis. The adverse effects of higher soil temperatures within the range 13–18°C when air temperature was kept at 7–12°C in increasing blasting is an important observation which probably has an explanation in the different patterns of respiration and translocation within the bulb. The interaction between light and temperature in relation to carbohydrate status would also repay detailed study.

VI. Forcing of lily

Using "bought-in" bulbs, lily forcing is fairly straightforward. Bulbs are stored on receipt in the autumn at 1°C for at least a month and are then removed as required because the bulbs can safely be held at this tempera-ture for up to nine months. Bulbs planted in pots in the winter can be grown in a glasshouse whilst those planted in spring or summer can be left outside until the shoots are about 8 cm high before transfer to a glass-house. Temperature must be kept low (not above 13°C) at night when the plants are growing but this can be raised to 16°C just before anthesis. Easter lily flower buds become visible on the stem apex about six weeks before Easter, when normally forced.

Recent work in the U.S.A. has indicated that the growth of non-vernalized Easter lilies to anthesis is accelerated by 30 or 45 long days given immediately after shoot emergence (Waters and Wilkins, 1967). Long days had little effect on non-vernalized lilies of three cultivars. Previous to this report the Easter lily had not been considered as responsive to photo-period, although Smith and Langhans (1962) had produced flowers 3–7 days earlier in long days than in short days, at temperatures between 10 and 27°C (Fig. 79). The effect of carbon dioxide supplementation in glasshouses, and effects of long days on the growth and flowering of Easter lilies has also been investigated at Minnesota University (Wilkins, Waters and Widmer, 1968; Wilkins, Widmer and Waters, 1968). There were

earlier indications that floral induction occurred due to natural photoperiod in non-vernalized 'Georgia' lilies grown in Florida (Waters and
Wilkins, 1967), with floral differentiation being accelerated by up to seven
weeks. Experiments on effects of long days on vernalized and unvernalized
lilies of three cultivars showed that long days accelerated floral differentiation and the flowering of non-vernalized lily bulbs, but the effect of long
day decreased as the length of the vernalization treatment increased. A
number of questions are posed by these results: Is the long day inductive
effect reversible, as Miller and Kiplinger (1966b) found with vernalization?
Is there a fixed number of photoperiods necessary for irreversible induc-

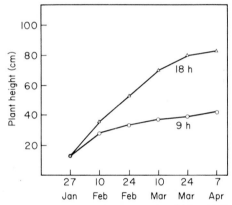

Fig. 7.9 Effect of photoperiod on height growth of 'Croft' Easter lilies grown in
9-hour and 18-hour photoperiods (after Smith and Langhans, 1962).

tion? What effects have different forcing temperatures on photo-induced
plants? Can bulbs be successfully treated with the appropriate photoperiod before planting?

Both carbon dioxide enrichment and long days decreased the period to
bloom in non-vernalized 'Ace' lilies (from 265 to 222 as carbon dioxide
levels increased from 300 to 2000 vpm, and from 265 to 168 as long days
were increased from 0 to 45 at 300 vpm carbon dioxide). Carbon dioxide
had little effect (4 days' earliness) on vernalized 'Ace' lilies, and long days
advanced flowering only slightly. The lily 'Nellie White' was, however,
responsive to carbon dioxide enrichment and photoperiodic treatment
even when vernalized, the maximum response to carbon dioxide in natural
daylength being 13 days.

Night-break treatments of four hours of incandescent, red or far-red
radiation during natural cooling hastened flowering by 22, 15 and 8 days,
respectively, compared with natural daylength. Further night breaks during
the forcing period had no further effect (Einert *et al.*, 1969). The earlier

date of anthesis was due to more rapid flower initiation which was accompanied by a decrease of 2 flower buds and 7 leaves per stem for every week of earlier anthesis. Four days' earliness was also obtained by planting the bulbs so that the bulb tip was at soil level instead of the more usual 12 cm depth (bulb half-exposed), but there was no effect on flower number. Benefits due to deeper planting were ascribed to improved stem rooting.

It would appear that there is still scope for improving the growth of lilies by investigations of the interactions of temperature (both vernalization and post-vernalization), photoperiod and growing conditions, especially light and carbon dioxide.

The form of the final product, the potted plant near anthesis, can be considerably affected by treatment given to the bulb or the young plant. Many of these effects are related to the amount of growth which occurs before the flowers are initiated. This then prevents further leaf formation. Early vernalization leads to early initiation, and short plants with few leaves. Delayed flower initiation produces tall, leafy plants which are less attractive commercially. Stuart (1967) illustrates the extremes of morphology exhibited by 'Ace' lilies given only 14 days at 1–2°C compared with those which had 102 days. The former had 18 flowers and 228 leaves, the latter 2 flowers and 69 leaves. The ideal is between these two extremes, although there is demand for two types of pot lilies, a tall form when lilies are used as a background material in flower arrangements, and a dwarf form for table decoration (Fig. 7.10). The short forms can to some extent be achieved by using dwarfing compounds.

Because the date of anthesis is important in Easter lilies, and because the date of Easter varies, it is important to have a method for varying the rate of plant growth. Such a scheme has been developed empirically by Box (1963) for naturally-cooled southern grown 'Georgia' lilies. It is not recommended for other cooling methods nor for bulbs produced in other areas. The plants are kept at 10°C from 1 January to 15 February. The appropriate night temperature is obtained from:

$$T_{(N)} = \frac{2260}{(DF)} + 30$$

where (DF) is the number of days from 15 January to the desired anthesis date. Day temperatures should be 5–7°C above the night temperature, and appear less critical than night temperature in determining anthesis date.

This method has recently been adapted for forced potted lilies by the preparation of programmes suitable for producing a saleable product by Easter, irrespective of the date of this holiday. Natural low temperatures are used for the pre-glasshouse phase which ends at the end of the calendar year, and differences in the glasshouse-phase duration are taken up by different temperature régimes. Progressive increases in temperature are used to achieve early anthesis.

Workers at Michigan State University have described forcing of lilies as a compromise between speed of growth and development, the numbers

Fig. 7.10 Forced Easter lily cultivar 'Nellie White' showing the dwarf habit desired for pot plant sale. (Photo. A. N. Roberts, courtesy of Oregon State University.)

of flowers and the number and length of leaves, because naturally-cooled lilies have more flowers and leaves than pre-cooled ones (De Hertogh *et al.*, 1969). To improve the quality of forced lilies, these workers investigated the effect of 17°C before the start of cooling on 'Ace' and 'Nellie White' lily bulbs of various sizes, and found a significantly increased number of leaves and flowers with no adverse effect on time to flower or on plant height.

Plant height is markedly affected by photoperiod, plants in 18 h days are 1·5–2·0 times the height of those in a 9 h day. This is an effect on internode elongation, rather than any change in node number. A long photoperiod can be achieved commercially with a "night break" using 60 W incandescent lamps spaced 120 cm apart and a similar distance above the plants, from, commonly, 10 p.m. to 2 a.m. or for 5 sec min^{-1} cyclically. Effects of photoperiod on extension growth are shown in Fig. 7·9, and the interaction between photoperiod and duration of low temperature in Table 7.13.

Taller plants than desirable result from both very dense spacing in the

Table 7.13

Interaction between low-temperature duration and photoperiod in Easter lily 'Ace', flowers per 10 plants (after Langhans and Weiler, 1967).

	Photoperiod during forcing	
Weeks at 4°C	9 hours	9 hours + night break[1]
0	0	1
1	0	1
2	0	8
3	2	10
4	9	10
5	6	10
6	10	10

[1] Night break of 4 h at 20 f.c.

glasshouse and insufficient light because of dirty glass or poor glasshouse transmission. Temperature during forcing has little effect on height within the range 10–27°C, but there are reports of dwarfing following very low temperatures during the mid-forcing period. There seems little scope, however, for height control by temperature manipulation in the forcing house. An indication of the amount of extra stem height obtained by reducing light in central Mississippi to 50% of full sunlight is given by Einert and Box (1967) who grew control plants 39 cm tall and half-shaded plants 48 cm tall. For lily 'Enchantment' light is more important than temperature for flower bud development; about 30 cal cm^{-2} day^{-1} is needed to prevent bud blasting and about 60 to prevent flower abscission, which are independent processes (Kamerbeek, 1969c).

Easter varies between 26 March and 22 April and considerable skill is required to produce Easter lily flowers at the saleable stage at the right time. A scheme has been developed by the Michigan State school for bringing plants into the glasshouse on a fixed date (20 December) irrespective of the date of Easter and following different glasshouse temperature to flowering, e.g. for early Easters 17°C until 20 January, 18°C to 20 February and 20°C until flowering. For a late Easter, 17°C is maintained throughout. This scheme, which is directly related to the widely-used "natural-cooling" procedure, is called "controlled-temperature forcing" (De Hertogh and Einert, 1969).

Effects of treatments have been observed on leaf length, especially those at the base of the shoot and because up to 50 leaves are initiated between anthesis of mother plant in July and bulb lifting in September, it might be expected that lifting date influences leaf expansion. Regular increase in the length of lower leaves was found with later lifting over the period July–September, and this trend was opposite to that of stem length (Blaney and Roberts, 1966c). In the "controlled-temperature forcing" method of De Hertogh and co-workers, lower leaves were distinctly longer than those of bulbs pre-cooled in peat, and in lilies grown by "natural cooling" leaves are longer than in pre-cooled plants. Commercially, longer leaves lead to a more attractive product.

Although most Easter lilies are forced in the spring, it is possible to bring bulbs to flower late in the same year as the bulbs were lifted. For maximum earliness, freshly-lifted mature bulbs should be stored for 5–6 weeks at 7–10°C and planted immediately to take advantage of light conditions in the autumn (Stuart, 1953). Effects of vernalization were investigated for Easter lily by leaf removal and different temperature treatments (Roberts and Blaney, 1968). Eighty-eight and 58-leaved plants from bulbs receiving 4 and 12 weeks at 4°C vernalization treatment were defoliated in a number of patterns to remove different proportions of young and old leaves during successive stages of extension. It was found that young expanding leaves were essential for the continued extension of the main axis, especially at the time of flower initiation in partially-vernalized plants. These young expanding leaves allowed rapid leaf unfolding, internode extension, the complete development of flower buds and maintained main-axis dominance. The removal of young leaves when about a third of the complement was unfolded enhanced the development of the daughter bulb, but most of the initiated flowers aborted.

It was concluded that the correlated inhibition of the daughter axis especially in the partly-vernalized plants is largely dependent on the young expanding leaves until the developing flower buds form a strong sink.

VII. Growth of *Narcissus* and tulip at high temperature

When the low-temperature treatment is completed in both *Narcissus* and tulip, they can be transferred to a higher temperature in the growing room, cellar or a glasshouse to bring the plants to anthesis as rapidly as possible. The rate of subsequent growth is rapid, when a temperature of 18–20°C is maintained. A great deal of work has not been done on factors affecting rapid growth in the glasshouse, but it is known that the time for which tulip bulbs are in the glasshouse at these temperatures is about 3–3·5 weeks under normal conditions. If longer periods of low temperature than the minimum are given before transfer to the glasshouse, then this duration is further reduced. For each 2·5°C below 18–20°C anthesis is delayed about a week, and the skilled grower can manipulate glasshouse temperature to achieve anthesis at convenient times, to avoid flower picking at the weekends and to encourage or delay anthesis to suit market demands. Care must be taken to ensure that air temperatures do not rise above 20°C, especially when sunny days occur. For *Narcissus*, slightly lower temperatures are recommended, 15–20°C.

Temperatures can be manipulated to encourage longer stems in the Single and Double Early tulips and Mendel tulips. An initial 16°C raised gradually to 20°C assists in producing longer stems. Later-flowering tulips, including Darwin and Triumph types, are usually kept at 13°C initially because higher temperatures result in weak stems and poor flowers. Later the temperature can safely be raised to 16°C and then to 18°C or even 20°C at a late stage when the insertion of the lowest leaf is about 4 cm above soil level. When the flower shows the first sign of colour, a lower temperature will provide better flowers with deeper colour. *Narcissus* are usually given 13°C for the first few days after transfer to the glasshouse before the temperature is raised to 16°C or even 18°C, which must be considered a maximum. Some cultivars must be kept at 16°C because of undesirable side effects of the high temperature, e.g. 'Helios' produce much leaf to the detriment of the flower at 18°C and 'Fortune' cups lose much of the attractive dark colour of the cup above 16°C. It is not always possible commercially to follow the recommended rise in temperature because a second "round" of bulbs is frequently kept under the staging supporting the first round, so they can obtain some of their high temperature concurrently with the first round. Contrary to popular belief, darkness is not essential for the early period in the glasshouse, although some form of darkening is frequently used for the shorter, early tulip cultivars (Single and Double Early, Mendel) to give a more acceptable stem length at anthesis, and if a second round is kept under staging, this is usually a dark enough situation to achieve extra elongation. *Narcissus* crops are never shaded.

There is little information on the effects of photoperiod on extension growth in *Narcissus* and tulip, although for lilies, long days are known to increase stem length considerably. A similar effect has been observed in controlled environment cabinets with the tulip 'Rose Copland' (Fig. 7.11), but no attempt has been made to utilize night breaks or extended days on a commercial scale, although this would appear a convenient method if it also works with the short-stemmed early cultivars.

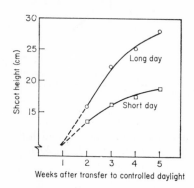

Fig. 7.11 Effect of daylength on the rate of extension growth of shoots of tulip 'Rose Copland' grown at 10°C and two daylengths (8 and 16 h) with light flux density adjusted to give the same daily total. Each point a mean from about 30 plants.

VIII. Growing bulbs in artificial light

Tulips are frequently grown in artificially-lit cellars or sheds, and it is argued that it is less expensive to provide lights in a well-insulated structure than to heat a poorly-insulated glasshouse. The quality achieved under artificial illumination is, however, less good: both leaves and flowers are usually paler in colour than the glasshouse-grown product. Tungsten lamps are usually used to give 100 W m^{-2}, usually with 40 W lamps arranged so they can be kept 30–40 cm above the growing tips of the leaves. Lamps are usually switched on for 12 h each day, and there is obvious scope here for photoperiodic treatments. Incandescent light accelerated floral differentiation and date of anthesis of Easter lilies by up to 5 weeks compared with control plants, although the number of flowers was reduced. The degree of response was affected by the intensity, duration and the date of lighting (Waters and Wilkins, 1966).

Preliminary experiments on carbon dioxide enrichment of *Narcissus* and

N

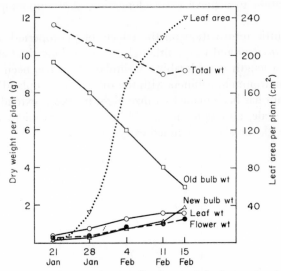

Fig. 7.12 Changes in dry weight distribution and leaf area in the tulip 'Paul Richter' after transfer to a glasshouse at 18°C on 20 January. Each point a mean from 18 plants.

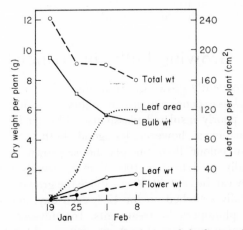

Fig. 7.13 Changes in dry weight distribution and leaf area in the *Narcissus* 'Fortune' after transfer to a glasshouse at 28°C on 18 January. Each point a mean from 18 plants.

tulip forcing houses showed that very little, if any, benefit results and that the cost of the carbon dioxide makes the operation uneconomic. The flowers were assessed for quality by measurements of stem length and flower diameter, and flowering date was recorded.

IX. Dry matter changes in tulips and *Narcissus* in the glasshouse

When tulip bulbs are transferred to the glasshouse there is a rapid transfer of dry matter from the bulb to the shoot, which is very similar to but more rapid than the processes which occur in the field in spring (Fig. 7.12). Total bulb weight falls over the whole period from housing to anthesis, and about three-quarters of the mother bulb weight is lost over the same period. Similar data were collected for *Narcissus* 'Fortune', (Fig. 7.13) which again emphasize the rapid mobilization of reserves in the bulb for the growth of the shoot.

Chapter 8

Physiology and metabolism

"... the processes which go on inside a bulb are very
difficult to test."   K. Goebel, 1905

1. BULB METABOLISM

2. THE METABOLISM OF THE ROOTED PLANT

I. Bulb metabolism

Information on metabolic changes in stored bulbs is neither extensive nor
comprehensive. The *Iris* has been studied more than other bulbous plants,
especially in the Netherlands and Israel. This is probably because the
bulbs can be stored for long periods at 25°C as "retarded" bulbs which
can be removed from storage when required; other bulbs store less well

for long durations, so that their study is much more seasonal and short term. Inevitably an account of stored-bulb metabolism will be disjointed and no clear theme will appear; this must be blamed on the general lack of information, and because much of what is known has been obtained by observation rather than by critically designed experimentation.

Two of the most obvious changes which occur in stored bulbs are a loss of water and a loss of dry weight. In bulbs which have initiated a flower before the start of storage (e.g. *Narcissus*), or which initiate a flower shortly after the start of storage (e.g. tulip), flower differentiation continues during storage and is followed later by extension growth of the shoot. In other bulbs (e.g. *Iris*) where flower initiation occurs after replanting, leaf production occurs in storage. There are no external indications of these activities, however. Little is known about anatomical or biochemical changes during this period; knowledge is restricted to measurements of extension growth.

I. Weight losses and respiration

Kamerbeek (1962a) found that over 355 days at 25°C, bulbs of *Iris* 'Wedgwood' lost 2·7% of the bulb dry weight and 29·2% of the original water. The loss of fresh weight was not uniform throughout the period, however; it was more rapid over the first month or so and linear afterwards.

In an investigation of dry weight changes in 10 cm bulbs of the tulip 'Paul Richter', no difference was found between two temperature régimes: (a) 2 weeks at 20°C followed by 10 weeks at 17°C and (b) 12 weeks at 20°C. A single equation therefore described the dry weight changes occurring in both sets of bulbs (Fig. 8.1). About 0·6% of the bulb dry weight was lost per week, or expressed as a (negative) relative growth rate, $-0·0007$ g g^{-1} day^{-1}, a value considerably lower than that found for the growing bulb during the winter phase (0·0023 g g^{-1} day^{-1}). The difference between the two values reflects the difference between respiration rates which are largely associated with bulb maintenance in one case and with active growth of roots and shoots in the other.

The general pattern of respiration in stored *Iris* 'Wedgwood' bulbs has been described by Rodrigues Pereira (1962). Bulbs averaging about 20 g, stored at 25·5°C, had an oxygen uptake of above 0·40 ml O_2 h^{-1} shortly after lifting at the end of August but this decreased by about half over two weeks and then remained nearly constant until the following March. Kamerbeek (1962a) also found very little change in carbon dioxide production after the initial high values shortly after lifting. Although respiration rates increased slowly over a whole year, the change was small, and Kamerbeek considered this a steady-state condition. Halevy and Shoub

(1964a) studied the maturation of *Iris* 'Wedgwood' bulbs in relation to respiration. In Israel, bulbs lifted in the last half of April were sufficiently mature for the earliest forcing but were immature if lifted two weeks earlier in the northern regions of Israel. Respiration rates showed a marked decrease in April from a peak value of above 14 μl O_2 mg N^{-1} h^{-1} to about 11 μl which could be a sign of bulb maturation. Respiration rates were determined on buds or growing apices at 30°C by standard Warburg manometry, so the rates cannot be compared with those of

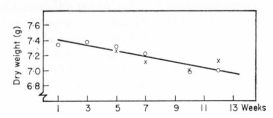

Fig. 8.1 Changes in the dry weight of 10 cm 'Paul Richter' tulip bulbs stored at 20/17°C and 20°C (circles 20°C, crosses 17°C) over a 12-week period starting in early September. Equation of fitted line, $y = 7.44 - 0.036x$.

Kamerbeek or Rodrigues Pereira, who used whole bulbs and expressed their results on a fresh weight or dry weight basis.

The initially high respiration rates in the intact bulbs at, or shortly after, lifting could have been due to a number of factors, such as: respiration of soluble carbohydrates; an increase in the respiration of the whole bulb following transfer to a higher temperature for storing the bulbs or for the measurement of respiration; or to carbon dioxide output from between the bulb scales consequent on the expansion, and subsequent leakage of gases within the bulb after the increase in temperature.

Kamerbeek (1962a) compared respiration rates of *Iris* bulbs with those of other plants. At 25 or 30°C the rate of carbon dioxide output was about 6μl CO_2 mg fresh weight^{-1} h^{-1}, equivalent to about 20μl on a dry weight basis. This rate is similar to that found in stored potatoes, but lower than in many other non-storage tissues.

II. Respiration of *Iris* bulbs

A. Effect of temperature on respiration rate of *Iris*

At 25–30°C the *Iris* bulb is in a steady-state resting condition; the activity of the growing apex is very low, there is almost complete cessation of extension growth, and the respiration rate is also low, consuming glucose at about 0·008 mg g fresh weight^{-1} h^{-1} (Kamerbeek, 1962a).

At temperatures higher and lower than those which support a steady-state resting condition, respiratory activity (measured either as carbon dioxide output or oxygen uptake) was increased. Transfer from 25°C to 15°C resulted, after six days, in the attainment of another steady state at a higher level, but at 40°C, where respiration was greater than at 15°C, a steady state condition was not reached in six days. Both the low-temperature and high-temperature induced respiration rates were reversible because transferring the bulbs back to 25°C resulted in a slow decrease of respiratory activity towards the original steady-state "resting" level.

Kamerbeek (1962a) analysed theoretically the effects of transfer of bulbs

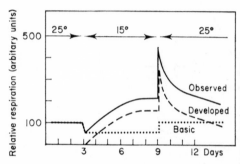

Fig. 8.2 The effect of temperature changes on *Iris* bulb respiration as interpreted by Kamerbeek (1962a).

from a steady-state at 25°C to 15°C and to 40°C. The respiration rate at 15°C is a resultant of the addition to the "basic respiration" of a "developed respiration". At 15°C a respiratory increase develops which is related to growth activity, but which is reversible (Fig. 8.2). Interpretation of the effects which occur in a transfer from 25°C to 40°C and back is more difficult, although a basic respiration and a developed respiration are again postulated. The basic respiration is higher at 40°C than at 25°C.

This general pattern of *Iris* bulb respiration was confirmed by Halevy *et al.* (1963) who found that heat-curing at 31°C reduced oxygen uptake in growing apices to a quarter of that at harvest time. A temporary increase in respiration occurred when each new leaf developed, and when bulbs were transferred to 13°C, a sudden increase in respiration corresponded with the differentiation of the first flower, and a second peak corresponded with the differentiation of the second flower. An increase in respiratory activity coinciding with the formation of leaf and flower primordia was also noted by Rodrigues Pereira (1962).

Effects of transferring *Iris* bulbs from one temperature to another were also observed by Rodrigues Pereira (1962). Bulbs were transferred from storage at 25·5°C to storage at 2, 13 or 31°C, whilst a control set was retained at 25·5°C. After two weeks, when the respiration rates were constant, the bulbs were transferred to 20°C and the respiration measured. The respiration rate of bulbs transferred from 31 or 25·5°C to 20°C decreased until a minimum was reached after a few hours, when it increased again to a new constant level 50 to 100% greater than the original level after about 24 h. With an increase in temperature from 2 or 13°C to 20°C a new higher steady-state was reached after about 24 h (Fig. 8.3).

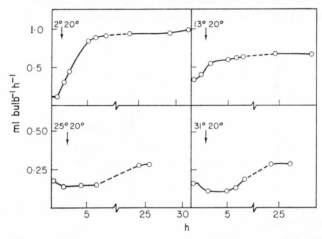

Fig. 8.3 Effect of changes in temperature on respiration rates of *Iris* 'Wedgwood' bulbs. All bulbs initially at 25·5°C until 10 March, then at 2, 13, 25·5, or 31°C until 25 March then to 20°C (at arrow) where respiration changes were measured as carbon dioxide evolved. Oxygen uptake showed similar responses (after Rodrigues Pereira, 1962).

These results were interpreted as confirming previous observations that the metabolism of *Iris* bulbs is inhibited by temperatures above 20°C. A number of authors have already commented upon the situation in bulb plants that, unlike most other tissues, an intermediate temperature of 5–15°C results in higher rates of respiration than higher temperatures (Algera, 1947; Forward, 1960).

The results of Rodrigues Pereira (1962) were confirmed by those of Kamerbeek (1962a) who concluded, on the basis of measurement of oxygen uptake and carbon dioxide evolution, that:

1. At 25°C the respiration rate is low and associated with the steady-state "resting" condition. At temperatures below 25°C respiratory

activity increases. The optimum temperature for this increased activity is 15°C, and the increased activity was thought to be due to the establishment of a new respiratory pathway or to the removal of some inhibitor of the process.

2. Respiratory activity is lower at 30°C than at 25°C, but above 30°C activity increases again.
3. The lethal temperature is near 40°C. Above this temperature respiration increases rapidly and above 45°C the respiratory mechanism is rapidly and irreversibly damaged.
4. Most respiratory changes induced by changes in temperature are reversible when the bulbs are transferred back to 25 or 30°C.

B. Structural factors and respiration of Iris bulbs

The *Iris* bulb is a comparatively bulky structure and the respiration rate of the whole bulb measured by conventional methods gives only an imprecise picture of the processes occurring. Little is known about the location of respiratory activity within the bulb—how much do the growing apices contribute to the total respiration and how much do the bulb scales?

The *Iris* bulb is tightly enclosed by 2–4 thin membranes which are the remains of dead leaves. It appears that these are a barrier to gaseous exchange, because when they were removed by Rodrigues Pereira (1962) the respiration rate increased from 0.4 ml O_2 bulb^{-1} h^{-1} to a maximum of 2.0 ml O_2 h^{-1} after about 24 h and then slowly decreased to reach a steady rate of about 0.8 ml O_2 bulb^{-1} h^{-1} after about 7 days. Kamerbeek (1962a) also observed a large increase in respiration following removal of the tunics. A peak occurred after 24 h, following which the respiration rate continued to fall over the next 22 days. In time this would almost certainly have reached the original level. This effect was observed with oxygen uptake as well as carbon dioxide evolution. Clearly the tunics have an important effect on gaseous exchange, which is more than a mere release of entrapped carbon dioxide.

Results such as these cast doubts on the validity of respiration measurements made on shoot apices. Halevy et al. (1963) were obviously aware of this but their results were obtained with excised shoot apices, the respiration rates of which were determined at 30°C. Their tests indicated that although significant differences were obtained between respiration rates measured at different temperatures, differences due to previous treatment were also significant.

The effects of oxygen supply to the bulb were examined by Kamerbeek (1962a). In 10% oxygen, respiration was about 25% lower than in air, and in 100% oxygen, it was 15–20% higher. Kamerbeek concluded that an oxygen deficiency in the bulb was unlikely in normal circumstances, although it appears that the rate of respiration is limited by oxygen concentration in air. A respiratory quotient (RQ) of 1·1 was demonstrated, which remained constant despite large changes in respiration rate. Fermentation was therefore unlikely even at high rates of respiration. These conclusions are similar to those reached by Burton (1950) in his detailed consideration of oxygen diffusion in the potato tuber.

C. Substrates

Sugar concentration has been found to limit the rate of bulb respiration in many cases where this factor has been examined. Kamerbeek (1962a) found that storage of *Iris* bulbs at nine temperatures between 0 and 40°C for six days, treatments which would produce widely differing respiration rates, had no effect on the percentage of sucrose. It is possible however that prolonged temperature-treatment would change the content of soluble sugars, so Kamerbeek calculated the expected changes in the substrate pool for given rates of respiration. About 28 mg of soluble sugars were present g fresh weight^{-1} and at 25°C Kamerbeek estimated that about 0·18 mg g fresh weight^{-1} would be consumed daily. During the six days after transfer to 40°C about 9·7 mg sugar g fresh weight^{-1} would be consumed. It was therefore unlikely that respiration was limited by substrate concentration, considering the relative amounts present and consumed. At the sites of respiration Kamerbeek thought that substrates could still be limiting respiration rate, because of low rates of transport of substrates within cells or between cells, but no specific information is available on this point for bulbs.

D. Respiratory quotient

Kamerbeek found RQ values to average 1·1 at 15°C, which was surprising because the reserves in an *Iris* bulb are almost entirely sugars and storage carbohydrates, and it is unlikely that substrates other than sugars are used in respiration. No explanation was suggested which could reasonably account for the RQ being slightly, but significantly, higher than unity.

E. Respiration and development in *Iris* bulbs

It might be expected that respiration rates would show marked changes as the apex was transformed from the vegetative to the floral condition. This was investigated by Rodrigues Pereira (1962) using conventional

Warburg manometry on small sterile portions of base plate bearing apices (fresh weight about 125 mg) excised from bulbs. Figure 8.4 shows that the respiration rates of discs increased to a peak shortly before the apex became reproductive and then decreased as differentiation proceeded. A secondary peak corresponded with the initiation of the gynoecium.

Kamerbeek (1962a) showed that in the absence of oxygen, no primordial growth occurred. Maximum growth of the first leaf occurred in 10% oxygen, the growth rate being lower in air and in pure oxygen. It was

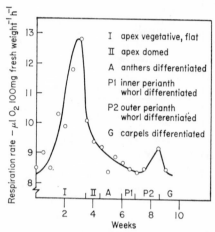

Fig. 8.4 Respiration rates of apices of 'Wedgwood' *Iris* bulbs during flower initiation at 13°C (after Rodrigues Pereira, 1962).

suggested that the oxygen concentration around the shoot could be as low as 10%, and that the higher growth rate at low oxygen concentration was an adaptation to the conditions within the retarded bulb. Primordial growth differs from respiration in response to oxygen concentration; highest respiration rates were observed in 100% oxygen.

III. Carbohydrate changes in bulbs

Halevy (1963) and Halevy *et al.* (1963) followed changes in carbohydrates in 'Wedgwood' *Iris* bulbs lifted early in May, stored commercially until early June and then stored at 5, 10°C or in uncontrolled conditions (common storage) (mean 24–26°C in July–September, 20°C in October). Periodic samplings showed that both total soluble sugars and starch, expressed as a percentage of fresh weight, increased over the first six weeks of storage, this was attributable to a decrease in water content over the same period (Fig. 8.5). Starch hydrolysis was greater at the two lower temperatures; total soluble sugars showed a concomitant rise, new leaves were formed and flower initiation occurred in storage. Both starch hydrolysis and apical activity were slower at 5°C than at 10°C, but the differences were small suggesting that the major effect was between 25°C and 10°C.

The initiation of starch hydrolysis was observed by Rodrigues Pereira

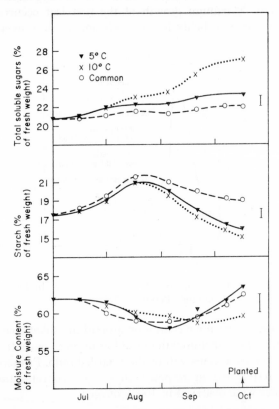

Fig. 8.5 Effects of storage temperature on total soluble sugar, starch and water content of 'Wedgwood' *Iris* bulbs stored at 5°C, 10°C or in a commercial store (24–26°C to September, 20°C in October). Standard errors shown as vertical bars (Halevy *et al.*, 1963).

(1962). At 13°C, hydrolysis started in the scales and soluble and insoluble carbohydrates accumulated in the apical region. A considerable increase in carbohydrate occurred in the young shoot within two weeks if the growing point had become reproductive, but only small changes were observed when the bulbs remained vegetative. No abrupt changes in metabolism occurred as the apex became reproductive; many changes in carbohydrates appeared two weeks before the identification of morphological change and continued for some time after initiation.

At 2°C *Iris* bulbs contained more soluble sugar than at 31°C, in both scales and shoots. Rodrigues Pereira (1962) was unable, however, in his experiments, to confirm the conclusion of Algera (1947) that concentrations of sucrose and reducing sugars in tulip and hyacinth increased rapidly as temperature was lowered, and that the response could be rapidly reversed by transfer to a higher temperature.

Carbohydrate changes in the tulip bulb in store

In the developing bulb before lifting, starch increased until it constituted 70–80% of the dry weight in cv. 'Murillo' (Algera, 1936). The starch then decreased during storage, at a rate dependent on temperature. Lower temperatures decreased the starch and increased the percentage of non-reducing sugars from about 5% to about 13%. During the storage period there was very little change in the reducing sugar concentration, although later, following planting, the concentration increased rapidly.

IV. Peroxidase and catalase activity in *Iris*

Interest in enzyme systems arose from the work of van Laan (1955) who investigated the effects of curing and pre-planting low temperatures on enzymes in iris bulbs. He found that the activity of dehydrogenases, catalases and amylases was correlated with the treatments given to the bulbs. The curing process initially increased dehydrogenase activity, although this effect was later reversed, decreased catalase activity, and completely inhibited amylase activity, whilst pre-cooling increased dehydrogenase, catalase and amylase activity.

Enzymic activity was later studied in Israel by Halevy *et al.* (1963) on apices taken from three batches of *Iris* bulbs stored at (a) 25°C, (b) 2°C or (c) in a commercial store for 10 days followed by 10 days heat curing at 30°C, 2 weeks at 25°C then 10°C. Enzyme activity was low at 25°C and 2°C. Both catalase and peroxidase showed slightly increased activity in the middle of the storage period followed by a decline, the rise coinciding with the start of slow leaf formation. No flowers were formed at either 2°C or 25°C (Fig. 8.6). In treatment (c), the heat-curing process did not appear to affect enzyme activity, neither did transferring the bulbs to cold storage. Despite a three-fold increase in respiration rate, during the first two weeks of cold storage, catalase and peroxidase activity only increased to about 150% of the basic level. When flowers were initiated, further marked increases in activity were recorded with a peak near the mid-period of flower differentiation (Stage P1).

The role of catalase and peroxidase in the metabolism of *Iris* bulbs is not clear; in many plants their activity is often related to the growth rate and to respiration, and this link is seen in *Iris* too. However, as noted by Halevy *et al.* (1963) there are certain exceptions to this apparent correlation. Enzyme activity was similar at 2 and 25°C but respiration was signi-

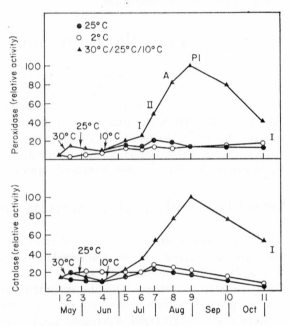

Fig. 8.6 Relative activities of catalase and peroxidase in apices of 'Wedgwood' *Iris* bulbs stored at various temperatures. Symbols on the peroxidase curve indicate stages of flower differentiation which occurred only in the 30/25/10°C treatment (for key see Fig. 8.4). Standard errors shown as vertical bars (Halevy *et al.*, 1963).

ficantly lower at 25°C; when leaves were initiated or developing, respiration, but not enzyme activity, increased, and during flower differentiation only a moderate increase in respiration accompanied the very large increase in enzyme activity.

Halevy *et al.* (1963) concluded that whilst changes in starch hydrolysis and respiration are mainly concerned with growth, the fluctuations in enzymic activity appear more closely related to stages of development at the apex.

V. Changes in *Iris* bulb metabolism during maturation

The correct time for lifting bulbs is one of the difficulties faced by the grower. A visual assessment of bulb maturity can be made from the appearance of the above-ground parts and the bulbs themselves. These are not always a reliable indication, however, especially after hot, dry periods which can accelerate bulb maturity more than the senescence symptoms usually associated with maturity. Halevy and Shoub (1964a) investigated changes in the composition and metabolism of 'Wedgwood' *Iris* as maturity approached, with a view to devising a simple test to determine maturity. *Iris* bulbs are normally lifted in Israel in the second half of April; the investigation extended from mid-February to mid-May.

Respiration increased in the shoot apex until early April, then fell rapidly, whilst that of the scales fell throughout the three months, rapidly at first but more slowly later. Catalase activity of the bulb scales was a better guide to maturity because it increased until mid-April, then decreased abruptly as the leaves started to desiccate. If the determination of catalase activity in other growing areas confirms that this factor is related to maturation, then the method could be more widely used. Meanwhile, its use is restricted to growers in Israel. In Washington, Kimura (1967) failed to find the expected decline in catalase activity in *Iris* bulbs sampled before and during normal harvesting periods.

VI. Respiration in other bulbs

In comparison with *Iris*, little work has been done on other flower bulbs, and very few measurements have been made. Dolk and van Slogteren (1930) studied the effects of temperature on the respiration rate of hyacinth bulbs because of the development of a hot-air treatment at 38°C for controlling *Xanthomonas hyacinthi*, the cause of yellow disease. Carbon dioxide output was linearly related to temperature up to 40°C, which was the approximate lethal limit.

Payne (1967) showed that respiration in *Lilium longiflorum* cultivars decreased over the first three weeks of storage at 4°C to a low steady-state value but the respiration rate of bulbs kept at 21°C rose simultaneously with sprouting of the bulbs. The transfer of bulbs from 21° to 4°C decreased the respiration rate to that observed in bulbs kept at 4°C throughout. No evidence was found of any major change in respiration rates of bulbs stored at 4°C which could indicate physiological changes occurring as vernalization progressed.

Tulip and hyacinth bulbs show patterns of respiration after lifting similar to that of *Iris*; the rate decreases after lifting and then remains constant for some time. If the temperature is lowered, respiration falls, but less than one would expect assuming a Q_{10} of 2, because the soluble sugar concentration is higher at lower temperatures (Algera, 1947).

Algera, in his extensive work on hyacinth and tulip respiration and carbohydrate metabolism, concluded that in both genera there is a clear relation between respiration and sucrose concentration in the bulb, and that cooled bulbs, which contain more reducing sugars than uncooled bulbs, have a higher respiration rate. During the summer the concentration of reducing sugars in the tulips is low, and respiration depends on the rate at which they are formed. In winter the concentration of reducing sugars is higher and a direct relation exists between their concentration and the rate of respiration. Less sucrose is present in the hyacinth than in the tulip but the concentration in the bulb increases with low temperature as in the tulip. The tulip contains inulin in considerably smaller quantities than sucrose, but the hyacinth contains a very high inulin concentration (and a much lower starch concentration) than the tulip. Temperature has little effect on inulin concentration.

The effects of temperature and harvesting date on respiration have been reported for 'Rose Copland' tulip bulbs (Rees, 1968b). When respiration was measured at 25°C, early in the season (mid-June) the rate fell from an initial value of about 50 μl O_2 uptake g fresh weight^{-1} h^{-1} to a steady-state rate of 5–10 μl O_2 over about 14 days after lifting. Later in the season initial values were lower but the steady-state values were progressively higher; a lifting date in mid-September gave initial values of about 30, falling to about 13 μl O_2 uptake g fresh weight^{-1} h^{-1}. There was evidence for an initial rise in respiration rate after transfer of the bulbs to the respirometer, after allowing for a period of temperature equilibrium. Bulb-to-bulb variation was not very great and the same pattern of respiration was shown by all bulbs.

When tulip bulb respiration rate was measured at 15°C, the same general pattern was obtained as at 25°C, early-season high rates were 30–35 μl O_2 uptake g fresh weight^{-1} h^{-1} which decreased to 10–12 μl O_2 after 6–8 days (Fig. 8.7). Later in the season the high initial values after lifting were not observed, unlike the situation when respiration was measured at 25°C. Bulbs lifted in mid-July and placed in the respirometer at 35°C had a much higher respiration rate (40 μl O_2) than similar bulbs whose respiration was measured at 15°C (10–12 μl O_2 uptake g fresh weight^{-1} h^{-1}), but this high rate decreased to 50% in three days.

There are indications that effects of short periods of high temperature can be important in bulb behaviour; three of these, observed empirically, are (1) preventing hot-water treatment damage to *Narcissus* flowers (see Chapter 6); (2) the acceleration of anthesis in tulips and *Narcissus*; and (3) the initiation of flowers in borderline-size *Iris* bulbs. The widely

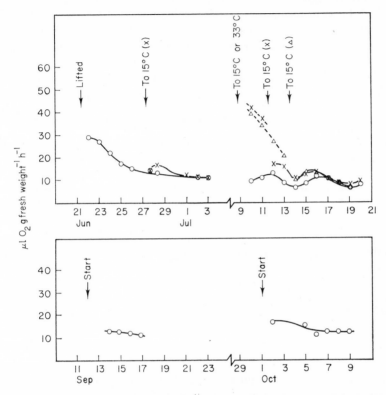

Fig. 8.7 Rates of respiration of 'Rose Copland' tulip bulbs measured at 10°C or 35°C (dotted lines). Each point a mean of at least 3 bulbs. Circles, bulbs at 15°C; crosses and triangles, bulbs at 35°C before transfer to 15°C.

different responses in the different bulb genera is indicative that some basic aspect of bulb metabolism is affected by high temperature, and it was thought that this might be reflected in the respiration rate. The transfer of bulbs from 25°C and 35°C for two days and then back to 25°C resulted in a higher respiration rate at 25°C (respiration was not measured at 35°C) —32 μl compared with 18 μl O_2 uptake g fresh weight^{-1} h^{-1}, but this increase due to the 35°C-treatment fell to the same level as the control bulbs within about four days.

Similar results were obtained when the respiration rate was measured at 15°C. The storage of bulbs at 2, 4 or 5 days at 35°C before transfer to

o

15°C had no great effect on the respiration rate measured at 15°C, a slightly higher rate decreased to that of the control within a few days (Fig. 8.7).

These results cast serious doubts on the measurement of respiration at temperatures higher than those at which the bulbs were stored. There is a transient burst of respiratory activity which does not decrease to a steady-state value for some days. It also seems unlikely that a few days' treatment at 35°C has any long-lasting effect on bulb respiration, as measured on intact bulbs. There may be an important effect on the respiration of the apex but this could well be obscured by respiration of the bulb scales.

Cutting a tulip bulb in half increases the respiration rate at 15°C from

Table 8.1

Effects of different peeling treatments on the steady-state (after 7 days) respiration rate ($\mu l\ O_2\ g^{-1}$ fresh wt h^{-1}) of bulbs of tulip 'Rose Copland' in two experiments.

Treatment	Expt. 1	Expt. 2
1. Whole bulb	8·57	6·34
2. Bulb with tunic removed and discarded	17·3	11·2
3. Bulb with tunic + 1 scale removed and discarded	37·7	28·4
4. Bulb with tunic + 2 scales removed and discarded	37·5	21·5
5. Scales only treatment 4	40·3	43·3
6. Bulb with tunic + 1 scale removed, but in respirometer	37·4	21·7
7. Bulb with tunic + 2 scales removed, but in respirometer	38·6	42·2

about 10 to 50 $\mu l\ O_2$ uptake g fresh weight^{-1} h^{-1}. The respiration rate of apices accounts for about a quarter of that of the whole bulb, and is similar to that of a halved bulb on a unit fresh weight basis. The effect of the covering structures was therefore examined in an experiment where various bulbs or bulb parts were included in the respirometer. The steady state values for respiration ($\mu l\ O_2$ uptake g fresh weight^{-1} h^{-1}) are shown in Table 8.1. Respiration rates can be expressed either in terms of the original bulb fresh weight or the weight of material in the respirometer; the latter is preferable in most respects and has been used in Table 8.1. The usual decrease in respiration was observed, especially in the first three days of the determination. Considering only steady values after a week, removal of the tunic approximately doubled respiration, and a further doubling resulted from the removal of one more scale. The removal of the second fleshy scale did not increase respiration further. The effects of replacing the removed scales into the respirometer with the bulb were not clear. In most cases, but not all, no further increase in respiration on a unit fresh weight basis occurred if all the parts were included in the respiro-meter, and this may have been due to the high rate of respiration of the excised scales. It must be concluded that the covering structures have an important effect on the respiration rates of the whole tulip bulb, and that excised scales have a respiration rate similar to the centre part of the bulb.

There is no indication why the respiration of the bulb is decreased by the covering structures; presumably they increase the resistance of CO_2 and O_2 diffusion, although Kamerbeek (1963) has argued that in *Iris* this is not likely. If, in an interpretation of bulb behaviour, we wish to examine changes in respiration occurring at the apex, then there is little to be gained from excising and measuring its respiration under conditions quite different from those occurring *in vivo*.

The bulb respiration of a number of tulip cultivars was measured by Nezu and Obata (1964) over 120 days' storage during which the tempera-ture fell from about 30°C to about 10°C. Values obtained were between 4 and 10 μg CO_2 evolved g fresh weight^{-1} h^{-1}, in reasonable agreement with those quoted above. The respiration rate decreased as temperature fell and with time.

Bould (1939) measured the respiration rates of *Narcissus* bulbs at 25°C, and found the pattern to be similar to that in tulip. An initial rate of 25 μl CO_2 evolved g fresh weight^{-1} h^{-1} in late July fell to between 5 and 10 μl by mid-August and remained at this level until early October before rising to about 12 μl by early November. In general the rates were below those for tulip throughout the period of measurement. Respiration was somewhat higher in both *Narcissus* and tulip bulbs grown in minus-N culture solutions.

VII. Effect of ethylene on respiration

A quantitative enhancement of the respiration rate of 'Wedgwood' *Iris* has been observed following treatment with ethylene (Kamberbeek, 1969b). When bulbs were kept at 30°C after lifting, the respiration rate was minimal and sprout inhibition was virtually complete. This basic respira-tion was stimulated by ethylene. After a four-hour lag the rate increased to reach a peak 24 h after treatment, irrespective of the ethylene concentra-tion. Respiration then decreased but increased to a second lower peak after 3 or 4 days before falling gradually. The stimulation was proportional to the ethylene concentration between 0·05 vpm and about 3 vpm; concentra-tions below the lower limit had no effect and above 3 vpm, no additional effect. Both carbon dioxide evolution and oxygen uptake were stimulated. The relation of these observations to other findings is not known but doubt is cast on the validity of changes in respiration with time when measured in respirometers where there is no control of the ethylene which may be produced.

VIII. Dormancy

Few studies have been made of factors affecting bulb dormancy, the reasons for dormancy or how dormancy can be overcome. Possibly, this is because little advantage can be gained from the early breaking of dormancy in bulbs which are normally planted in the autumn and have to pass through the winter before active aerial growth can occur.

In *Lilium longiflorum*, Wang (1969) has studied the effects of scale removal and various temperature and chemical treatments on dormancy and concludes that the main factor responsible for dormancy resides in the daughter scales. The ratio of new scales to old was shown to be a useful index of bulb maturity; bulbs were considered mature when the ratio approached unity. The removal of old scales had little effect on dormancy, but removing three-quarters or all the new scales broke dormancy and accelerated emergence. The concentration of growth inhibitors was higher in new scales than in old ones, but the amount decreased with storage whilst growth promoters increased. One of the inhibitors resembled abscisic acid, whilst one of the promoters was similar to indol-3yl-acetic acid. Dormancy can also be overcome by storing bulbs at 4°C, by hot-water treatment of bulbs at 38°C for 1 h, by heating soil before flowering to 24°C or by using gibberellic acid, indol-3yl-acetic acid, ethrel or ethylene. However, some of these procedures were deleterious to flowering, e.g. cold storage reduced the number of flowers produced.

The beneficial effects of warm storage of tulip and *Narcissus* bulbs may be an effect on dormancy, but this has not been adequately studied.

Sprouting and flowering time of 'Croft' Easter lilies was followed for bulbs harvested from mid-May to mid-October from soil heated to about 21°C for six successive 3-month periods from 15 February to 15 May, 15 March to 15 July etc., and from unheated soil (Blaney and Roberts, 1966b). Non-vernalized bulbs grew progressively earlier after harvests from mid-May to mid-October. All vernalized bulbs from heated soil except the last two periods flowered earlier than the controls. These results were interpreted as showing that the daughter bulbs in late winter and spring are not deeply dormant because warmth induces sprouting and precocious flowering. Dormancy deepens as the season advances, and after anthesis in July the daughter bulb dormancy slowly breaks normally but vernalization is necessary for early flower initiation. Warmth before anthesis produces a response similar to vernalization later.

2.   The metabolism of the rooted plant

Few studies have been concerned with the metabolism of rooted bulbous plants, as opposed to "dormant", unrooted bulbs. Other species have been more convenient, more easily available or more quickly grown from seed. Some work on bulbous plants has been done, it is suspected, because they happened to be available in a glasshouse, in winter, when the researcher had a bright idea. This lack of information on the metabolism of bulbous plants means that this part of the chapter will consist of small items of un-related information which do not fit into any pattern except the "general" one of conventional text-books of plant physiology which emphasizes similarities between plants, not their differences.

I. Soils and soil factors, root growth

Tulips grow in a wide range of soils, as experience throughout the world has indicated. Although much of tulip growing is practised on sandy and silty soils, they can also be grown on light clay. Lincolnshire soils used for tulip growing are characterized by low clay contents, rela-tively high organic matter contents and high proportions of fine sand and fine silt. The preference for light stone-free soils is due to the greater ease of mechanized handling. Soil pH is not critical either, although 6·0–7·5 is considered optimal (Schenk, 1969), and lime is frequently used in tulip growing to raise the pH to 6·0. Daffodils have been successfully grown at a pH as low as 4·9 (Gibson, 1935) and lime is not usually added to soils for *Narcissus* growing.

The peculiarities of the tulip root systems are a finite, comparatively low number of roots, which do not branch nor bear root hairs and are limited to a depth of about 65 cm. These factors contribute to the tulip's sensitivity to water stress, especially in times of rapid growth or high transpiration rates. In some parts of the world, as in Japan, irrigation of bulb crops is regularly practised or soil moisture is controlled by adjusting the water table as in Holland. In some soils there are dangers of poor drainage or of soil capping affecting bulb yield by allowing the decay of the root system due to reduced oxygen supply (Van der Valk and de Haan, 1969).

For the tulip cv. 'Apeldoorn', root production related to bulb size and shape have recently been studied in Holland (Schuurman, 1971). Root initiation ended shortly after emergence of shoots from the bulbs and root number was constant after this time. Bulb size had a positive effect on root number weight and rooting depth, independently of bulb shape.

Observations of root penetration into different soil types (clay, sand and brick-earth) were made at G.R.C.I. using a trench with glass walls inclined at a small angle to the vertical so that the roots grew against the glass, where their positions were recorded. Tulip ('Rose Copland') and *Narcissus* ('Fortune') bulbs were planted in mid-September, and root penetration was observed at 10 cm within 2 weeks, and at 20 cm by 20 October. The roots continued to grow to the lower edge of the glass at 66 cm before the end of the season in the three plots of *Narcissus*, and in the brick-earth and clay soils for tulip. In the sandy soil maximum penetration by tulips was only 35 cm.

The occupation of 0·25 in² (1·61 cm²) squares of the glass was also studied throughout the season for *Narcissus* and tulip roots. For *Narcissus*, occupation by roots increased rapidly until the end of January, then slowed down, but continued until lifting time, whilst tulip roots grew at a steady rate (as measured by occupation of squares) until about March then slowed down until lifting time. There was little difference in the percentage occupation of squares with the three soil types but the tulip roots occupied 62% of the possible squares compared with only 33% for *Narcissus*. These observations, although not extensive, do indicate that tulip roots occupy available space more intensively than do *Narcissus* roots, probably because tulips have more roots per bulb.

If roots of *Narcissus* and *Iris* are cut off, new ones are developed from the base plate, and not as secondary roots from the primary ones. Roots of *Narcissus* 'King Alfred' and *Iris* 'Alaska' were removed three times at 15-day intervals (mid-October to mid-November) or three or four times at one- or two-month intervals from November to the end of February (Yasuda and Fuji, 1963). As the number of root excisions increased, the number of roots formed was reduced. Root length was not affected but some of the *Narcissus* failed to flower.

Poor growth of tulips in the field can frequently be attributed to inadequate root growth, often caused by inadequate aeration which may be a result of soil compaction or waterlogging. Wiersum (1971), however, considers tulips to be less sensitive to poor aeration than some other crops, and has demonstrated survival for 8 days under anaerobiosis at 10–25°C. Indeed the bulb itself is more sensitive than the roots. Increasing the soil mechanical resistance and lowering the aeration level both retard root growth. For silt soils a minimum air content of 10 vol% at field capacity is considered a minimum for good root growth.

II. Water relations and stomata

Kraaijenga (1960) showed that the water status of the plant was important in determining bulb growth in the field. The increase in circumference of a growing tulip bulb was found to be determined by external factors, a number of bulbs growing in the same, varying, environment show closely similar patterns of growth. Growth occurs at night but is almost at standstill in the day. To investigate transpiration concurrently with bulb growth water loss from a *Hippeastrum* bulb in a glasshouse was followed with a recording balance. Observations showed that stomata of *Hippeastrum* were closed from shortly after sunset to early the following morning.

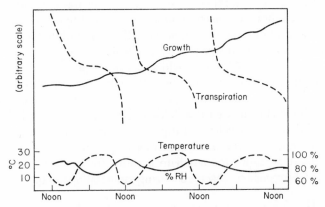

Fig. 8.8 Changes in transpiration, bulb growth, temperature and relative humidity over three 24-h periods starting at noon on 3 June 1956 (Kraaijenga, 1960).

Transpiration rates of tulips in the field measured with a specially constructed balance gave average figures of 5 mm day^{-1} for 'Krelage's Triumph' and at least 8 mm day^{-1} for the larger plants of 'Golden Harvest'. These figures agree reasonably well with lysimeter data although the photographs of the apparatus suggest that the experimental plants were not surrounded by enough guard plants.

The simultaneous observation of transpiration and growth showed that the latter occurred only when transpiration was slow, and as it increased growth decreased (Fig. 8.8). A further observation was that growth was stimulated by the first rain after a dry period. There was no apparent relation between daily growth and factors such as temperature and radiation. Bulb growth was also regulated by the duration of the period without, or with only very slow, transpiration. This effect is not always negligible because stomata are not always completely closed at night. A practical consequence of this work suggested by Kraaijenga is that the provision of windbreaks can reduce night transpiration and thereby encourage bulb growth. He suggests the use of tall trees, but the reduction in light caused by shelter belts would probably outweigh benefits gained by reducing transpiration. No evidence was produced to indicate that there was any long-term ill-effect of transient decreases in bulb growth rate, which occurred during the day in any case.

Effects of light intensity on stomal numbers were investigated by Pazourek (1970) in the experiment of Wassink (1969) on *Iris* described later in this chapter. Stomatal frequency decreased with lower light intensities, and also showed differences between successive leaves; the frequency increased up to the third or fourth leaf then decreased to the highest leaf. The total number of stomata in a leaf was constant in higher light intensities, but decreased significantly at low light, suggesting that light affects the differentiation of guard mother cells and that leaf expansion is not the sole cause of differences in stomatal density.

Tulip stomata belong to Loftfield's "potato-type" where the stomata are continuously open except for about three hours after sunset, and daytime closure occurs only when the leaves are badly wilted. Shaw and Maclachlan (1954) estimated that, although chlorophyll a and b could be demonstrated in guard cells of tulip, the chlorophyll concentration was very low so that even the maximum rate of photosynthesis in the guard cell was about 50 times too small to account for the maximum rates of osmotic pressure change observed during stomatal opening.

III. Mineral nutrition and salt uptake

A. Mineral nutrition

Investigations on the mineral nutrition of bulbous plants have mostly been done only on tulips, although it is recognized that all bulbous ornamentals are susceptible to root damage because of high salt concentration on soil or containers used for forcing. Instructions for forcing contain recommendations not to use fresh kipper boxes, nor recently creosoted forcing boxes, and there is some danger to five-degree tulips planted in the glasshouse border following a heavily-manured tomato crop. Field crops of bulbs often do not receive fertilizer at planting because fertilizers are given to other crops in the rotation, and it is usually necessary to continue experiments on nutrition for more than one season in order to "accumulate" the deficiency because of the reserves present in the bulb. For a *Narcissus* crop which it is intended should remain in the ground for two years before lifting, a fertilizer dressing to maintain nitrogen and phosphate and to increase potash levels is required, e.g. 75 kg nitrogen, 55 kg phosphorus and 260 kg potassium ha^{-1} (Anon., 1970a). Similar requirements are frequently quoted for tulip.

The most comprehensive of the early studies on bulb nutrition was that of Bould (1939) who grew *Narcissus* 'King Alfred' and tulip 'Farncombe Sanders' in sand culture watered with complete nutrient solution, with solutions lacking in either nitrogen, phosphorus or potassium or all three elements. In the first year of the experiment, few symptoms appeared in *Narcissus*, apart from paler leaves and slightly-delayed emergence in the minus-nitrogen treatment. Flower stem length, flower quality and anthesis date were unaffected by treatment, but minus nitrogen (but not minus phosphorus or minus potassium) reduced bulb weight compared with the full nutrient treatment. In the second year when bulbs from the first year were replanted, omission of any nutrient element delayed shoot appearance by a few days, but no marked deficiency symptoms were apparent, although growth was less good than in the first season.

For the tulips, absence of potassium and phosphorus had little effect on foliage apart from a slight marginal chlorosis and a bluish-green colour respectively. In the absence of nitrogen, however, leaf area was reduced, leaves were of more upright habit and yellow-green in colour. Near the time of senescence, the leaves and stem developed reddish tints typical of nitrogen starvation. Omission of the various elements had no effect on flower stem length or flowering date and had only a small effect on flower size and quality (omitting potassium had no effect on flower size or quality). Omitting nitrogen or potassium or all nutrients (but not phosphorus) decreased bulb weight compared with the full treatment. In the second year, tulips showed foliage symptoms similar to those of the first year but, as might be expected, they were more marked. There was little effect of withholding potassium, however. Flower stems were shortened by omitting all three elements separately with potassium having least effect (about 5 cm) and nitrogen the greatest (8–9 cm) compared with the full-nutrient flowers which were about 52 cm tall. Flowering was delayed about three days in the minus-nitrogen plants. Bulb weight increase was reduced by all treatments; minus phosphorus was most marked in the second year, and omitting potassium had least effect.

Specific effects of nutrition on daughter bulb production were found by Cheal and Hewitt (1963) in the two tulip cultivars 'Golden Harvest' and 'Elmus' grown in sand culture. Effects of nitrogen were dominant, but the levels giving optimum bulb yields were different in the two cultivars. Effects of potassium and magnesium deficiency were smaller, and significant interactions were found between nitrogen and potassium. It is likely that in the large bulbs (11 or 12 cm) used in the experiment, reserves

of nitrogen, phosphorus, potassium and magnesium were adequate for the
developing plant throughout the growing season but in the smaller bulbs
(7 cm) reserves, especially of nitrogen, were much more limited and the
external nutrient supply during growth would have been of sufficient
importance to modify the pattern of development as well as explaining the
observed changes in growth. Nitrogen particularly affected the distribution
of daughter bulb weights, higher levels giving more of the large-size bulbs
(above 20 g), and also more very small bulbs (below 5 g).

This work was continued for a second year using the healthiest, heaviest
bulbs from each treatment. The symptoms developed in the second year
were similar to those described by Bould (1939), and magnesium-deficient
plants had necrotic areas which appeared after flowering, on the two lowest
leaves. "Topple", a collapse of the stem, occurred under low nitrogen high
potassium treatments in both cultivars. Nitrogen was again the element
showing most effect; nitrogen deficiency decreased bulb yields, leaf area,
stem length and flower size and retarded flowering. Most of the nitrogen-
deficient bulbs were small and non-flowering. Deficiencies of phosphorus,
potassium and magnesium were more serious than in the first year, and
generally reduced leaf area and bulb yields, and sometimes reduced stem
length and flower size.

More extensive studies of low and intermediate levels of nitrogen and
potassium were reported for sand culture experiments and field-grown
crops by Cheal and Winsor (1968) and by Winsor and Cheal (1969). In the
former, the response to nitrogen occurred over the whole range examined
(0–16 meq nitrate litre^{-1}) and lowering the nitrogen level to 4 meq nitrate
litre^{-1} had a great effect on leaf area and bulb weight than the complete
omission of potassium. Bulb yield, leaf area and leaf fresh weight increased
markedly with increase in nitrogen level. For maximum growth in sand
culture, the nitrogen content should not be less than 1·6–1·7% nitrogen in
the bulb or 3·8–4·1% nitrogen in the leaves. A similar experiment where
potassium was varied from 0 to 8 meq potassium litre^{-1} showed little
growth or yield response.

The work was continued for five seasons in an experiment where
nitrogen, phosphorus, potassium and magnesium were included factorially
at two levels. All healthy bulbs over 9 cm grade were replanted each year
to follow cumulative effects of treatment. The weights of bulbs lifted were
increased by potassium, but as each factor was included at two levels no
optimal content of potassium could be reported for bulbs or leaves. There
were no indications of excessive potassium so it is suggested that leaves
and bulbs should contain at least 1·9–2·2% potassium and 1·2–1·4%
potassium respectively. In the absence of fertilizers, the crop was limited
less by shortages of nitrogen than of potassium. Where growth is not

limited by other factors, the values quoted for nitrogen in the sand culture work may not be excessive, but where other nutrients are inadequate growth is depressed by excess nitrogen, and Winsor and Cheal suggest values not greater than 3·6–3·7% nitrogen in the leaves and 1·4–1·5% nitrogen in the bulbs except under the most favourable growing conditions in the field. It was concluded that, despite the generally considered view that the tulip is not particularly responsive to manurial treatment in the field, the yield response obtained, despite the absence of obvious deficiency symptoms, was sufficient to warrant further work on tulip manuring.

A survey of nutrient levels in above-average tulip crops grown in Lincolnshire was made in 1969 (Harrod, unpublished; Anon., 1970b). Eight holdings on light silt soils where the three cultivars 'Apeldoorn', 'Rose Copland' and 'Elmus' were grown, were surveyed and leaf, soil and bulb samples were analysed, the first two when the flowers were showing some colour.

Data for the plant analyses are shown in Table 8·2 where the mean

Table 8.2

Mean values of analyses of material from 8 above-average tulip crops in Lincoln-shire. Mid-stream leaf samples were taken and samples of 10 bulbs larger than 11 cm (Harrod, unpublished, and Anon., 1970b).

| | | % in dry matter | | | | | |
		N	P	K	Mg	Ca	dry matter
'Apeldoorn'	leaf	3·73	0·31	2·48	0·34	1·21	—
	bulb	0·94	0·18	1·05	0·06	0·03	41·7
'Rose Copland'	leaf	4·06	0·32	1·78	0·37	1·42	—
	bulb	1·19	0·21	1·14	0·08	0·04	48·3
'Elmus'	leaf	3·20	0·23	1·77	0·23	1·00	—
	bulb	0·91	0·21	0·98	0·07	0·04	49·4

values conceal a fairly wide variation in nutrient levels, but there is no close relation between soil levels and those in the crop.

These figures may be compared with the levels recommended by Winsor and Cheal (1969); in most cases the leaf and bulb nitrogen and potassium levels of these commercial crops are below those recommended as upper limits. The average levels show wide variation with cultivar, however, so that levels suggested for one cultivar are not necessarily valid for another. Provided soil nutrient level is satisfactory, Harrod concluded that levels in leaf and bulb are not readily related to either soil analysis levels nor to added fertilizers.

The redistribution of nutrients in the tulip cv. 'Blizzard' was followed in an experiment by Schmalfeld and Carolus (1965) using potting soil of low fertility with no added nutrients. Plants were harvested to follow nutrient movement. Mineral nutrient first moved from parent bulbs into leaves and daughter bulbs, and large quantities of nitrogen, phosphorus and potassium were subsequently redistributed to daughter bulbs as the foliage matured. It was suggested that allowing leaves to mature and senesce naturally should ensure maximum nutrient redistribution to daughter bulbs.

Changes in the rates of uptake of nitrogen, phosphorus and potassium by tulip bulbs follow those of water absorption, being low in winter and increasing as the above-ground parts grow. Nitrogen is absorbed in greatest quantity, even in the pre-emergence stage, followed by potassium with phosphorus least. Small bulbs (about 2 g) were found to absorb more water and nutrients than large bulbs (15–16 g) and it appeared that they were more efficient users of water and minerals (Hagiya and Amaki, 1966).

For lilies grown in Georgia, responses to added lime are generally obtained and a general recommendation for field-grown lilies in Oregon is to apply 57 kg of nitrogen, 113 kg phosphate as P_2O_5 and 79 kg potash as K_2O ha^{-1} on soils receiving 6000–9000 kg ha^{-1} of lime. Superphosphate is applied before planting, part of the nitrogen and potassium are supplied at planting and the remainder as side-dressings in the spring (Blaney and Roberts, 1967).

B. Salt uptake

Narcissus roots have been used in classical studies of solute absorption because they are non-branching and usually have no root hairs (poorly-developed root hairs do occur in some ill-defined circumstances). Steward and Millar (1954) used Cs^{137} to show that, contrary to previous opinion that dividing cells would have the highest accumulation, most accumulation occurs at the point of most rapid cell growth by enlargement, i.e. in the root just behind the root apex and not at its tip. Behind the apex smooth decreases in ion concentrations occur, especially when the cells are absorbing according to their growth, and not primarily to replace a deficit caused by translocation to the shoot.

Ions accumulate at the base of *Narcissus* leaves and in the sheathing leaf bases where the intercalary meristems occur, and Steward and Sutcliffe (1959) suggest that the role of the dicotyledonous plant cambium in accumulating ions and diverting them from a longitudinal path in the xylem to the growing and accumulating lateral organs is fulfilled in monocotyledonous plants by intercalary meristems at the bases of the leaves. This speculation can be extended to monocotyledonous forms without linear leaves where an intercalary meristem at the bases of the stem or scape could be envisaged as performing the same function.

In *Cucurbita* the average concentration of a particular ion in the root system of a plant grown in water was lower than in each short internode, so that each leaf accumulated ions from the subtending internode. Thus the order of bromine concentration was leaf > stem > root. For Cs^{137} in *Narcissus* the order was different, being roots > axis > sheathing leaf base > growing leaf. Cs^{137} is stored primarily in the roots of *Narcissus*. Steward and Sutcliffe emphasize that a major factor in the formation of storage organs is the redistribution and storage of salts and other solutes. Remarkably little is known about the metabolism of these changes, although the stimuli initiating the changes are thermoperiodic or photoperiodic in some cases.

IV. Chemical composition

Vickery *et al.* (1946) describe comprehensive investigations of changes in *Narcissus poeticus* grown either in distilled water, or in culture solutions with nitrogen as nitrate ion or as ammonium ion in a glasshouse in the dark. All the data cannot be quoted here but selected ones can be used to indicate what orders of magnitude might be expected for some constituents (Table 8.3).

The major component of the bulbs is starch, with protein a very much smaller proportion of the total. The plants grew better on nitrates than ammonium salts, although the latter could be used in nitrogen metabolism. There was no large effect of the growing medium on the amounts of asparagine and glutamine, however. The plants grown without an external supply of nitrogen lost 15% of their nitrogen during development, probably as a result of interaction between amino acids and nitrous acid, as had been proposed by Pearsall and Billimoria (1939).

Organic acids are present in low concentration in comparison with other plants such as tobacco and rhubarb. Malic, citric, oxalic and succinic acids account together for only about half the total organic acids present.

A number of investigations have been made of the anthocyanin pigments of tulips, and some workers have also observed changes in amounts as the flower colour develops. From 'President Eisenhower', Halevy (1962) isolated six anthocyanins from the perianth parts; five of these were identified as delphinidin 3-glucoside, delphinidin 3-rhamno glucoside, pelargonidin 3-glucoside, pelargonidin 3-rhamno glucoside and a new isomer of the last.

Cultivar 'Bartigon' and its mutants also contain pelargonidin and cyanidin 3-glycorhamnosides in nonacylated form, the difference in colour in the

Table 8.3

Total nitrogen and protein of *Narcissus poeticus* plants after 28 days in a glasshouse (Vickery *et al.*, 1946).

		Planted bulb	Plants given	
			NO$_3$-N	NH$_4$-N
Total nitrogen	leaf		7·4	5·3
(g per 50 bulbs)	bulb	10·8	5·8	7·2
	root		2·8	1·4
	total		15·9	14·0
Protein	leaf		3·8	2·6
nitrogen	bulb	5·5	3·0	3·6
(g per 50 bulbs)	root		0·9	0·7
	total		7·7	6·8
Per cent of protein of planted bulb used			46·0	34·8
Total organic	leaf		166	94
acids	bulb	342	280	301
(meq per 50 bulbs)	root		73	29
	total		519	424
Starch				
(g per 50 bulbs)	leaf		0·4	0·5
	bulb	301	127	201
	root		0·1	0·1
	total		128	202
Total soluble	leaf		32	19
carbohydrate	bulb	66	49	55
(g per 50 bulbs)	root		3	3
	total		84	76

mutants being due to different proportions of the anthocyanins. Red and salmon-pink flowers contain a preponderance of pelargonidin glycoside and the pink flowers contain more cyanidin glycoside (Solecka, 1967).

Earlier work had indicated that tulips could be divided into two groups according to their anthocyanin content. One group contained pelargonidin and cyanidin pigments, and the other delphinidin derivatives, sometimes with cyanidins free from pelargonidins. Cultivar 'Pride of Haarlem' apparently belongs to a third group containing all three pigments, and a fourth is represented by 'President Eisenhower' which has only delphinidin and pelargonidin derivatives (Halevy, 1962).

Narcissus pigments are mainly carotenoids, and the red coronas of some cultivars are a rich source of β-carotene. Orange and yellow cultivars contain similar amounts of total carotenoids, but considerably less β-carotene. In the red fringes of coronas of *N. poeticus recurvus*, carotene comprises $16\cdot5\%$ of the dry weight, but a more usual figure for coronas of less red colour is 2% of the dry weight (Booth, 1957).

V. Translocation

One of the few studies dealing with translocation in bulbous plants is that of van Die *et al.* (1970) who investigated the fate of C^{14} labelled assimilates following the supply of $C^{14}O_2$ to single leaves at various heights along the axis of flowering plants of *Fritillaria imperialis*. The leaves on the flowering shoot are arranged in five orthostichies, and these are more or less independent pathways of translocation to the nectaries which were sampled for nectar using self-filling micropipettes. Dye-injection did, however, reveal a few connections between an individual leaf and adjacent orthostichy bundles. Following the sampling of the nectaries, the plants were divided into three fractions: the bulb, the leafy shoot, and the terminal part of the shoot with flowers and the distribution of 70% ethanol soluble activity assessed. The bulb contained relatively high amounts of activity when the treated leaf was in the lower half of the leafy shoot part, but small amounts of activity were detected in the flower-bearing part. When the treated leaf was high up the stem, about 25% of activity was in the flower-bearing part and only about 5% in the bulb.

These results clearly demonstrate that the flower-bearing part of the shoot is an important sink for photosynthates, attracting material from the upper leaves of the leafy shoot part as well as using its own products. The bulb is able to attract small quantities of assimilates from the terminal leaves, however, despite the proximity of the flower to this source. The authors also conclude that the glucose and fructose in the nectar are derived from sucrose, which is the translocated sugar in this species as in many others.

VI. Effects of light and temperature

Effects of light intensity on the growth of the tulip in full light and under different shades which reduced the light intensity to 75, 37 and about 12%

of full daylight have been studied by Wassink (1965). Wassink considers that the absence of effects of light intensity on some aspects of development (such as the development of the aerial parts) and their presence in other aspects (such as the growth of daughter bulbs) implies that the main achievement of the adult plant is to build up new bulbs and that the aerial parts develop mainly at the expense of the old bulb. The energy relationships between the tulip plant parts can be represented by:

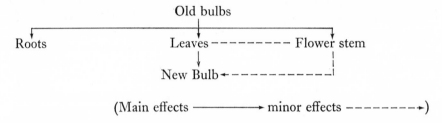

At the lowest light intensity new bulb weight was only about 40% of that in full light; daughter bulb weight increase was clearly and strongly dependent on current photosynthesis.

In addition to effects of light intensity through the photosynthetic process, Wassink (1965) also observed effects on leaf shape when this was characterized by length-breadth ratio. Most of the effect was obtained between darkness and 12% full light, and much less from 12% to 100%. Narrow leaves resulted from very low light (L/B = 10·3 for leaves 1 and 2 in darkness, compared with 3·9 for 12% daylight and 2·0 for 100% daylight). Leaf area, in contrast to leaf shape, showed relatively little effect of light intensity. There was an optimum of 37% daylight for maximum leaf area but the areas at all intensities did not differ by more than 20%. Leaf length and breadth responded to the changes in light intensity in opposite ways. Leaf length showed a clear inverse relationship with light intensity whereas leaf breadth was directly related to light intensity, although this was pronounced only below 37% daylight.

Stem length was less affected by light intensity in the tulip than was stem dry weight. The longest stems resulted from 37% full daylight, whilst 100% daylight gave the shortest stems. Complete darkness gave even faster elongation but this was not continued for as long as in the plants in the other light treatments. This observation could have been expected from grower observations that reduced light increases extension growth in forced tulips. Anatomical observations of stem transverse sections showed that vascular bundle dimensions were correlated with diameter, but that the number of vascular bundles was not affected by the light-intensity treatment.

Preliminary observations in different daylength did not give any convincing indications of effects on the growth of daughter bulbs nor any other part of the plant.

Wassink has also studied effects of light intensity on dry-matter production and morphogenesis of *Iris* 'Wedgwood' (Wassink, 1969). Responses of the various plant organs were expressed as the ratio of dry weights at 12% and 100% of full daylight. This quotient was 4·4 for bulbs at the end of the season, and higher earlier. For leaves and stems the quotient was about 2 with lower values earlier in the season. This difference in the response of leaves and bulbs reflects the deposition of food reserves in the bulbs as the season progresses. Leaf area and leaf weight showed very little light dependence. Because leaf area was almost unaffected by treatment, differences in dry weight accumulation reflected changes in photosynthetic rate with different light intensities, an eight-fold increase in light resulting in only about a three-fold increase in total dry weight, and about 4·5 times more bulb weight. Bulbs are a larger part of the total dry weight at higher light intensities.

As in the tulip, leaf shape showed a decrease in length/breadth with increasing light. Stem length and leaf area responded similarly to changes in light intensity, and average stem weight/length responded to light intensity in a very similar manner to the curve of total plant weight. Stem length and leaf area are probably a result of a compromise between available assimilates and morphogenetic semi-etiolation effects induced by lower light.

Bulb yields in tulip in relation to a number of weather factors have been examined at Lisse from records of fourteen growing seasons and from weekly samples within a season (Kraaijenga, 1960). The only positive correlation with weather and seasonal variation in yield was obtained with sunshine hours in late April and early May. Negative correlations were, however, obtained with a number of factors at various times of the year. The increases in weight of the new bulbs was positively correlated with temperature until May and negatively thereafter. The development of the leaves was closely related to temperature—a warmer Spring resulted in faster and earlier leaf expansion—but foliage weight was not related to final yield because leaf area duration was as important as the leaf area developed per plant, and yield was in many cases determined by the date of senescence of foliage. From these observations it is possible to predict that ideal growing conditions for high yield would be provided by an early and consistent rise in temperature in spring until the end of April and that temperatures should remain low for as long as possible after this date. It is comforting to find these relatively crude observations and correlations confirmed in studies done in controlled-environment facilities (Fortanier,

P

1968), quoted by Schenk (1969), and Sisa and Higuchi (1967b). The optimum temperature for bulb development lies between 12 and 15°C under low light. If the temperature rises rapidly after flowering, and this frequently occurs in natural conditions when water is in short supply, early death of the above-ground parts occurs and the already short growing season is further curtailed. When dry, hot winds, which are a feature of some countries like Israel, occur in the post-flowering period, senescence and death of the aerial parts set in very rapidly and dramatically curtail the growing season. Early senescence can be exploited commercially if bulbs are required for early forcing, and bulbs are grown in northern Italy or the south of France for a single season for this purpose. The decreased yield compared with bulbs grown in more traditional areas is more than compensated by the extra value of the very early flower crop.

Frost injury can occur to bulbs in the ground during the winter, and mulches of reed and straw are used in the Netherlands as a protection against frost injury. In preliminary experiments on the causes of injury, winter hardiness was found to decrease in the order tulip, hyacinth, *Narcissus* and *Iris*, but in all species temperature below −1°C had a harmful effect on leaf formation (van der Valk, 1971). In bulbs' natural habitat, snow cover may prevent very low temperatures at bulb depth. In the U.K. soils seldom freeze to a sufficient depth to damage bulbs, but in the severe winter of 1962/3, 'Elmus' tulips showed "feathering" of the perianth parts caused by the abnormally low temperatures.

In most tulip cultivars, droppers are formed only by very small bulbs, but in the Darwin Hybrid cultivars they are formed by large, flowering-sized bulbs, a feature which can make mechanical lifting very difficult. In an attempt to control dropper formation in Japan, effects of storage temperature have been investigated (Tsutsui and Toyoda, 1970). Dropper formation was found to be affected by temperature only after mid-September, and the higher the storage temperature up to 25°C, the more was dropper formation inhibited. In the Japanese tulip-growing areas, dropper formation is encouraged by the rapid fall in soil temperature from early October, but by storing the bulbs at 25°C and delaying planting until mid-November, dropper formation can be almost entirely eliminated. It was concluded that the retardation of early growth inhibits dropper formation, and has very little adverse effect on subsequent bulb production.

It is well known that low temperatures allow the development of more intense colours in *Narcissus* cultivars which have orange-coloured coronas, e.g. 'Fortune'. Outdoor-grown flowers are usually much darker than forced flowers, especially if these are grown at high temperatures. Exposure of inflorescences of 'Grand Soleil d'Or' to low temperatures when only one floret is open results in the development of deeper corona colours. A temperature of 2°C for 15 days gave the deepest colours but appreciable increases were obtained after only a few days (Smith and Wallis, 1967).

VII. Carbohydrate metabolism

Chen (1969a) determined the carbohydrate contents of both the photo-synthetic and storage organs of *Narcissus tazetta* at four stages of plant development both under natural growing conditions in Hong Kong and when incident light was varied. The photosynthetic parts are the above-ground parts of the foliage leaves and the flower stalk, and the storage organs are the leaf bases, bulb scales and the base of the scape which form the bulb.

Samples for analysis were taken on four occasions: dormant before planting; when the first foliage leaves were fully expanded and the plants were in full flower; at full leaf development when the flowers had died; and finally when the aerial parts of leaves and scapes were senescent. Samples were taken of the outer protective scale, the innermost fleshy scale leaf, and the first foliage leaf, and estimates were obtained of hexose, sucrose and starch content.

Starch was abundantly stored in all the storage organs, particularly in the leaf bases under high light intensity, although the level was relatively stable in the green part of the leaf and the scape and relatively unaffected by light except at high intensity. Starch also occurred in both the bundle sheaths throughout the whole blade and in the guard cells, contrary to earlier suggestions that starch is present only in the guard cells of the epidermis (Barton-Wright and Pratt, 1931; Parkin, 1912). Its presence cannot be detected by the ordinary Sach's test, however, but blade sections must be stained directly with iodine solution. Sucrose was continuously exported from the leaf blade and scape into their bases where it was stored. Sucrose decreased in the blade and the green part of the scape in the dark, but increased as light was increased. Hexose levels were low in all parts of the dormant bulb but increased with maturity and exceeded those of sucrose except in high light intensity. At the time of above-ground sene-scence, sugar disappeared almost completely. Storage organs were gradu-ally depleted of carbohydrate in a centripetal manner so that the outer bulb scales were the first to atrophy and become thin and membranous. Even at this stage, however, these scales contained nearly 10% residual dry weight of starch while sugar content was below 1%.

Chen (1969a) concluded that with the *Narcissus*, like other plants, sucrose is the first formed sugar of photosynthesis in the leaf and the free hexose present in cells does not participate in sucrose or starch synthesis.

The newly-formed sucrose may become the precursor of the polysaccharide continuously synthesized in leaves, but the proportion exported will increase as the leaf matures and senesces, so that the interrelations between carbohydrates in the leaf can be expressed by:

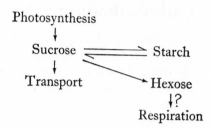

This sequence can also occur in storage organs where sucrose is again the key sugar.

Chen (1966) also described how starch was localized in the leaves and flower stalks of *N. tazetta* in relation to stages of development. Starch first appeared in the newly vacuolated parenchyma of the leaf primordia when these were only 0·5 mm long and became localized in the leaf bases when sheath and blade were differentiated. The high sucrose content in the sheath which was sufficient to allow starch formation is a result of the translocation of sucrose upwards into the sheath from the stem plate during the primordial stage of the leaf, or downwards from the blade when the foliage leaf is photosynthesizing. The intercalary meristem which separates sheath from blade appears to act as a physiological and anatomical barrier; when the cells of the meristem are dividing actively, no starch is laid down, and it is tempting to correlate the absence of starch with a high metabolic activity.

Little further is known of photosynthesis or carbohydrate metabolism in bulbous plants. The results of work described earlier on dry matter accumulation suggest that rates of photosynthesis are similar to those of many other crop plants, and that crop growth rates are limited mainly by the short growing season.

VIII. Protein synthesis and nitrogen metabolism

Narcissus was used in an early investigation of protein synthesis (Pearsall and Billimoria, 1938, 1939), which established that in the *Narcissus* leaf only the young meristematic and vacuolate tissues are capable of protein synthesis, and that this capacity is lost by the time the tissues are fully grown and are green. Subsequently it was confirmed that for a range of leaf types, protein synthesis is a function of the younger leaves, which usually ceases by the time the leaves are half-grown and it was suggested that the growing leaf is capable of synthesizing protein whilst the mature (but by no means senescent) leaf is not. The basal, white, semi-meristematic part of the leaf is unusual in comparison with most meristems in containing less protein than the mature distal part of the leaf.

Changes in leaf protein during the forcing of *Narcissus* indicated that the leaves were increasing their protein content at the same time as the flower was developing in the pre-emergence stage, although the oldest parts of the leaves had lost the capacity for protein synthesis. For the whole leaf, the protein nitrogen content remained approximately constant (220–260 mg (1100 g fresh weight)$^{-1}$ in basal parts and 300–420 for distal

Table 8.4

Amino, imino and keto acids and their derivatives which occur free in ornamental bulbous plants (extracted from Steward and Durzan 1965).

β-Alanine	Isolated from *Iris tingitana*
α-Aminoisobutyric acid	Free in *Iris tingitana*
(-)-β-Aminoisobutyric acid	*Iris tingitana* bulbs
L-γ-Methyleneglutamic acid	Tulip
γ-Methyleneglutamine	Tulip
γ-Amino-β-methylenebutyric acid	Tulip
m-Carboxy-α-phenylglycine	*Iris* bulbs
m-Carboxyphenyl-L-alanine	*Iris* bulbs
Glyoxylic acid	Tulip
α-Ketoglutaric acid	Tulip
γ-Methylene-α-ketoglutaric acid	Tulip
Dimethylpyruvic acid	Tulip

parts), irrespective of the amount of leaf development, or whether flowers had appeared or not. Further, no gains in protein were observed in leaves of plants when flowers were fully open, or when the flowers had withered. At or shortly after flower withering, leaf growth ceased and their protein content fell—the first sign of leaf senescence was usually a yellowing of the leaf tip, a sign of decreasing protein content. Pearsall and Billimoria suggested that the maintenance of the nitrogen content of the *Narcissus* leaf during flowering development may be a result of its organization; the meristem at the base of the leaf is less permeable than mature cells and acts as a regulator to the movement of materials, as also suggested by Chen (1966). The role of vascular strands through this region is obviously important, and it is interesting that although xylem vessels are well developed here at an early stage, phloem development occurs much later. It may be speculated that the different flowering/senescence pattern in the tulip, compared with *Narcissus* is perhaps due to the absence of any physical barrier to translocation in the tulip leaf; the failure to maintain a high protein content in the leaf would then lead to its more early senescence.

In work on effects of light on the nitrogen metabolism of *Narcissus* leaves, Pearsall and Billimoria (1939) showed that there were three ways in which light operated. These were by increasing the rate of absorption of inorganic nitrogen, by accelerating nitrate reduction and by increasing the rate of production of organic nitrogen.

The tulip plant contains several compounds discovered by chromatography (Table 8.4), and large quantities of arginine occur in the bulb, amounting to about 60% of the total nitrogen of the bulb as free arginine or as a prolamine-like complex. In complete contrast the aerial expanded green leaves contained none or only a very low level of arginine (Zacharius *et al.*, 1957).

Changes in the size and composition of the pool of soluble nitrogen compounds at flower initiation and subsequently during flower differentiation and growth have been studied by Steward and co-workers. The total amount of soluble nitrogen increased at the expense of the arginine-rich reserves, but as the flower developed, it showed a distinctly different metabolic pattern with more glutamine, asparagine, and alanine, and Barber and Steward (1968) showed in later work using electrophoretic separations on acrylamide gels that the separate organs each has a distinctive pattern of soluble nitrogen compounds, although these are nearly all, basically, modified leaves. It is difficult to distinguish between differences in protein pattern which are the result of morphogenetic change and those determining morphogenetic change. Changes were, however, observed in shoot apices before and after floral induction, and Barber and Steward consider that the protein complement responded to the conditions that induce flowering before the floral organs had developed. It can be claimed, however, that the critical period for determining the fate of the apex (vegetative or floral) is after the production of the first leaf. If a second leaf is formed, then the apex will go on to form a flower, i.e. it is "committed" to flowering. It can be argued then that some irreversible change occurs in the tulip apex long before floral initiation is morphologically apparent, i.e. floral "evocation", and a more detailed investigation of proteins at this early stage could be rewarding. The observations made, however, do support the views that differentiation and morphogenesis are accompanied by the formation of organ-specific proteins and enzymes. The protein changes in the growing point which anticipate the formation of floral

organs, and which are presumed to be causally related to ensuing development, are thought to owe their formation to specific mRNA's which
originate when genes are de-repressed by floral stimulus.

Serological analysis has been used to investigate protein changes in tulip
bulb scales in relation to low-temperature treatment of bulbs (Higuchi and
Sisa, 1967). By using the precipitation obtained from the antigen-antibody
reaction using a double-diffusion method, six precipitin bands were
detected in 'Mozart' and eight in 'Zwaneburg'. Low temperature reduced
the bulb-scale protein levels in both cultivars, by the loss of some proteins
and a decrease in others. These results were considered as useful indicators
for investigations of the low-temperature treatment of bulbs and for
selecting cultivars suitable for forcing.

IX. Senescence and dormancy

Little is known about factors affecting senescence in bulb plants. High
temperatures after flowering can have important accelerating effects on
the process, especially in more arid countries where very rapid senescence
can occur. In more temperate countries, high temperatures, low humidity
and low soil moisture are closely interrelated and no work has been done
to establish which of these factors is important in causing senescence, if,
indeed, any one is of overriding importance.

It is equally difficult to consider dormancy. When the above-ground
parts have senesced and died back, there are no active parts above ground
level, so that superficially the plant is dormant. Below ground there is
some activity, however, because apices can be actively initiating flowers or
flower initials and daughter bulbs are growing within the mother bulb.
There is some controversy about root growth during this period. Some
species and cultivars have apparently only a very short period between
the death of the old roots and the appearance of new ones. This seems to
occur especially in *Iris* and in *Narcissus tazetta*.

This dormancy, if this term can be used, is a form of summer dormancy
because it is a result of the plant's avoidance of the severe summer conditions of heat and water shortage in the native habitat. Normal growth is
resumed only after the plant has passed through a low-temperature period
of winter, which ensures that the plant is active in the spring.

In Easter lily, effects of a number of factors on bulb dormancy have
been studied; these included bulb scale removal, vernalization, heat
treatment and chemicals. It was concluded that daughter scales are the
main cause of bulb dormancy and the ratio new scales/old scales gives an
index of bulb maturity such that bulbs are mature when the ratio approaches unity. Dormancy can be overcome by cold storage treatment, by

hot water followed by cold storage, by soil heating before flowering, or a treatment with gibberellic acid, indol-3yl-acetic acid or ethylene (Shyr and Blaney, 1968).

X. Hormones and growth retardants

It is now well known that hormones play a major role in directing the movement of organic metabolites and in establishing sinks. It is much less clear how the four major groups of plant hormones (gibberellins, auxins, cytokinins and dormins), interact to control the growth of even a relatively simple structure like a tulip plant.

It is likely, however, that all four groups of hormones are involved in bulb growth, with auxin being produced by the stem apex stimulated by gibberellins formed by the young leaves, and this gibberellin stimulating internode elongation. Growth ceases probably either because of the formation of inhibitors (dormins) by the old leaves or because of a falling off in cytokinin supplied from the root system. In bulb plants the dying of old leaves and of roots means that supplies of hormones are cut off and are resumed only when new organs are formed during the developmental cycle. Flower formation, in *Iris* 'Wedgwood' at least, seems to be controlled by gibberellin-like substances.

Little work has been done on the occurrence of growth substances in ornamental bulbous plants. A number of workers have applied some auxin, gibberellin or kinetin—often in desperation—but results are usually negative, have not been followed up in detail and are widely scattered through the literature, so that no coherent picture emerges. An exception to the above is the work by Aung and De Hertogh (1967, 1968) on the presence of gibberellin-like substances in tulip, and the relation between gibberellin content in free and bound forms with low-temperature treatment.

The concentration of free gibberellin-like substances was found to increase with the duration of cool storage at 9°C up to 13 weeks, whereas bound gibberellin-like substances decreased slightly after 4–5 weeks at 9°C then showed a gradual rise in concentration after 8 and 13 weeks. The free gibberellin-like substances increased about 370-fold, while the bound increased 8-fold compared with bulbs stored at 17°C. At 5°C, free gibberellin-like substances showed no significant change in concentration. It is suggested that, in addition to the release of gibberellin-like substances from the bound to the free form, there is also some synthesis during development at low temperatures.

Root development in bulbs plays an important role in changes of endogenous gibberellin-like substances, and roots may either be sites of synthesis or may provide water or precursors for gibberellin production in other organs such as the scales or the shoot.

Changes occurring in free and bound gibberellin-like activity of 'Ralph' tulip bulbs at 13°C and 18°C have been followed after flower initiation and a 5°C pre-cooling treatment of 9 weeks' duration. At 18°C the content of free gibberellin increased by 67% over the initial amount, but the bound gibberellin decreased rapidly after an initial small rise. At 13°C free gibberellin declined markedly whilst bound gibberellin increased two-fold. Later, however, when these plants were transferred from 13°C to 18°C the free gibberellin increased to the initial level and the bound gibberellin decreased to a low level (Aung et al., 1969b). These results suggest that a temperature-sensitive interconversion exists in tulip bulbs between free and bound gibberellin and that synthesis or transformation occurs during development.

Further work by Aung et al., (1971b) showed that endogenous gibberellin content is affected by water and temperature; gibberellin was increased 39-fold by treatment at 17°C when wet compared with those treated at 17°C dry, and an 89-fold increase was obtained when bulbs were treated at 9°C wet compared with 9°C dry. The highest gibberellin content followed 9°C wet, but the removal of the base plate of bulbs grown at 9°C wet or 17°C wet considerably reduced the gibberellin level.

Preliminary work has suggested that gas-liquid chromatography of trimethylsilyl ethers of methyl esters of partially-purified extracts of tulip bulb organs on a 3% OV-1 column could be used to identify gibberellins. For tulip 'Elmus', fleshy scales contain gibberellins A1, A5, A8 and A9, the shoot contains A1 and the roots contain gibberellins A5, A9 and A13 (Aung et al., 1971a). These observations are tentative but could well be a useful basis for resolving what is obviously a complex situation.

Original work on tulips has been extended to other bulbous ornamentals by Aung et al., (1969a). Gibberellin-like substances have been found in free and bound forms in bulbs of all the widely-grown genera (Table 8.5). Although the precise roles of gibberellins in bulb development are not known, their presence suggests they are involved in the developmental physiology of the bulbs; in Iris they are apparently involved in flower initiation and flower stem development and in tulip in flower stalk extension.

Recent work by van Bragt (1971) on terminal buds containing a complete flower growing on agar medium with nutrient and vitamins showed that buds isolated from bulbs previously stored at 5°C for 12 weeks grew better than those from bulbs not cooled. Bud growth was promoted by exogenous gibberellin.

In Narcissus tazetta, application of gibberellin and indol-3yl-acetic acid to root tips over ten days was found to have very little effect on cell behaviour. The gibberellin did not prevent the division of root tip cells, but induced differentiated cells to divide. Mitosis was unaffected by gibberellin and no chromosomal changes or polyploidy were observed. Auxin caused differentiated cells in the roots to divide, but long treatment durations prevented the division of root tip cells. Auxin but not gibberellin caused the enlargement of cortical cells above the root tip (Leivonen, 1958).

The tulip stem above the uppermost leaf is derived from the apical

Table 8.5

The content of free and bound gibberellin-like substances in ornamental bulbous plants (Aung, De Hertogh and Staby, 1969a)

Plant	Free	Bound
Hyacinthus orientalis		
cv 'Marconi'[3]	$1 \cdot 1 \times 10^{-3}$	$2 \cdot 8 \times 10^{-2}$
Iris 'Wedgwood'[2]	$3 \cdot 2 \times 10^{-2}$	$3 \cdot 0 \times 10^{-4}$
Lilium longiflorum		
cv. 'Ace'[4]	$1 \cdot 5 \times 10^{-3}$	$4 \cdot 6 \times 10^{-2}$
Narcissus tazetta		
cv. 'Geranium'	$1 \cdot 6 \times 10^{-3}$	$3 \cdot 0 \times 10^{-2}$
Tulipa gesneriana		
cv. 'Ralph'[2]	$3 \cdot 2 \times 10^{-4}$	$1 \cdot 3 \times 10^{-2}$

[1] Iris assayed by dwarf-pea assay, others by barley endosperm half-seed assay.
[2] No cold treatment, bulbs stored in 17°C.
[3] Rooted and with well-developed scapes following low temperature. Flowers excluded from extraction.
[4] After flowering, flowers excluded from extraction.

meristem and each cell of this part of the stem is derived from cell divisions in the subapical region. Removal of the flower prevents stem elongation, but this can partly be replaced by auxin or gibberellin applied in lanolin to the tip, or completely replaced by the two together (Sachs, 1961).

Changes in endogenous hormones in Easter lilies were investigated at the University of Kyoto, Japan, by Tsukamoto (1971). After a hot-water treatment at 45–48°C for one hour, the bulbs were stored at 30–33°C for one week before transfer to 13°C for two weeks followed by 8°C for five weeks. Scale samples were taken from inner, mid and outer regions of cooled bulbs and from others stored at room temperature. Using the *Avena* coleoptile straight-growth test, no differences in the amounts of growth-promoting or inhibiting substances were found with different positions within the bulb before chilling, but promoters clearly increased in the outer scales of bulbs given low temperature, and at the same time, the inhibitor level decreased. At room temperature, however, although the inhibitor level decreased, the amount of promoters did not increase. A similar situation could exist in other bulbous plants, with growth being promoted by a change in the balance of inhibitors and promoters, the change being affected by environmental changes, especially temperature. In tulip, for instance, abscisic acid has been identified in bulbs before the start of pre-cooling (Aung and Rees, unpublished), and the interaction between abscisic acid and gibberellin could be the key to plant behaviour in relation to low-temperature treatment.

Application of gibberellic acid as a soil drench to Easter lilies before flower initiation and in combination with various low-temperature treat-ments failed to affect leaf or flower number, or the number of days to anthesis, but 1000 ppm GA3 reduced the number of flowers initiated. It is suggested that the most sensitive stage occurs just before flower initiation. The relationship between gibberellins and cold treatment in this lily is not clear, but preliminary experiments suggest that different gibberellins affect different processes (Kays et al., 1971).

Ornithogalum arabicum has also been used for investigations of changes in endogenous gibberellin levels during development both when the bulbs were in storage and in the field (Halevy et al., 1971). A sequence of temperatures to promote earliest flowering was used; 33°C (for preparation and retarding) followed by 20°C (for flower initiation) then 13°C (to enhance flower elongation). High gibberellin activity was found in the new leaves within the bulbs and in the base plate, but considerably less in the scales. After transfer to 20°C, gibberellins decreased markedly and re-mained low during flower development, but increased sharply on removing the bulbs to 13°C. Later at 13°C, the level declined but rose again as the flower stems emerged in the field.

In an attempt to separate effects of development on gibberellin content from those caused by temperature changes, changes were followed in bulbs at 20°C after an initial two months at 33°C. Gibberellin activity was fairly high in the buds and scales of completely vegetative bulbs at the end of the period at 33°C, but the activity declined sharply at both sites a week after transfer at 20°C, but a rise in activity in the bud occurred after the initiation of the pre-floral stage, accompanied by a further decline in the scales. Later, when flower initiation was in process, a slow but steady increase was seen in both bud and scales.

Changes in gibberellin level in *Ornithogalum* are related to both tempera-ture of storage and to the stage of development of the bud. Like many other observations on endogenous growth substances, this work is still at the observational stage; attempts at interpreting the significance of the changes must await more knowledge of the mode of action of gibberellins in relation to morphogenesis.

Buds of *Iris* 'Wedgwood' also contain gibberellin-like substances, which are either formed or accumulated by immature leaves (Rodrigues Pereira, 1964, 1965). Halevy and Shoub (1964) found that exogenous gibberellin injected into bulbs of 'Wedgwood' and 'Prof. Blaauw' *Iris* resulted in earlier flowering by up to 19 days but had little or no effect on length of leaves or flower stem. Spraying plants seven times with 10^{-2} molar gibberellin solution hastened flowering and also increased foliage growth in both cultivars. In 'Wedgwood', stem elongation was increased by gibberellin sprays. The replacement of part of the cold requirement by gibberellin was clear; other workers' failure to obtain a response could possibly be because the gibberellin was not applied at the best time. The most sensitive stage was after the initiation of the flower bud but before the completion of flower differentiation.

Early attempts to replace the cold requirement of tulips by root absorption or injection of gibberellic acid have, however, proved unsuccessful (De Hertogh, private communication; Rees unpublished). More recently however, it has been found that gibberellins can substitute for the first half of the usual 12-week treatment of five-degree tulips 'Apeldoorn', and for part of the second six weeks. Pre-planting application was more effective than post-planting and gibberellin A4 + 7 was more effective than gibberellin A3. However, neither of the two gibberellins substituted completely the effect of 12 weeks at 5°C, and the final length of the flowering stem was unaffected by gibberellins. A further interesting point is that very large doses of gibberellin were required (1–50 mg per bulb) suggesting either the effective gibberellin is present only in small quantities in the commercially-available gibberellins or that the applied gibberellin was being rapidly broken down or was not reaching the required site (van Bragt and Zijlstra, 1971). Endogenous growth regulators appear to be involved in a number of phases in the growth of bulbous plants. Certainly gibberellins are involved in the low-temperature requirement and in subsequent extension growth; in some instances they seem to affect flower initiation. Auxins are also involved in growth, especially of subapical meristems of the flower scapes. Very little is known about the involvement of growth substances in bulbing process or in the dormancy of daughter bulbs. It is disappointing that studies on bulbs using exogenously applied growth substances have not proved more rewarding especially as the commercial potential of replacing by the growth substance the long period of low temperature necessary for forcing most bulbous plants is very attractive and could revolutionize bulb forcing as we know it today. The need for more work on growth regulators in bulbous plants is obvious, and pressing.

There is increasing evidence that ethylene is important in tulip development, often producing serious adverse effects on growth and flowering. Many of the symptoms produced have been known for a long time, but it is only recently that the key position of ethylene has been recognized. Symptoms of physiological disorders caused by ethylene are described in Chapter 9.

Ethylene can be produced in quite high concentrations, especially by tulip bulbs infected with *Fusarium oxysporum*. At about 20°C, over 0.1 cm^3 per bulb per day has been measured, and as 0.1 ppm ethylene can damage bulbs, the importance of ventilating bulb stores is obvious. At lower temperatures ethylene production by infected bulbs is considerably slower. Other ethylene sources such as flowers and fruit must not be allowed to affect stored bulbs (Kamerbeek and de Munk, 1965).

Even at very low concentrations ethylene slows down growth, and there appear to be susceptible stages of development. One of these occurs immediately after lifting when the shoot within the bulb is extremely small and another is at pollen tetrad formation about four weeks after the completion of flower differentiation. The stunting of perianth extension growth produces the so-called "open" flowers where the anthers are exposed, allowing mites to enter the flower, to feed on the anthers and infect them with fungal and bacterial spores which grow, kill the flower and shoot tip, producing the disease called *kernrot*.

In the absence of mites, typical *kernrot* symptoms do not develop but the resulting flowers are smaller and shorter stemmed than normal. Anther necrosis results from ethylene damage after the completion of flower differentiation, and anthers of cultivars which are normally black or dark coloured remain pale yellow at anthesis. Perianth parts are frequently green at anthesis or the whole flower becomes dried out or "blasted".

Ethylene damage can also occur in the glasshouse, especially at temperatures above 14°C during the first week after transfer. Ethylene concentrations in forcing boxes of up to 10 vpm have been demonstrated, the concentration decreasing with distance from the deliberately-planted *Fusarium*-infected bulb. Shoot height in neighbouring plants was decreased by 5 cm and all flower buds dried out within 25–35 cm of the infected bulb. Root symptoms were also evident; these averaged 0.9 mm in diameter compared with the usual 0.6 mm for healthy roots, appeared twisted and were abnormal in bearing short root hairs (de Munk and de Rooy, 1971).

There is some evidence of damage to flowers by endogenous ethylene production by anthers of healthy bulbs during meiosis. This can be increased by high temperatures and can lead to flower death, either accidentally as in "heating in transit" (see Chapter 9) or deliberately as in *blindstoken* (see Chapter 6).

Ethylene has been extracted from bulbs of a number of species (Staby and De Hertogh, 1970) at concentrations which would be expected to have physiological significance. Values uncorrected for dissolved ethylene (1 vol of ethylene dissolves in about 9 vol of water at 20°C) ranged from 0·04 ppm in hyacinth to 0·21 in both lily and tulip, with *Narcissus* and *Iris* intermediate at 0·16 and 0·07 ppm respectively. Further studies on tulip, where internal gases were trapped over 0·5 M sodium chloride solution to decrease ethylene solubility in water, showed a wide range of ethylene levels from 0 to 19 ppm depending on cultivar. The ethylene concentration was, however always lower in bulbs treated with the systemic fungicide "Benlate" than in the water controls, suggesting that fungi normally associated with bulbs are at least partially responsible for the gas.

Ethylene has been reported to accelerate flowering of 'Wedgwood' *Iris*. After storage for 5 days at concentrations of 1, 5 and 10 ppm, bulbs produced flowers up to 8 days earlier than the controls. Treatment later in the season, after storage at 10°C for 42 days, was less effective, leading to the suggestion that ethylene may play a role in flower initiation and development that augments the accelerating effects of vernalizing temperatures (Stuart *et al.*, 1966).

The production of a substance called tulipalin (α-methylene butyrolactone) by the outermost scale of the tulip bulb is of interest in the prevention of fungal attack, especially by *Fusarium oxysporum* f. *tulipae* (Bergman and Beijersbergen, 1971). Extracts of the outermost scale contain tulipalin only until it is transformed into the papery brown tunic, but not afterwards. The substance is fungitoxic *in vitro*, and its presence coincides with the normal time of infection which is during the last few weeks before lifting. There appear to be large differences in the concentrations of tulipalin in different cultivars, which may reflect their sensitivities to attack.

In vivo spectrophotometric assays have shown the presence of high levels of phytochrome in actively or developing regions of bulbs of *Narcissus*, tulip, *Hippeastrum*, hyacinth, *Iris* and lily, whilst storage parts such as scales have much smaller quantities of phytochrome (Koukkari and Hillman, 1966).

In recent years a number of growing retardants have been used for producing short-stemmed lilies. The compounds CCC (chlormequat chloride) and Phosfon (chlorphonium chloride) have been used with some success, but the results have not been consistent and further work on the time and method of application and dosage rates are needed before the method is commercially worthwhile. Ill-effects noted include browning of leaves, especially at low light and at close spacing, and weak stems (in 'Ace' when the retardants are applied to plants 15 cm tall). Current recommendations are to apply Phosfon when the plants are 30 cm tall (Adelman, Tayama and Kiplinger, 1970). In experiments in England on the *Lilium tigrinum* hybrids 'Cinnabar', 'Enchantment' and 'Harmony', plant height was effectively reduced by cycocel applied as a soil drench of 57 ml pot^{-1} of a 2·5% a.i. solution when the plants were 8 cm tall. Height was reduced, on average, by 7–8 cm (Anon., 1969).

Sporadic attempts have also been made with *Narcissus* and tulip in order to produce short, attractive pot plants using commercially-available cultivars, but results have been discouraging. The alternative cultivars of normally dwarf stature e.g. *Tulipa praestans* 'Fusilier' are more expensive than the commoner cultivars. It is possible to force potted *Narcissus* and tulip to give short stems by restricting the low-temperature period, but this also leads, unfortunately, to uneven growth of individual plants within the pot and a poor quality product. Further work is obviously needed in this field of bulb growing, and this should be encouraged by reports of some success with CCC at 6% as a soil drench, although flowering was delayed and flower size decreased slightly.

In preliminary work using cycocel on five-degree 'Apeldoorn' tulips cooled for 12 or 18 weeks, stems were shortened by about a third but at the expense of delayed flowering, smaller perianth parts (especially after 18 weeks' cool treatment) and an increase in the number of blind flowers. The quantities of cycocel used were 6·25 g per 250 ml water per 5 litre pot containing 6 bulbs, applied four days after planting and repeated the following day (van Bragt and van't Hoff, 1969).

Ethrel (ethephon), which releases ethylene at the site of application, has been used in the field and on forced bulbs to prevent excessive stem elongation. Although few experiments have yet been done, it appears more promising than other conventional growth retardants for *Narcissus* and tulip. Tulip stem elongation was considerably retarded without affecting vase life by concentrations of 200–400 ppm applied to the soil two days after transfer to the glasshouse or as a foliar spray shortly before flower picking in the field. Similar results were obtained with *Narcissus*.

Effects of CCC on isolated buds and scales of *Iris* 'Wedgwood' grown in a nutrient medium have been observed; the older of the two leaf primordia left on the explant elongated, but a competitive interaction with gibberellic acid could not be established, although CCC inhibited, and the gibberellin promoted, elongation. CCC did not retard flower formation and promoted the production of gibberellin-like substances in excised scales. Flowering was promoted by gibberellic acid (Rodrigues Pereira, 1970).

CCC is generally accepted to be an inhibitor of gibberellin synthesis; it is therefore not surprising that it has little effect on tulip stem elongation when gibberellins themselves appear to have little effect on flower stem elongation (van Bragt and van't Hoff, 1969).

XI. Aspects of development

A. Germination

Authoritative works on the different kinds of germination behaviour shown by seeds of bulbous plants are those of Chouard (1926, 1931) who distinguished two chief types, hypogeal (e.g. *Narcissus pseudonarcissus* and *Endymion natans*) and epigeal (e.g. *Scilla bifolia* and *Tulipa gesneriana*). An intermediate form, where the germinating seed remains at the soil surface was considered more closely related to the hypogeal than the epigeal, where the seed is carried well above the ground. In the hypogeal form, the cotyledon remains below ground and the first leaf, produced by the apex, grows out through the side of the cotyledon and emerges above ground. This first leaf may be narrow and tubular or enlarged and spatulate. In the epigeal type of germination, the cotyledon is emergent, green and photosynthetic, and is not usually accompanied by a leaf, although this occurs in some cases (Fig. 8.9).

Bulb formation occurs early in the life of the seedling, possibly as a result of leaf emergence or the restriction of the above-ground parts to a single structure, either cotyledon or leaf. No information is available on external factors affecting bulbing, such as photoperiod. As many bulbous plants have a cold requirement for germination (and this may be of many weeks' duration), growth will only occur in the spring when daylength is increasing.

Although seeds of *Narcissus* and tulip have a low-temperature requirement for germination, there are no indications of optimum temperatures nor durations for rapid germination. Seed boxes after sowing are usually kept outdoors in the winter or in cold frames, and germination occurs, rather unevenly, in the spring. In some experiments on tulip seeds (Fortanier, personal communication) 5°C has been successful, but not 8°C, but other batches of seed have germinated successfully after 5, 8 and 10°C. A further feature is that effects of one week of cold treatment can be nullified by one subsequent week of high temperature. Two weeks of cold treatment can be nullified similarly, but not four.

Sisa and Higuchi (1967a) investigated a number of factors concerned with tulip seed germination. They concluded that the seeds were not dormant, but required low temperatures for germination, the optimum being 5°C, at which temperature the process takes 40–45 days. Above 10° germination was delayed. Seeds would germinate 50 days after pollination and the germination pattern hardly differed from that of fully-matured seeds.

These results are in broad agreement with those of Russian workers who

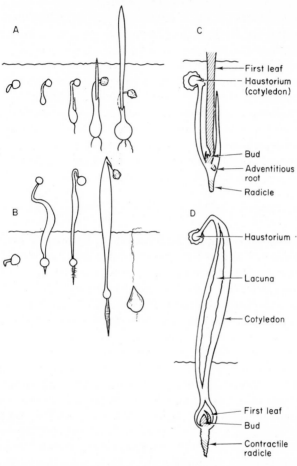

Fig. 8.9 Diagrammatic representation of (A) hypogeal and (B) epigeal germination in bulbous plants, and sections of seedlings exhibiting (C) hypogeal and (D) epigeal germination (after Chouard, 1926).

quote optimum temperatures for tulip seed germination of 2–5°C (Popcov and Buč, 1968) or who describe high germination percentages at 4°C with seed of wild tulip species compared with no germination at 25–30°C (Abramova, 1968).

Following germination, Sisa and Higuchi's seedlings kept at 13°C

Q

started to show senescence after 70 days and were then transferred to 23°C to hasten senescence and ripen the daughter bulbs. The total period from sowing to harvesting the daughter bulbs was 135 days. Daughter bulb weight increased with the duration of the period at 13°C until about 70 days then levelled off at about 490 mg per plant.

Immersing the seeds in a mixture of naphthalene acetic acid and gibberellin had no effect on germination, but larger bulbs resulted from treating seedling leaves with naphthalene acetic acid and gibberellin either separately or together during the growing period. The increase was 30% compared with the control. Kinetin, on the other hand, reduced bulb weight per plant by about 10% (Sisa and Higuchi, 1969b).

Some members of the Amaryllidaceae produce large seeds which contain sufficient water to allow germination without any water being supplied. These seeds germinate readily on the laboratory bench or in seed packets. Water represents a high percentage of the fresh weight of these seeds, usually over 80%, and the heavily cutinized or suberized boundary layer of the seeds prevents water loss. High water contents in seeds have been observed in *Amaryllis, Crinum, Haemanthus, Clivia, Nerine* and *Brunsvigia* (Isaac and McGillivray, 1965).

Juvenility is important in bulbous plants because it extends over a number of years, and as a plant breeder must base his selection on flower appearance, a long wait is very frustrating. *Narcissus* normally flowers in the fifth year, but there is some varietal variation, some flowering in the fourth year and others requiring six years. Leaf number increases from one in the first three years, to two in the fourth year and three or more in the fifth year. The seedling bulb can be compared with daughter bulb units of similar size, which also show variation in leaf number, but the seedling bulb is round in transverse section, unlike the daughter bulb unit which is flattened because of pressure from other, older bulb units. The tulip bulb only has a single leaf until flowering starts four to seven years after germination; the seedling leaf is thread-like and tubular and changes its shape in successive seasons to the typical large dorsiventral structure.

Annual increments of bulb growth in the seedling tulip are small because of the low leaf/total weight ratio, limited activity by a single leaf and the annual increase in bulb number which prevents the more rapid formation of single bulb. Death of above-ground parts is endonomic, and cannot be much extended (Fortanier, 1971). Shortening the life cycle to nine months is practical, and a reduction to six months a possibility which would allow the growing of seedlings in the southern and northern hemispheres in alternating half-yearly cycles and thereby hasten development to maturity.

The long time-lapse between germination and flowering is a serious handicap to tulip breeders. This has led to a programme of work in the Netherlands aimed at developing methods of early selection of characters such as productivity, forcing ability and disease susceptibility. Germination rate was found to be maternally controlled and therefore of no value for selection, but shoot growth is useful as an indication of forcing ability and the rate of bulblet formation is showing promise as a criterion of productivity which is being tested on large populations (van Eijk and Toxopeus, 1968).

Juvenile leaf form recurs in tulips where the main shoot of a bulb is killed by late high-temperature treatment or by attack by *Botrytis tulipae* which can cause a split in the base of the bulb which permits the entry of fungi which kill the shoot. In these conditions, and in other ill-defined cases which presumably have a physiological origin, the outermost scales of all the daughter bulbs elongate to form a cluster of narrow green above-ground leaves. Occasionally the next-to-outer scale of a daughter bulb also elongates in this way.

B. Post-harvest physiology

Many bulb flowers, especially hyacinths and lilies, are sold as pot plants, but where flowers are cut before marketing, problems arise of how best to improve the quality of the product so that the purchaser obtains as long a life as possible from the flowers. Important factors are the stage of development at cutting, and post-harvest treatments such as storage, packing methods and treatment after purchase by the consumer.

The average vase life of *Narcissus* is 7–8 days at 16°C and 65% R.H., but this varies considerably with cultivar from 5 to 12 days. Many trumpet cultivars have a shorter vase life than those of *N. cyclamineus*, *N. jonquilla*, *N. tazetta* and *N. poeticus*. Appearance of the flower is unfortunately no guide to keeping quality, as some flimsy-looking flowers have good keeping qualities and more robust-looking ones do not last well (Fry, 1967). It is recommended that flowers are picked before the buds have opened so that they are fully open after purchase. Double-flowered types must however be picked only after the flowers are three-quarters open otherwise they fail to absorb water and the flowers do not open fully.

Near anthesis the upright flower has an intact spathe, but as the flower develops the spathe is split and the angle between the pedicel and peduncle decreases to 45°. This stage is called the green goose-neck stage and is followed by a considerable enlargement of the flower accompanied by the development of colour (called fat goose-neck). Picking before the goose-neck gives small short-lived flowers, and for best quality the fat goose-neck is the best stage for cutting (Wallis, 1966). For marketing, however, the green goose-neck stage is most satisfactory because the flowers can be packed satisfactorily and post-purchasing development is trouble-free. It is not considered necessary to stand the flowers in water before despatch to the market, as they rarely wilt appreciably and recover rapidly when they eventually are stood in water. If it is required to open the flowers, temperatures of 10–16°C are most suitable; higher temperatures can reduce the vase life and lower temperatures prevent the opening of flowers of some cultivars (Anon., 1970a).

Most *Narcissus* cultivars can be stored for 14 days at 1–2°C without losing more than a quarter of their potential vase life. Flowers are best picked in the goose-neck stage and stored in water, or dry in polythene wraps. Higher storage temperatures shorten the vase life. Flower diameter decreases with increased duration of storage, but is unaffected by storage temperature (Wallis, 1968). Attempts to increase vase life with additives such as silver nitrate solution or senescence inhibitors such as benzyl adenine have not been successful (Wallis, 1969).

Narcissus cv. 'King Alfred' were found to keep best in an atmosphere of 100% nitrogen at a range of temperatures, but, although the respiration rate of the flower increased by about 900% when the flowers were moved from 0°C to 21°C, no relationship was found between carbon dioxide output and vase life (Parsons, Asen and Stuart, 1967). Little commercial use has been made of controlled-atmosphere storage for bulb flowers.

Like *Narcissus*, there are varietal differences in the keeping quality of tulips. 'Copland' cultivars last 9–11 days at 16°C compared with 6–9 for a number of Darwin Hybrid cultivars.

It is generally recommended that flowers should be cut when they are completely coloured with no green remaining, and the period between cutting and placing them in the vase should be kept as short as possible. For up to five days dry storage at 0–5°C, keeping quality will not be affected; for periods longer than this the flowers must be protected from drying by airtight packing or by giving the flowers water. If the precautions against drying are adequate, tulips can be kept for two weeks at 0–5°C without seriously impairing quality. Storage in atmospheres of carbon dioxide or nitrogen does not improve keeping quality compared with storage in air.

Removal of the white base of the shoot where flowers have been picked with bulbs attached, and also when flowers have been brought in from cold glasshouses, can aid water absorption otherwise restricted by blocked xylem vessels.

The temperatures of the room where the flowers are displayed is vitally important; vase life falls non-linearly from about 17 days at 10°C to 5 days at 25°C and 3·5 days at 30°C. These figures are averages for a large number of cultivars. Between 10 and 20°C a rise of 1°C reduces vase life by about a day. Light has very little effect on keeping quality, nor has relative humidity above 40% unless accompanied by high ventilation rates.

Only in some cultivars is the addition of sugars to the vase water beneficial, but at 20°C vase life can be doubled in some cases. In other cases no benefit ensues, and the infiltration of intercellular spaces ("water stalks") occurs in sensitive cultivars. Most of these observations were made by Hekstra (1966).

Less information is available on the post-harvest physiology of the *Iris* than in other bulb plants.

Picking is best done for most cultivars as soon as colour is visible, and before the flower starts to open, but difficulty is sometimes experienced with 'Prof. Blaauw' if it is cut in the tight bud stage. Cut flowers may be stored safely for 4–5 days either dry or wet at 2°C and dry at 5 and 9°C. Dry storage can lead to limp flower stems which require water for some hours to recover. Keeping quality deteriorates if storage is prolonged beyond 4–5 days. *Iris* flowers have a vase life of about 5–6 days.

It is possible to store early-maturing plants of Easter lilies at either −0·5 or 2–10°C protected from full sunlight by shading until the earliest buds are in the white "puffy" stage. Plants can be stored for up to 14 days (Culbert, 1967).

Some changes occur in the post-harvest phase of flower growth. Elongation and growth of stems or pedicels occurs in both *Narcissus* and tulip, in some cultivars especially and these features can affect the aesthetic appeal of flowers.

For tulip, preliminary investigations have shown that all cultivars tested continued to grow after harvesting, and that elongation occurring in the uppermost internode accounted for about a half of the total growth, and was most rapid during the first day after cutting. If the flower was removed, internode growth was inhibited; removal of the flower accompanied by de-leafing increased stem growth, but if the flower was left intact, de-leafing had no consistent effect. The gynoecium had the greatest effect of all the floral parts, but the perianth also had some effect on stem elongation (Benschop and De Hertogh, 1971).

C. Tissue culture

Monocotyledonous plants are notoriously difficult to grow in tissue culture, but some success has been obtained with a modification of White's medium supplemented with coconut milk and 2,4-D. On this medium, tissue from *Endymion* bulbs displays a capacity to retain organization and proliferates into a mass of tuberized shoots with some callus tissue, but attempts to subculture the callus have so far been unsuccessful. Limited success has also been obtained on the same medium using *Crinum* bulb scale tissue (Mullin, 1967). Successful culture of lily tissue has also been reported recently, using a Linsmaier and Skoog medium which is higher than other media in mineral salt content, especially salts of nitrogen and potassium (Sheridan, 1968).

Chapter 9

Physiological disorders

"Blaguro ychydig oedd ei chyfran,
Rhoi un wên ar wyneb anian;
Llef o'r nef yn Hydref waedda—
'Darfu'th waith,'—a hitha drenga."
Alun, 1851

A number of disorders of bulbs occur for which there are no known or no recognized causal organism. Sometimes the response is due to unfavourable environmental conditions which may be well defined as are the methods of avoiding the trouble. It may, however, be more difficult to determine the cause because a number of factors could result in very similar conditions. Some disorders are sufficiently specific to warrant common descriptive names, e.g. tulip "topple", whilst others, such as a failure to flower in apparently healthy, large-sized bulbs can be due to failure of flower initiation, or the abortion of the flower at any one of a number of stages of development, as a result of a variety of causes.

Every season a physiologist dealing with bulbs will receive a number of requests for advice on abnormalities, but in many cases no clear diagnosis can be made. This is partly because the time-scale involved can be of many months' duration and if relevant records of treatment are forgotten, detective work becomes impossible. Dissection of plant material can often give indications of where troubles originated, especially in cases of flowering failure, where the presence of a small aborted flower could pin-point when trouble was experienced. This can sometimes show that trouble originated before the bulbs were purchased from a grower or wholesaler.

The purchaser can then seek redress for the shortcomings of the bulbs he bought.

Most physiological disorders affect flowering, causing a complete failure of flowering or the production of poor quality material, e.g. short stems, or deformed or distorted flowers. Many of these abnormalities can be traced to the grower's failure to follow the complex but well-understood forcing schedules. As indicated in Chapter 7, short stems occur if the low-temperature period in *Narcissus* and tulip is too short, and in severe cases necrotic or pigment-free areas occur at the tips of the perianth parts in tulips, or the flower may even die. It is also well known that hot-water treatment for eelworm control when applied early can severely damage *Narcissus* flowers, causing a severe splitting of the paracorolla and a narrowing of the perianth parts to give "starry" flowers. These symptoms can be avoided by warm-storing the bulbs before the hot-water treatment.

Disorders of the vegetative parts are less common, but can cause considerable concern. Fasciation occurs sporadically, especially in *Narcissus*, but is seldom severe. Failure of rooting also occurs commonly, sometimes because adverse storage conditions produce a very dry and hard base plate. In *Narcissus* and tulip this results in the upward growth of roots within the outer scale or even between the scales to emerge near the neck of the bulb. If a large part of the root system is affected in this way the resulting plant can be stunted and the flower may be lost.

Frost and hail can cause damage, or plants may die in waterlogged field conditions but the alert grower is usually aware of these hazards, even if he is not in a position to do much about them.

I. Disorders of *Narcissus*

A. Grassiness

A common complaint of field-grown *Narcissus* is that called "degeneration" or "grassiness". Few flowers are produced and large numbers of leaves appear from the bulb which tends to split and produce many daughters. A number of factors can cause this condition but the most likely are the killing of the main shoot by bulb fly or bulb scale mite, or by too-severe hot-water treatment, which stimulates the initiation and growth of new laterals. Another occurrence is the contamination of a stock by rogue plants of another cultivar which may produce more leaves than the true-to-type cultivar. Observations by Moore (1939) on true-to-type 'Golden Spur' and grassy plants contaminating the stock, showed that true 'Golden Spur' remained true and the stocks did not show degeneration due to the actual deterioration of the individuals within the stock.

Where the grassiness is caused by injury to the growing shoot and the stimulation of the growth of laterals, it would be expected that the trouble would disappear in the next few seasons, when the small bulbs would grow, provided that subsequent generations are not similarly affected.

Other causes, such as genetic instability or virus infection, cannot be ruled out as causal agents of grassiness in some cases.

B. Soft rot

A soft rot of *Narcissus* bulbs frequently occurs when large quantities of fresh bulbs are kept in unventilated spaces where temperatures rise to 30°C or above. The loss of such quantities of bulbs especially if in transit from a grower to a purchaser can be very embarrassing. From data on respiration rates, it can be calculated that fresh bulbs produce about 1×10^6 J h^{-1} and considerable quantities of water—ideal composting conditions when ventilation is poor. These conditions can occur shortly after lifting, during transit and also during and following hot-water treatment.

The breakdown of bulb tissue occurs rapidly; in one instance twelve tons of bulbs were lifted and immediately stored at 34°C for four days in an unventilated store. Ten days later five tons of the bulbs were rotten. No fungi were found but bacterial infection was present. Similar bulbs not heat-treated remained healthy.

C. Bullhead condition in 'Cheerfulness'

Up to 10% of flowers in a crop of the double *Narcissus* 'Cheerfulness' may fail to emerge from the spathe, which remains dry and membranous resembling a drumstick. Inflorescences composed of a single flower are most frequently affected.

A normal flower of 'Cheerfulness' has six perianth parts, a paracorolla, six petalloid anthers and a normal gynoecium, the "double" appearance being due to the presence of petalloid anthers. The bullhead form has extra perianth parts, the paracorolla is frequently dissected and has petalloid styles which fuse with the wall of the corolla tube above the ovary, and ovary development is poor. The corolla tube elongates late in flower development, a few days before the perianth parts start to show colour. The corolla tube in the bullhead forms fails to elongate, the spathe is not split and remains dry, papery and enclosing the malformed flower (Fig. 9.1). The cause is not known, but marked plants produce bullhead flowers again in the following season, suggesting either a virus or genetic cause.

Fig. 9.1 "Bullhead" form of *Narcissus* 'Cheerfulness', in longitudinal section: left—almost single form; centre—bullhead; right—normal form with doubling due to petalloid anthers. Note fusion of petalloid styles and the failure of corolla elongation. (Photo. courtesy G.C.R.I.)

D. Hot-water treatment damage

A range of symptoms can be caused by hot-water treatment of bulbs, although it is well known that if the correct procedures are followed over 90% of the flowers produced are marketable. Damage symptoms can be found on roots, leaves and flowers, and bulb yield may be affected if damage is severe. Severe root damage can occur if the treatment is late, when root initials are present near the surface of the base plate. Some or all the roots are killed, no new roots are produced and the plant spends a whole season with a restricted or absent root system until new roots are produced the following autumn. The absence of an efficient root system means that the above-ground parts of the plant are poorly developed, its water status is in considerable jeopardy and the aerial parts senesce rapidly. The plant usually survives, however.

Leaf damage is expressed as a speckling of the tips, roughening and, in severe cases, distortion. This has been demonstrated experimentally in bulbs stored at temperatures which may (depending on season) be near ambient, but are certainly too low to prevent hot-water treatment damage. Flower damage ranges from complete flower loss, although scapes may survive, to reduced flower size, or split and distorted perianth parts and paracorollas.

To avoid these troubles, bulbs should not be stored below 16°C immediately before hot-water treatment (see Chapter 6) and the treatment should be given sufficiently late to avoid flower damage, and sufficiently early to avoid root damage. Recommended times are immediately after flower differentiation is completed for avoiding flower damage, if the bulbs are not given a warm-storage period before hot-water treatment. The widespread use of warm storage has allowed successful early hot-water treatment without damaging flowers.

E. Other *Narcissus* disorders

Narcissus poeticus 'Flore Pleno' (Double White) is commercially a very useful cultivar because it flowers late (in May in the Tamar Valley in south-west England, where it is most widely grown in the U.K.). Two conditions give trouble, the first is a "reversion" to single form and the second is in death of the flower bud. The former condition is sometimes thought to be due to stock contamination by a single form of the same cultivar but this has yet to be established. Flower death is commonest on warmer slopes and growers' observations suggests that extremes of temperature between day and night, hot, dry weather during the growing season or a wet autumn are contributory factors. All these could operate through poor water relations, aggravated by a poor root system and also affected by edaphic or topographic factors. Research on some of these aspects is in progress.

II. Disorders of Tulip

The most commonly encountered troubles with tulips are those which cause a failure to flower. Flowers may not be initiated at all, so that although a bulb is of flowering size it contains only the single leaf of the non-flowering plant. A few bulbs, perhaps amounting to 1% have no flower, but only a single large leaf as in a small bulb, and the reason is not known. Occasionally specimens are encountered where three normal leaves are present but no flower is initiated, the apex being occupied by a long narrow thong-like leaf. Again, the causes are not known.

A. Blind flowers

More commonly, flower initiation occurs normally, but the flower fails to complete its development and aborts at some stage after initiation. The abortion may involve the flower alone or only part of the flower (Fig. 9.2). Anthers are very frequently affected and may be straw-coloured or partly so in cultivars which normally have black anthers. If the perianth parts are affected, the damage is a slight to pronounced ragged edge to the perianth tip in cultivars where it is normally smooth and entire. If more severe, the perianth parts have white necrotic or green tips depending on the amount of chlorophyll present late in the development of the flower. Even more

Fig. 9.2 Range of flower and shoot damage in tulip 'Apeldoorn'. From left to right: (a) normal plant; (b) plant with flower which has died late in development; (c) flower death at early stage, flower is small white object in centre; (d) loss of complete shoot except basal leaf; (e) loss of complete shoot; Note the development of laminae on many daughter bulbs when the shoot is extensively damaged. This occurs in plant (a) to a small extent. (Photo. courtesy G.C.R.I.)

severe damage can kill part or the whole of the shoot; if the whole shoot is killed, then only the above-ground parts are the single leaves produced as prolongations of the scale tips of the daughter bulbs. A number of these narrow thin leaves appear from each mother bulb. An intermediate condition where the whole stem above the top leaf including the flower is necrosed and very reduced in size, is called *kernrot* (stem rot) in Dutch.

The cause of these flower distortions has long been known, but seasonal differences in the extent of the damage and also differences due to cultivar make generalizations difficult. Most of the trouble is caused by high temperatures before planting and, as bulbs are often being transported during this stage, the troubles have been called "heating in transit" and have been investigated and recognized since the early days of Dutch bulb exports. The condition in a severe form (where the whole flower is killed but not for the shoot or leaves) is similar to that aimed at in the *blindstoken* treatment for increasing bulb weight by killing the flower in bulbs before field planting.

Some or all of these symptoms can also be induced in forcing small bulbs, from forcing too early or at too high a temperature. Wide fluctuations in temperature adversely affect flowers, and poor rooting (due perhaps to a failure to keep the rooting medium moist) can also contribute to failure.

Van Slogteren (1936, 1937) induced damage of this type by treating bulbs for two weeks at 25 or 30°C during August, September and early October. The bulbs were stored with and without low temperature (9°C) and high temperature (25°C) pre-treatment. Almost 70% of flowers were lost after the low-temperature pre-treatment. Two weeks at 25°C were ineffective in killing flowers until applied in early September. Later treatment was progressively more deleterious until the end of September, after which treatment had less effect. Bulbs not pre-cooled showed no damage symptoms until mid-September and the numbers of damaged flowers increased with later treatment to about 20% by mid-October. High-temperature storage delayed the danger period for flower damage caused by two weeks at 30°C from early September to early October, but after the critical time both the warm stored (25°C for 8 weeks then 17°C) and those not warm stored (20°C then 17°C) produced no flowers.

Investigations of *kernrot* at Lisse showed that the first symptoms occurred before meiosis, i.e. shortly after the completion of flower differentiation. Occasional cases of damaged anthers have been observed, when the surrounding anthers are healthy. Damaged anthers appear glassy and necrosed, and the necrosis spreads into the adjacent parts (Kamerbeek and de Munk, 1965).

There is mounting evidence that *kernrot* has a complex origin. The condition is commonest when ventilation is poor, and when some bulbs are infected by *Fusarium oxysporum*. While it seems likely that ethylene production and its accumulation are important factors, it does not directly lead to *kernrot*. Low concentrations of ethylene reduce shoot growth and especially the growth of perianth parts, resulting in the development of an open flower within the bulb (see also Chapter 8). This apparently allows the entry of mites (*Tyrophagus* and *Rhizoglyphus*) which feed on the anthers and leave wounds which are contaminated by fungal and bacterial spores. The growth of these infections leads to *kernrot*, and the extent of the final damage is a function of the growth rate of the pathogen and the time of infection (Kamerbeek, 1969a; de Munk, 1971).

B. Topple

Topple, also called "wet stem" or "water neck", occurs in forced tulip crops when the flower stem collapses and falls over late in the flower development or even after the flowers are picked and are on the way to market (Fig. 9.3). When the flower is near anthesis, a glassy water-soaked area appears on the peduncle, usually in the top internode, but sometimes

Fig. 9.3 Topple in tulip 'Apeldoorn'. Note the collapsed stems above the uppermost leaf. (Photo. courtesy G.C.R.I.)

below this. Liquid may exude from the area and soon afterwards the tissue shrinks inwards, so that ridges and wrinkles appear on the outer surface. It has long been recognized that the condition can be avoided by keeping forcing-house temperatures low, and, also, that the condition is nutritional because adding calcium salts to the plants' water controls topple.

In a recent account of topple, Algera (1968) states that the first symptoms are a slower rate of protoplasm flow within the cell and a decreased cellular activity. First the nucleus becomes hyaline, then the cytoplasm becomes lumpy and disorganized and finally the cells shrink and the stem collapses. Observations indicated that in most cases infiltration begins at a point just below the zone of most rapid growth. The zone affected depends partly on temperature during development because the zone of rapid growth moves upwards from the lowest to the uppermost internode during development. As infiltration starts, permeability increases, possibly because of a disturbed balance of permeability-regulating ions. Infiltration is promoted by potassium, sodium and ammonium ions and inhibited by calcium and magnesium ions. Toppled internodes contain considerably less calcium than healthy ones and it is apparent that the calcium status of the plants is closely related to topple. Algera postulates that calcium deficiency occurs locally in the rapidly elongating stem because of the low mobility of this element and that the nuclear and plastid membranes and plasmalemma break down; this then leads to increased permeability, the vacuole contents are lost and the cells die. As a result the stem loses turgor locally and collapses.

The condition has also been observed in *Iris* and lily where it is called "limber neck".

C. Blauwgroeien

Some tulip cultivars develop brown necrotic spots in the bulb scales of new bulbs, and which are apparent only in the scale underlying the tunic. The condition has been described in preliminary investigations by Kamerbeek (1958). Early symptoms are the occurrence of small colourless glassy spots in the bulb-scale parenchyma. Neither fungi, bacteria nor virus have been isolated from affected scales, and bulb growth rates are correlated with the numbers of affected bulbs, larger, faster-growing bulbs being most affected. Adding salts of boron, copper, cobalt, magnesium, manganese and zinc were without effect, indicating that a nutritional deficiency is unlikely to be the cause. While the true cause of the condition is not known, it is believed to be a physiological disorder. Further investigations (Kamerbeek, 1962b) confirmed the linear relation between bulb weight and disease incidence, and indicated that factors preventing rapid bulb growth also reduced the numbers of diseased bulbs. In experiments to demonstrate this effect, shading of bulb plots to 75% or 50% of full light, considerably reduced or even eliminated the disease. The period of maximum response to shading was during the last week of April and the first two weeks of May.

A hypothesis developed by Kamerbeek to explain the origin of the necrotic spots involves the loss of cell sap (and possibly sugars) into the intercellular spaces of the parenchyma leading to necrosis. The condition is aggravated by environmental factors which tend to increase transpiration. There are some similarities between *blauwgroeien* and topple.

D. Chalking

Stored tulips often develop dry hard white spots which resemble chalk. These areas frequently coalesce until the whole bulb becomes hard and stone-like. The condition is called *verkalking* (chalking) or *huidziek* (skin disease) in Dutch. A number of factors contribute to chalking, such as mechanical damage, lifting immature bulbs, storing bulbs wet or in poorly-ventilated humid conditions, or exposing bulbs to strong sunshine for some hours after the removal of the tunic.

Fungi have been isolated from affected bulbs, especially when browning of bulb scale tissues has occurred, but it is believed that these are secondary infections, since dipping bulbs in fungicides failed to prevent chalkiness.

The general consensus of opinion among advisers is that chalking results from poor handling techniques, and is not commonly encountered by good growers with suitable bulb-storing facilities.

E. Hard base

Some tulip cultivars exhibit "hard base" where the bulb has no prominent root ridge. When these bulbs are planted, the roots are unable to penetrate the tunic, and frequently grow upwards between the tunic and the next fleshy scale to emerge at the nose of the bulb. This occurs particularly in forced bulbs and more so in five-degree tulips where the tunic has less time to disintegrate than in autumn-planted field-grown crops. Cutting through the tunic just above the normal root-emergence area allows the roots to grow normally. The condition is aggravated by early lifting and heat treatment which tends to give a thicker tougher tunic than normal, although there has been a tendency to produce such apparently "good-looking" bulbs for the retail trade.

F. Thieves

Tulip "thieves" are aberrant plants with withered and small bulbs which rarely flower. These bulbs can be separated from normal bulbs by a flotation process. Normal methods of pre-sale grading of bulbs separate off for sale large bulbs and tend to concentrate thieves in the remaining unsold stock.

G. Watersoaking

Under certain conditions intercellular spaces of tulip leaves become infiltrated with liquid so that the leaf appears blotched with dark areas. This is frequently observed after bulbs are transferred to a glasshouse from a frozen standing-ground and also in high-humidity conditions in glass-houses following watering. The condition appears alarming but there is no evidence of permanent ill-effects, and normal leaf appearance is resumed when conditions allow more rapid transpiration. 'Elmus' and 'Rose Copland' are both susceptible cultivars. The infiltration is similar to that occurring in early stages of topple but the tissues recover because the cell permeability is not irreversibly affected.

H. Knuckling

A condition occurring in some tulips (especially 'Copland' cultivars and sports) and especially when large bulbs (above 13 cm) are being forced is the emergence of the shoot in a doubled-over position with the leaf tip retained in the bulb. The shoot tip may become free during growth but in the worst cases it does not and a deformed flower results. Although knuckling occurs sporadically in both field-grown and forced crops, and can affect as much as a third of the crop, no explanation of the condition has yet been found.

I. Gummosis

Gum production in tulip, *Narcissus* and hyacinth has been described by Moore (1939), but until recently little information on causes was available. Bergman *et al.* (1968) described how a stream of air drawn over a culture of *Fusarium* and then over 'Apeldoorn' tulip bulbs caused the latter to produce large quantities of gum. Because it is known that the fungus produces ethylene, air containing a small quantity of the pure gas was passed over bulbs and also produced gummosis. A concentration of only one vpm is

R

sufficient to produce considerable gumming in 'Apeldoorn'. These observations stress the need for keeping any *Fusarium*-infected bulbs away from healthy ones and to ventilate bulb stores adequately to prevent any accumulation of such volatiles. The occurrence of gummosis on apparently healthy bulbs in the field suggests that in some conditions ethylene can be produced and accumulate on or near bulbs in soil in the absence of infection by *Fusarium*.

Gummosis has also been observed in muscari and hyacinth.

III. Disorders of Hyacinth

A. Loose-bud

This term, or the more descriptive *spouwen* (spewing) or *cracher* (spitting) is applied to the ejection of the inflorescence shortly before flowering. The inflorescence is detached from its peduncle and is carried up by the leaves which then open so that the inflorescence falls to one side. Loose-bud may occur in outdoor-grown crops, but is commoner in forced plants, although there are large seasonal differences. Some cultivars are also more susceptible; these include 'First Bismarck' and 'Pink Pearl'.

A number of speculations on the cause of loose-bud have been made, frequently without an examination or even a consideration of the time at which the trouble starts. The position is further confused by the existence of two forms of the condition caused by physiological and mechanical factors. The former was examined in detail by Beijer (1947) who traced back the loose-bud condition occurring in outdoor hyacinths in January or February to events in December or January. The first visible symptom was found to be a sap infiltration of the base plate and the peduncle producing a water-soaked appearance, accompanied, in the most seriously-affected plants, by a narrow longitudinal cavity in the peduncle. From this cavity arise radial fissures which develop into small transverse cavities. Extension growth by the leaves at this stage carry up the inflorescence and pull upwards on the peduncle which fractures across one of the transverse cavities, to leave a stump of pedicel 1–15 mm long. The loose inflorescence is then carried up and for a time remains turgid because its lower end is surrounded by sap which fills the cavity between the ends of the peduncle. The break may occur early or late in growth; if the latter, then abnormal flowers can develop. After the emergence of the inflorescence from the soil, turgidity is soon lost and the symptoms of the disorder are apparent.

The cause of the infiltration is considered to be a disturbance of equilibrium between water uptake by the roots and the utilization and transpiration from the shoot, probably involving a high root pressure. Factors predisposing bulbs to loose-bud are: (a) a lack of high temperature during the summer treatment of the bulbs; (b) planting the bulbs too early; (c) too high a soil temperature in the glasshouse after planting; (d) too high a soil temperature in winter encouraging water and solute absorption; (e) too much available soil water; and (f) using in autumn ammonium sulphate fertilizer which affects cell permeability. Beijer points out, however, that high root pressure alone is insufficient to cause the disorder, and the contribution of low growth rates (and low water utilization) and low transpiration rates are important.

A mechanical form of loose-bud was later described by Beijer (1963). This differs in important details from the loose-bud described above which has been referred to as physiological (Kamerbeek, 1969a). The mechanical form of loose-bud has no tissue infiltration of the peduncle, and no split peduncle and associated transverse splits. The peduncle breaks at its base, no short stump is left attached to the base plate and the cavity is air-filled. The cause is believed to be entirely mechanical but is aggravated by sudden increases in temperature, e.g. when planted bulbs are moved into a glasshouse, although it can also occur when temperatures are fairly constant or are increased gradually.

B. Root failure

Moore (1939) described root failure in hyacinths where early shoot growth was normal but either no roots at all were produced or only a few which died very quickly. As a result, shoot growth soon halts followed by wilting then necrosis. Seasonal differences exist; the condition is more common after a cold summer and is aggravated by lifting the bulbs too early and early forcing.

C. Forcing failures

Forced hyacinths exhibit a range of flower abnormalities such as death of some flowers on the inflorescence before it is fully open or even a complete failure of the inflorescence. Troubles can usually be traced back to incorrect storage treatments.

IV. Disorders of *Iris*

A failure of *Iris* bulbs to flower can usually be attributed to one of two causes. Flower initiation may not have occurred, so that the plants have three leaves and are vegetative, or flowers may have initiated normally but dried out during forcing ("blasting").

A. Failure of initiation

The factors affecting initiation of *Iris* flowers have been described in an earlier chapter dealing with bulb storage. If the bulbs are sufficiently large then a high percentage will be expected to initiate flowers, and in border-line-sized bulbs a higher percentage of initiation can be obtained by early lifting and storing the bulbs at high temperatures (see Chapter 5).

B. Blasting

Kamerbeek (1963) showed some indications that the sugar content of the plant at the time of shoot extension was important, and investigated the effects of air and soil temperatures on the incidence of blasting. Soil temperature was closely related to blasting; at 13, 15 and 18°C the percentages of blasted flowers were 10, 45 and 73. Air temperatures were approximately the same for all the soil-temperature treatments and ranged between 7 and 12°C. Additional carbon dioxide supply had no effect on blasting, but light was important in some circumstances, especially in winter, because unlike *Narcissus* and tulip, the *Iris* plant is dependent on current photosynthesis for the complete development of the inflorescence. Troubles are frequently encountered in forced crops which near maturity in dull weather in winter, and also in outdoor-grown *Iris* in similar conditions. Flowers can also wither after they have been picked and arrive in the market in an unsaleable condition.

V. Disorders of lily

A. Bud blasting

Flower bud abortion may occur in Easter lilies at a late stage in flower development and the condition is called "bud blasting". The base of the flower bud becomes light green, then yellow and shrivelled, and finally turns brown but does not absciss. Buds of any size can be affected but they are usually between 2 and 50 mm. Buds smaller than 2 mm often fail anyway. It occurs especially in 'Georgia' lilies and reduces this cultivar's advantage of having more flower buds than any other cultivar in south-eastern United States according to Einert and Box (1967). They were also of the opinion that as flower number per inflorescence increases, so does the occurrence of bud blast, suggesting that competition for nutrients could be an important factor in the condition. Others have suggested that sudden moisture deficits increase abortion (Smith and Langhans, 1961) and as does a soil nitrate level above 50 ppm (Eastwood, 1952). Mastalerz (1965) demonstrated increased abortion by factors reducing carbohydrate supply to the developing flower buds (such as leaf removal, or cooling the bud pedicel). He found a direct relation between the percentage of blasted buds and the duration of darkness in plants shaded when the buds were between 6 and 12 mm long. Einert and Box (1967), however, failed to increase flower abortion by shading 'Georgia' lilies to 50% of natural sunlight in central Mississippi, but perhaps their light conditions were better than those used by Mastalerz.

Effects of light on bud blast in lily 'Enchantment' were observed when plants being forced at 21°C were kept for one week in darkness before return to the glasshouse (Schenk and Boontjes, 1970). High numbers of bud blast (27%) and bud abscission (72%) were observed in weeks 6–8 after planting, and work is in progress to test whether flower abortion in mid-winter can be prevented by high light treatment in the last month before flowering.

VI. Chemical injury

Chemical injury is sometimes observed in forced bulbs, caused by the contamination of the straw used in the standing ground by selective weed-killers which distort or yellow the bulb shoot as it grows through the straw. Cases of such damage are not well documented, and it is often very difficult to trace the chemical responsible.

Bulbs may also suffer damage from pre-emergence herbicides which are applied too late, i.e. at emergence. Paraquat causes yellowing of *Narcissus*, tulip and *Iris* leaves, and it is essential that these sprays be applied 12–14 days before emergence. At a rate of 1–2 kg ha^{-1} just after flowering the plants are killed, after the foliage becomes a pale greyish-yellow. High levels of pre-emergence herbicides can be harmful, and *Narcissus* damage has followed applications of alicep above 6 kg ha^{-1} active ingredient (a.i.) and yield reductions have been observed after 9 and 12 kg ha^{-1} a.i. Severe damage has been obtained with the soil-acting herbicide EPTC at 4 kg ha^{-1} a.i. on tulips, while terbacil at 0·75 kg ha^{-1} damages tulip flowers and leaves, reduces yield and kills a number of bulbs.

The post-emergence sprays prometryne and alicep reduce tulip yields at 4 and 9 kg ha^{-1} a.i. respectively, and damage *Narcissus* and tulip at 0·5 kg ha^{-1} a.i. Linuron sprayed before flowering at 0·5 kg ha^{-1} a.i. causes yellowing of *Narcissus* foliage, and the flowers produced when the bulbs are forced are slightly smaller and have shorter stems than those untreated. Alicep at 2 and 4 kg ha^{-1} a.i. before flowering causes green perianths and yellowing of tulip leaves.

Chemicals used to kill plants that are not lifted with the main crop can damage other stocks if spray drift occurs. TCA causes flower distortion, and must be used with care. After the leaves have died down weed-control chemicals can be sprayed, or sprays may be used to accelerate leaf senescence. Herbicides may also be applied to control weeds in a two-year crop. It is important that *Narcissus* foliage is dead, and preferably detached from the bulb by cultivation or flailing to prevent the translocation of the herbicide into the bulb. The avoidance of dalapon, TCA and chlorthiamid in particular is recommended because of the risk of bulb damage which can be extensive and persistent (Turquand, 1969).

Chapter 10

Pests and diseases of bulbs

> "When we reflect on this struggle, we may console our-
> selves with the full belief, that the war of nature is not
> incessant, that no fear is felt, that death is generally
> prompt, and that the vigorous, the healthy, and the
> happy survive and multiply."   Charles Darwin, 1859

Ornamental bulbous plants suffer from pests and diseases which are an
unavoidable and important facet of bulb-crop husbandry. Detailed descriptions of the pests and pathogens, their biology and measures for their
control are outside the scope of this book and reference may be made to a
number of publications such as the Bulletins of the Ministry of Agriculture, Fisheries and Food (No. 51 "Narcissus Pests"; No. 62 "Bulb and
Corm Production"; No. 117 "Diseases of Bulbs"; and No. 201 "Hot-
water Treatment of Plant Material") and to other standard works (e.g.
Hussey, Read and Hesling, 1969).

1. Bulb pests

Some pests are specific to bulbs or even to single bulb species; others are
of more general occurrence and can attack a wide range of host plants.
Pests of bulb plants will be considered by reference to the host plants.

I. *Narcissus* pests

A. Eelworm

Probably the most serious pest of *Narcissus* is the stem nematode (*Ditylenchus dipsaci*) which was described over a hundred years ago and is now widespread and important in all temperate regions of the world. Different isolates of the eelworm thrive on a range of different host plants, and it is known that there are perhaps 20 or more biological races, although there are no distinguishing features apart from host range. The tulip race attacks both *Narcissus* and tulip, but the *Narcissus* race cannot multiply in tulip. Adult eelworms are 1·0–1·3 mm long.

On leaves nematodes induce discrete, yellow, elongated swellings *spikkels* which sometimes contain very few eelworms. In heavier attacks the *spikkels* often coalesce to produce unevenly yellow, necrotic patches, often with leaf distortion and short, twisted or missing peduncles. Eventually, especially in forced plants, the leaf eventually rots. Severe symptoms can result from a few eelworms; a plant was reported as almost killed by 16 nematodes, and 50 usually cause a bulb to be rated as "very diseased" (Hesling, 1965). A population of 10 eelworms added to each kilogram of soil causes severe damage, and bulbs are entered within a week of planting in infested soil. The eelworms congregate in the basal parts of the leaves, multiplying many thousandfold in one season, but lateral spread in the soil is usually limited to a metre or so, and survival for longer than a year in moist soil is unlikely in the absence of a host plant. Severely-infested bulbs rot quickly and the eelworm population within such bulbs falls rapidly due to their migration, death, and the activity of predatory fungi, competitive mites and insect larvae. In the absence of *Narcissus*, other plants can act as hosts and will support a breeding population of eelworms until *Narcissus* are again available. At lifting time and in store, eelworm-infested bulbs often lack lustre and are soft in the neck region. When cut transversely, such bulbs often show the brown-ring symptom (one or more scales being brown in colour) which is useful diagnostically, although not specific to eelworm.

The introduction of the well-known hot-water treatment of bulbs to control eelworm about 50 years ago saved the bulb industry from ruin, but the method is far from ideal because of the small margin between a treatment lethal to eelworms and that damaging to the bulb. The heat-tolerance of the bulb is influenced by storage treatment (especially temperature) before hot-water treatment, as well as by cultivar and season.

Experimentally it has been shown that 5 h at 43°C is needed to control eelworms completely in a medium-sized bulb, but commercially 44°C for 3 h is usually quite effective. For physical, and possibly physiological, reasons, dry or re-wetted masses of eelworms, which congregate on bulbs in dry stores, seem particularly difficult to kill by hot-water treatment. During hot-water treatment careful control of temperature is essential; good quality thermometers and sensitive and reliable thermostats must be used. The water in the tank should contain a non-ionic wetter and formalin is commonly used to give a bath concentration of 1 in 200 of commercial 38–40% formaldehyde (formalin). The formalin is an effective nematicide and fungicide which prevents the dispersal of pests and diseases within the treatment tank.

Eelworm control is most effective when hot-water treatment is complemented by good hygiene during treatment and also during the growing season. The crop should be regularly inspected; infested plants and their neighbours should be removed and burned, and a nematicide applied to the infested area. Treated bulbs must be kept in clean stores completely isolated from untreated bulbs and unsterilized plant material, boxes, etc.

There is a risk of flower damage by hot-water treatment; this can be minimized by treating the bulbs at the right stage of flower development and by warm storage of bulbs before treatment. The best treatment date is when flower differentiation has been completed; earlier treatment damages flowers, whilst late treatment damages roots, especially if root initials have started to form. Bulbs are normally treated in July and August in England. Warm storage of bulbs before hot-water treatment eliminates the flower damage that used to be considered inseparable from hot-water treatment, but it is believed that warm storage acclimatizes the nematodes so that they survive hot-water treatment. Thus, only in stocks believed to be eelworm-free is it worth risking warm storage; warm storage before hot-water treatment should be avoided with eelworm-infested stocks and a more severe treatment used e.g. a temperature of 46°C. Eelworm-infested stocks are usually lifted early and treated without delay, the following season's flower crop being sacrificed.

The use of bulb dips of thionazin (diethyl 0–2 pyrazinyl phosphorothioate) held promise as a simple and effective method of eelworm control but these hopes have not been fully realized. Soaking bulbs at ambient temperatures in 0·23% thionazin solution for 2·5 h is generally less effective than hot-water treatment, although less flower damage occurs. Sometimes phytotoxic effects of shortening stems have been observed and bulb yield has been less good after thionazin treatment than after hot-water treatment. Another disadvantage of thionazin is its high mammalian toxicity.

Other eelworms (*Pratylenchus* spp.) attack only the roots and incite a root rot that can be serious. The root rot is largely due to the secondarily pathogenic fungus *Cylindrocarpon radicicola*. Control is by killing the eelworm in the soil using D-D (dichloropropane-dichloropropene) at 450 kg ha^{-1}.

B. Bulb flies

There are three narcissus flies, the large (*Merodon equestris*) and small (*Eumerus tuberculatus* and *E. strigatus*). All are widely distributed within Europe and North America and both probably originated from southern Europe.

The large narcissus fly resembles a small bumble bee 12 mm long. The adults appear from late April to late June and lay single eggs on or near the bulb. Eggs hatch in 10–15 days and the developing larvae enter the bulb through the base plate and feed on the scales until the following spring when they pupate in the soil before emerging as an adult in April–June, or earlier from forced bulbs. A small infested bulb may fail to produce a shoot but larger bulbs are rarely killed although the shoot may be killed or partly eaten so that leaves emerge on only one side of the apex. This loss of apical dominance encourages the emergence of large numbers of leaves, giving the plant a grassy appearance.

The small narcissus flies are about 6 mm long and resemble a large housefly, first appearing in the open in April. The adult flies lay eggs on damaged bulbs, frequently those damaged by stem nematode. When eelworm or other cause of primary damage is controlled, small bulb fly is not a problem. Eggs are laid in batches (never singly) and the larvae enter the neck of the bulb causing a more rapid destruction than *Merodon*. A number of generations occur in one season.

Some control of *Eumerus* sp. can be achieved by removing dying foliage and closing the soil crevices which normally allow the insects access to the bulb, especially the tubular hole left in the soil by the dying foliage. Early lifting is also a useful measure which removes the bulbs from the range of the flies.

Bulbs damaged by bulb flies should be destroyed and if infested stocks are not hot-water treated (which will kill the larvae of all narcissus flies) the bulbs can be soaked in 0·05% miscible gamma-BHC solution with wetter for 1 h. Fly attack can also be prevented by a 15 min pre-planting dip in 0·2% aldrin solution. Alternatively this chemical can be added to the soil just before planting.

C. Mites

Bulb scale mite (*Steneotarsonemus laticeps*) is a major pest of *Narcissus* in the U.K. The tiny mites (0·2 mm long) live between the bulb scales especially in folds or longitudinal furrows between the scales, and migrate on to foliage, or from infested bulbs to healthy ones. Infested bulbs are soft and can be recognized by the presence of brown patches at the scale angles. Plants from infested forced bulbs have abnormally bright green leaves which later turn yellow. The flower may be killed or the peduncle may elongate, bearing a dead flower still enclosed by the spathe. The peduncle characteristically has saw-tooth edges. Hot-water treatment is an effective control measure, as most of the active stages and eggs die following 43°C for one hour. Complete eradication can only be achieved by 43°C (4 h) or 44°C (3 h). Dipping bulbs in 0·2% thionazin solution with 0·1% non-ionic type wetter is as successful as hot-water treatment for 3 h at 44°C as a control measure. When bulbs are forced the infestation is often discovered too late for hot-water treatment, but 0·1% endrin or endosulfan applied as drenching sprays can save most of the flowers.

The bulb mite (*Rhizoglyphus echinopus*) frequently occurs in bulb stocks in western Europe. It is larger (0·9 mm) than the bulb scale mite, and is saprophagous, living in tissue-rot caused by other pathogens.

D. Other pests

Slugs can cause considerable damage to *Narcissus*, especially in prolonged damp weather. In winter the bulb base or the roots are attacked and the whole plant may be killed. Slugs are also attracted to the paracorolla especially *N. poeticus* cultivars and damage to these parts, often seen in gardens when flowers have been blown down by the wind, renders the flowers unattractive and unsaleable. Standard control methods using metaldehyde (30 kg ha^{-1}) or methiocarb pellets (6 kg ha^{-1}) are useful but underground attack is difficult to combat.

Caterpillars of the garden swift moth (*Hepialus lupulina*) can also attack bulbs and be locally important, but no effective control methods are available.

II. Tulip pests

A. Eelworm

Tulips are also susceptible to attack by the stem nematode, but only the tulip race of this pest is serious. Potentially it is a very serious pest because both flowers and bulbs are rendered unsaleable, and control is difficult because hot-water treatment of tulips is far less successful than with *Narcissus*. Infested bulbs are soft with discoloured outer fleshy scales, usually yellowish, but sometimes with pronounced brown rings as in *Narcissus*. Symptoms are more obvious on above-ground parts; stems are scarred, bent and often split, and shoots often die prematurely. Hot-water treatment of tulips is not satisfactory because it usually damages the plant, and it has been superseded by thionazin dips. Control of nematodes by thionazin in tulips is better than that obtained in *Narcissus* probably because tulips absorb more of the chemical and because tulips are lifted and treated annually. Careful inspection of stocks and removing diseased plants can almost eliminate eelworm; combined with control treatments this has led to very low levels of the disease in parts of England.

B. Aphids

Tulip bulb aphids (*Dysaphis tulipae*, and two other species) are occasionally encountered in bulb stores. These insects are grey-purple or olive-brown in colour and may be present in large numbers. Fumigation with nicotine is an effective control measure. Aphids may also be present on the growing crop and increase to levels necessitating control with a nicotine or malathion spray.

C. Other pests

Mice and rats can be troublesome, especially in standing grounds covered with straw, and care must be taken that the bulbs are not being damaged. Pheasants can also be troublesome in winter; the usual control measures are recommended.

III. *Iris* pests

Iris nematode (*Ditylenchus destructor*) attacks *Iris* bulb scales but the eelworm problems of *Iris* are less severe than those of *Narcissus* and tulip. Severe infestation results in stunted or killed bulb foliage and poor bulb yields, but *spikkels* are absent and no resistant "wool" stage is known. Current recommendations for hot-water treatment are to store bulbs at 23°C for 3–14 days followed immediately by hot-water treatment at 44°C for 2–3 h depending on bulb size. A dip in 0·23% thionazin with added commercial formalin (38–40% solution of formaldehyde) to give 0·5% formalin is usually effective.

IV. Pests of other bulbs

Hot-water treatment of other bulbs is also practised; these include grape-hyacinth which can be successfully treated at 45°C if the bulbs are warm stored at 34°C (4 days) immediately after lifting and before hot-water treatment. For *Scilla sibirica* warm storage at 25·5°C, soaking for 24 h, followed by hot-water treatment at 43·5 for 3 or 4 h were success-ful in killing eelworm without damaging the bulbs. Hot-water treatment of *Hippeastrum* to control eelworm root-rot is successful at temperatures between 40 and 50°C for 2 h. At 47°C and above, the first flower bud is lost, but subsequent flower bulbs are normal after treatment even up to 50°C.

2. Bulb diseases

Bulb crops appear to have at least their fair share of disease, especially those caused by fungi and bacteria. With increasingly sophisticated research methods, however, it is becoming apparent that viruses of bulbs are also very important—far more so than had been originally suspected.

Some control measures have been practised since the crops were first grown; roguing crops is well established and good growers have always taken a great deal of trouble with their stocks, inspected them regularly and have been ruthless in discarding any deviants, irrespective of the extent of the peculiarity or how few plants were affected. With increasing costs of labour and much more extensive mechanization, frequent and close inspection is becoming increasingly difficult, and stock health is in many cases less good than in previous decades. On the other hand, very much more information is available for the grower; life cycles of many of the pathogens are now known in detail and successful attempts have been made in some cases to attack any weak link in the life cycle. Further, wide ranges of chemicals for controlling disease incidence and spread are now available, techniques have been worked out for their effective application, and information obtained on suitable dosage rates and frequencies of application. These techniques are most useful for foliar diseases, and those which affect the bulbs. Apart from roguing and preventing virus spread by controlling aphids or other vectors, little can be done for virus diseases.

Because of early trade in bulbous ornamentals, and similarities of climate in the major bulb-growing areas of the world, most of the diseases are widespread whenever bulbs are grown, but there are some climatic effects such as the greater frequency of *Fusarium* rots in higher tempera-tures (i.e. nearer the equator, but also in temperate climates in seasons warmer than usual).

I. Fungal and bacterial diseases of bulbs

Most of the fungal diseases are specific to one species, or a group of species, and usually of one of two kinds—those affecting the above-ground parts, especially the leaves and flower, and those affecting the below-ground parts, the bulb, the base plate and the roots.

A. *Narcissus* diseases

Even within the small climatic differences found in the British Isles, there are differences in the kinds of diseases affecting *Narcissus*; leaf diseases are much more important in the warmer, moister, more maritime climate of south-west England than in the colder, drier eastern counties. Similar distribution patterns also occur elsewhere in the world.

(i) Leaf diseases of Narcissus

There are three common leaf diseases of *Narcissus*, which can reduce bulb yield through premature death. White mould, caused by *Ramularia vallisumbrosae* attacks leaves and peduncles, but not the flowers, producing greenish-white spots or streaks accompanied by white masses of fungal spores. Infections start from the black sclerotia which were produced in the leaves the previous year and which overwintered on the soil surface. The sclerotia are not very persistent so that in its first year a crop is usually not severely affected. Late-flowering cultivars are particularly affected. The rate of spread of the disease is determined by the weather; warm, damp conditions favour a rapid spread and complete death of foliage often weeks before normal. Good control can be obtained by spraying every 2–3 weeks with tank-mix zineb with petroleum oil emulsifier, starting when the foliage is about 7 cm tall.

Leaf scorch affects leaves, stems and flowers causing a burnt appearance especially to emerging leaves. Although widespread in western Europe and North America, leaf scorch is rarely of economic importance except in maritime districts with warm winters. The causal organism is *Stagonospora curtisii*. The primary infections occur in the leaf tips from fungus persisting on the neck of the bulb which infects the leaf tips as they emerge. Fruiting bodies develop on the leaf tips and on the secondary spotting which develops lower down on the leaves, and these extrude quantities of spores which are spread by rain splash. Spotting on the flower perianths is often inconspicuous but spots can develop after picking and during transit, making the flowers unsaleable on arrival at the market. The disease is more serious in the cool-stored, late-planted field crops which flower early.

Fire, a disease caused by *Sclerotinia polyblastis* occurs occasionally in south-west England, and in the Pacific north-west of U.S.A., causing leaf and flower spotting and premature leaf death The disease develops first on the flowers which show small, pale brown spots on the perianth and paracorolla near picking time. If conditions are sufficiently moist, the disease spreads rapidly, the flowers are killed and the leaves become infected. Under favourable conditions leaf death can be very rapid, and the fungus overwinters in dead leaves.

Control measures for these leaf diseases are based on a knowledge of the fungal life cycles. Removal of leaf debris can reduce the dangers from white mould and fire, and hot-water treatment reduces the fungal population carried on the bulbs in leaf scorch. Removal of flowers, whether for sale or not, prevents the spread of fire, and routine spraying with tank-mix zineb or Bordeaux mixture (which does however, damage leaves in some circumstances) is recommended at regular intervals during the growing season.

(ii) Bulb diseases of Narcissus

Basal rot is the most important bulb disease of *Narcissus*, which is caused by *Fusarium oxysporum* f. *narcissi*. Infected bulbs have a brown discoloration near the base plate which is soft. The rot spreads upwards into the scales which become brown, sometimes tinged with pink, and a whitish fungal mycelium appears between the scales or even on the surface of the bulb. Infection occurs through wounds caused during lifting or handling or when roots emerge or die. The disease spreads most rapidly above 18°C when conditions are moist, and in the last few weeks of growth spread may be rapid in susceptible cultivars. Careful lifting and handling help to prevent disease spread; bulbs of susceptible cultivars should be dried quickly and stored in a cool store below 18°C. Infected bulbs should be removed and a field which has produced a diseased crop should not be replanted with *Narcissus* for a number of years. It is also essential that a fungicide is used in any situation where bulbs are soaked (hot-water treatment, pre-soak bath, etc.) to prevent the spread of the disease, and formalin is widely used for this purpose.

White root rot (*Rosellinia necatrix*) is important on the Isles of Scilly but rarely on the mainland, and can affect also *Ixia*, *Iris* and tulip. Outer scales of affected bulbs are black and rotten, and white fungal strands are visible near the base plate. No adequate control measures are available, but diseased bulbs should be destroyed and infected fields avoided.

Smoulder is a fungal disease caused by *Sclerotinia* (*Botrytis*) *narcissicola* which attacks leaves mainly at ground level producing malformed yellowish shoots or a rot which is sometimes accompanied by a grey mould. Secondary infections occur on damaged leaves and sheaths and serious flower spotting may also occur. Lifted bulbs often have black sclerotia attached to the outer scales and infected bulbs sometimes rot in store, or fail to emerge in the spring. The disease is particularly damaging after a cold, wet spring when growth is delayed. Removal of infected bulbs is the only known control measure.

B. Tulip diseases

Fire occurs wherever tulips are grown, and can cause very severe damage or even a complete loss of crop in some circumstances. The causal organism is *Botrytis tulipae* and the disease has been known for about 140 years. Bulbs at planting often bear small shiny black sclerotia on or under the tunic, and the outer fleshy scales sometimes have small sunken lesions, but slightly-infected bulbs are easily overlooked and planted. Infected bulbs produce shoots which are stunted, brown and frequently only about 5 cm long, which are covered with sporulating mycelium. These shoots, called "primaries" or *stekers*, are not very conspicuous in the field. The conidia produced by these primaries are dispersed to neighbouring plants where they can produce non-aggressive lesions which remain as small dark spots. On flower parts these brown spots make the flowers of susceptible cultivars unsaleable. Aggressive lesions also occur on both flowers and leaves; these continue to enlarge to produce a mat of conidiophores and conidia. Prolonged periods of high humidity are essential for the formation of aggressive lesions; the major loss of crop in any one season is related to the number and extent of these aggressive lesions and the consequent loss of leaf area (Price, 1970). The disease is carried-over on the bulbs, and daughter bulbs are infected by contact with the infected mother-bulb or the flower stem, the position of the mother bulb infection determining whether the disease is transferred to shoot or daughter bulbs, or both. These observations suggest that control of the disease would be more effectively achieved by bulb-treatment such as systemic fungicides or fungitoxic fumigation rather than by leaf spraying with contact or residual fungicides, although the latter is important for preventing the spread of aggressive leaf lesions in the current season. A number of fungicides (such as dichlofluanid or a dithiocarbamate) can be used to control the spread of fire on leaves, but fortnightly sprays are usually necessary, starting from shoot emergence. Early removal of primaries must be practised. Some cultivars are affected by "split base" which is sometimes caused by the same organism. The cracks which develop in the base plate allow the entry of secondary organisms which rot the shoot. The daughter bulbs continue to grow but the bulb yield is poor and the flower yield non-existent in affected bulbs.

Grey bulb rot is a serious soil-borne tulip disease common, but rarely serious, in bulb-growing areas. The causal organism is the fungus *Sclerotium tuliparum*. Bulbs rot in the field and either fail to produce shoots or are very stunted and die before flowering. Characteristically, diseased patches with an occasional survivor are seen. Infected bulbs usually have a healthy base plate and roots, the rot affects the upper parts of the scales, which turn grey but remain firm. Sclerotia occur on the bulbs, or in the surrounding soil, and are white at first but become brown, then black and are up to 8 mm across. The control methods usually advocated are to burn infected bulbs and the surrounding soil, and to avoid planting other susceptible bulbs on the land for at least five years.

Fusarium rot of tulip bulbs is a current cause of great concern in Europe and North America, partly because the pathogen is favoured by changes in bulb growing such as mechanical handling which leads to bruising, partly because of the more widespread use of susceptible cultivars like the Darwin hybrid group and partly because a series of warmer springs in western Europe has favoured the rapid spread of the disease. The symptoms are a soft rot occurring in spots on the bulb; these are often pinkish in colour with light brown margins. Within a few days the bulbs are often completely rotten. In the early stages, infested bulbs smell sweetly like pear drops, but later on a sour smell is given off which gives the Dutch name *zuur*. One important feature of *Fusarium* infection is that ethylene produced by infected bulbs has a number of physiological effects on other healthy bulbs, such as gum formation, and effects on flower development (see Chapters 8 and 9). Little is known yet about effective control measures, but the use of systemic fungicides is increasing. The fungus can remain active in the Netherlands dune-sand soil for at least eight years, even in the absence of host plants.

Tulip bulbs are affected by a number of other diseases, such as storage rots caused by *Penicillium* spp., smoulder, caused by *Sclerotium perniciosum*, and black stem rot caused by *S. wakkeri*. Root rot is caused by *Pythium* spp., and *Pythium* (and possibly other fungi) also causes a bulb soft-rot of five-degree tulips. *Rhizoctonia* affects five-degree tulips and field-grown crops; leaves are retarded in growth, lose turgidity, turn pale yellow and sometimes die. Leaves often have a dead streak along the whole length of the blade. Lifted bulbs can be misshapen and show brown concentric rings in cross-section. Control measures involve soil sterilization to check the spread of the disease, and, because the disease can be transmitted from one crop to another, to avoid planting tulips after a susceptible crop, e.g. chrysanthemums.

s

C. Hyacinth diseases

Yellow disease of hyacinth caused by *Xanthomonas hyacinthi* has been known in the Netherlands for a century, and also has been reported from a large number of countries which import hyacinths. The bulbs rot either before or soon after planting and shoot emergence either fails to occur, or badly diseased, non-flowering shoots are produced. A transverse section of a slightly-infected bulb reveals small yellow spots arranged concentrically. These spots are longitudinal bands which eventually reach the base plate from whence they will infect healthy scales. Eventually other secondary organisms rot the bulb. The disease spreads very rapidly through wounds on leaves or peduncles from inoculum released by, and spread from, infected plants and carried by wind, rain splash or by human agency. High storage temperatures (30°C initially, but higher later) are used for suspected stocks; these encourage the development of the disease, so that the infected bulbs can be identified and discarded. Close scrutiny in the field can lead to infected plants being found early and the spread of the disease can then be prevented.

Bacterial soft rot, caused by *Bacterium carotovorum*, affects hyacinths at flowering time; growth is stopped, and leaf tips become yellow, shrivel and dry out. The scape rots near ground level, the inflorescence often falls over and the rot spreads to leaves and bulb scales leading from a rapid bulb collapse to a rotting, smelling mass. The removal and destruction of infected material and the sterilization of the soil are recommended. Hyacinths suffer from a root rot caused by *Pythium* spp, including *P. ultimum* and *P. violae*, which appears above ground as a loss of leaf turgor and tip death. Disinfection of soil using formalin or methamsodium is recommended for control.

Hyacinth foliage is attacked by *Botrytis hyacinthi* which causes a disease called fire. It can be serious in damp springs, and in these conditions it spreads rapidly and destroys foliage. Flowers are sometimes affected, but not the bulbs. The disease can be controlled by fungicidal sprays.

D. *Iris* diseases

Diseases of bulbous *Iris* have been well described and illustrated by Gould (1950).

Bulb rot of *Iris*, and especially retarded *Iris*, causes widespread losses in the Netherlands, the U.K. and elsewhere. It is caused by *Penicillium corymbiferum*, which colours the attacked parts blue-green because of the characteristic colour of the spore masses. The rot which follows is probably due to secondary infections, and the extent of damage depends on the original site of infection. If lateral, the rot does not spread beyond the outer fleshy scale and a short crooked shoot may be formed. It is now known that entry is through small wounds either caused by damage or due to root emergence. Good results have been obtained with fungicidal dips before planting, with measures which reduce bulb damage, with reduced humidity in stores, and when bulbs are despatched to the grower as soon as possible and planted on receipt.

Leaf spot (or fire) of *Iris* is caused by *Mycosphaerella macrospora*, a fungus which has also been named *Heterosporium gracile*, and *Didymellina macrospora*. It is world-wide and can be serious, especially in wet seasons, in regions of high humidity, and on crops which have been grown for more than one year on the same site. Small brown spots are the first symptoms, these appear early in the season but the disease is not usually noticeable until the flowers appear, when the leaf tissues collapse and die prematurely. The flowers are also affected and unsaleable. In the U.S.A. (where the perfect stage occurs) rotation of crops and the removal of dead foliage prevents reinfection from overwintered material, and regular spraying from leaf emergence helps to prevent spread. It is essential that a white-oil sticker be incorporated into sprays to ensure best results.

Ink disease is caused by *Bipolaris iridis* (syn. *Mystrosporium adustum*) which produces the characteristic black markings on the leaves which are responsible for the common name. It occurs all over the world where *Iris* spp. are grown and is of major importance on *I. reticulata*. On infected bulbs of this species, black crusty patches or streaks occur which may be small or may cover the whole bulb. After planting, the infected bulb can decay, leaving only the tunics containing black powder. In less severely infected plants, a shoot will emerge with black patches which may enlarge and kill the shoot before flowering time. The disease is particularly severe in second-year crops, and an underground transfer of the disease from mother bulb to daughter bulbs has been demonstrated. The control measures suggested include annual lifting, destroying diseased bulbs and crop rotation. Fungicidal spraying can also prevent spread within a crop.

Iris crops in the U.S.A. are also attacked by a blight caused by *Bacterium tardicrescens*. Watersoaked areas near the bases of the leaves and stems enlarge rapidly under moist conditions, turn brown and cause premature leaf death. The disease is serious only in wet seasons and when temperatures are high in midsummer. Bactericidal sprays help to prevent the spread of the disease in the crop.

Bulbous *Iris* are affected by crown rot due to *Sclerotium delphinii*. Infected plants are yellow, stunted and die prematurely from a rot of the bulb or of the shoot immediately above the bulb. The soil surface can become covered with sclerotia up to 6 mm in diameter, and these may also develop on the stem and on the bulb. Early lifting and the burning of infected bulbs is advocated. A *Fusarium* rot of *Iris* is also known, but the disease is not so severe as in *Narcissus* and tulip.

E. Lily diseases

Botrytis blight caused by the fungus *Botrytis elliptica* is called the lily disease in U.K. and has been known for almost a century. It is rarely serious in well-managed glasshouses but is a threat to field-grown plants (Dimock and Tammen, 1967). Small reddish-brown spots first appear on the leaves; these spots enlarge and can spread on to the stems, pedicels and flower buds, later killing the foliage. Moist cool weather, and coastal fogs, encourage the disease, but the drier glasshouse environment does not. Bulbs rarely become infected. Sanitation and a routine spray programme are advocated as control measures.

Two soil-inhabiting fungi attacking lilies are *Phytophthora parasitica* and *P. cactorum*, which cause a rot of stem and leaf tissue near the soil surface. Soil sterilization before planting is the usually-adopted control measure.

A root-rot complex involving *Rhizoctonia* and *Pythium* spp. has been described which cause symptoms ranging from a minor browning and the rotting of a few roots to the killing of the whole root system. A number of control measures are recommended to eliminate diseased material and prevent the disease being transferred to healthy plants. These are largely based on hygiene and sterilization and the use of fungicidal drenches after potting.

II. Virus diseases of bulbs

Viruses occur commonly in *Narcissus*, tulip and other bulbous ornamentals. Some cause serious disease, whilst others are much less important, although over a long period they can, if not checked, cause considerable economic loss. It is only in the past few years that virus diseases of bulbs have been sufficiently studied to obtain a broad picture of their occurrence, importance and mode of spread. The following account is largely based on two recent reviews; these are on *Narcissus* (Brunt, 1970) and on tulips (van Slogteren and Asjes, 1969).

A. *Narcissus* viruses

Until ten years ago a number of diseases affecting *Narcissus* had been recognized and variously described by their symptoms as "yellow stripe", "streak", "mottle" or "mosaic", but in most cases the causal organism had not been identified or characterized. The thirteen viruses known to infect *Narcissus* can be grouped conveniently by their mode of transmission (Table 10.1).

Some of these viruses, such as cucumber mosaic virus and the nematode-borne viruses, are well-known pathogens of other plants, but others are known only in *Narcissus*, e.g. narcissus yellow stripe (probably the most important *Narcissus* virus), narcissus white streak, narcissus latent, narcissus mosaic, jonquil mild mosaic and the Grand Soleil d'Or virus. Yellow stripe virus has, however, been isolated from *Nerine*.

The *Narcissus* species commonly grown show differential susceptibility to some of these viruses; thus narcissus white streak, narcissus mosaic and narcissus latent viruses have been found in only *N. pseudonarcissus*, the

Table 10.1

Viruses affecting *Narcissus* and their modes of transmission (Brunt, 1970).

Transmitted by		
Aphids	*Nematodes*	*Mechanically*
Narcissus yellow stripe	Arabis mosaic	Narcissus mosaic
Narcissus white streak	Strawberry latent ringspot	
Narcissus latent	Tomato black ring	
Grand Soleil d'Or virus	Raspberry ringspot	
Jonquil mild mosaic	Tobacco ringspot	
Cucumber mosaic	Tobacco rattle	

Grand Soleil d'Or virus only in *N. tazetta* and the jonquil mild mosaic only in *N. jonquilla*. Narcissus yellow stripe causes similar symptoms in both *N. pseudonarcissus* and *N. jonquilla* but does not occur in *N. tazetta*.

Aphids are responsible for the spread of six of the important *Narcissus* viruses. Of these, cucumber mosaic occurs in numerous other plants; the remainder are probably spread only from *Narcissus*. *Narcissus* crops are rarely colonized by wingless aphids but the plants are visited by substantial numbers of alatae, especially from mid-May until the end of the growing season in southern England. Aphids can acquire and transmit viruses within a few minutes; it is highly likely that these migratory aphids are responsible for the field spread of these six viruses.

In contrast to the aphid-borne viruses, those transmitted by nematodes occur in a wide range of cultivated and weed species and are well-known pathogens. *Narcissus* plants can easily be infected from these other host plants, and infected *Narcissus* plants can also act as reservoirs of infection for more susceptible crops. The nematodes responsible for the spread are probably species of *Trichodorus*, *Longidorus* and *Xiphinema*.

As bulb crops are almost invariably propagated vegetatively, this is an excellent method of spreading disease, and it is usual to find infected daughter bulbs when the mother bulb is infected, although this is not always, or necessarily, true. Care must be taken in the initial "bulking-up" period for new cultivars that infected material is not widely distributed. This is especially important because although some viruses can be eliminated from other plants by heat therapy no simple methods exist for eliminating viruses from infected plants, and the roguing and destruction of infected plants still forms the basis of any control programme. Control of insect vectors has proved difficult and sprays have sometimes led to faster spread of virus, probably because spraying temporarily induces greater activity in the vector. Control of eelworm populations in the field is not very feasible and is very costly.

B. Tulip viruses

Seven viruses are known to infect tulips; these are listed in Table 10.2.

The two transmitted by aphids are cucumber mosaic and the tulip-breaking virus. Cucumber mosaic induces "corky fleck" symptoms in the

Table 10.2

Viruses affecting tulip and their mode of transmission (after van Slogteren and Asjes, 1969).

	Transmitted by	
	Soil-borne	
Aphids	Fungus	Nematodes
Cucumber mosiac	Tobacco necrosis virus	Tobacco rattle virus
Tulip-breaking virus		Tobacco ringspot virus
		Arabis mosaic virus
		Tomato black ring virus

bulb scales, during storage and green or otherwise discoloured flowers with leaf flecking resembling fire. The virus is spread by winged aphids in the last weeks of the growing season, when aphid populations are highest, and affects late-flowering cultivars. Because of secondary infections by fungi and bulb mites many infected bulbs do not survive. The symptoms of "tulip breaking" have been well known since the sixteenth century when broken tulips were highly prized. Apart from some lily species, tulip-break virus is specific to tulips. The characteristic symptom is a white or yellow streaking of the perianth in pink, red and purple-flowered cultivars because of failure of anthocyanin formation in parts of the perianth which therefore remain the colour of the mesophyll. In other cases the anthocyanin colour is intensified and both types of symptom can occur together. The intensity of symptom development depends partly on the strain of virus infecting the plant; virulent and mild strains are recognized, but their relation to symptom expression is not clear. Leaf mottling may also be apparent in some cultivars infected with the virulent strain.

With the exception of tulip-breaking virus, all the other tulip viruses have a wide host range. Tobacco necrosis virus induces a disease known as Augusta after the cultivar in which it was found in the Netherlands in 1929, and causes brown necrotic streaks on leaves and stems, and sunken glassy spots which later turn brown on daughter bulbs. The virus is transmitted by zoospores of the fungus *Olpidium brassicae* which is commonly found on roots of weeds and crop plants, but not on tulip roots. Transmission to daughter bulbs occurs, but is unimportant commercially because the daughter bulbs are too small to be marketable.

Four tulip viruses are transmitted by nematodes but two of these (arabis mosaic virus and tomato black ring virus) are rare and relatively unimportant, and are symptomless in tulip. Tobacco rattle causes elongated chlorotic or transparent flecks along the veins of the leaves, dark streaks on flowers of cultivars with a red perianth and transparent streaks in flowers of white and yellow cultivars. The plants are also stunted. The virus is transmitted to the plant by nematodes of the genus *Trichodorus* which thrive in sandy soils. Another virus, tobacco ringspot, has been associated with veinal streak symptom, but symptom expression depends on environmental conditions and they do not always appear, especially in the field. The leaves show a vein banding, and if symptoms are severe, the main veins later become watery, brown and necrotic.

Control measures are similar to those advocated for *Narcissus*. The removal of plants showing symptoms is most important. Some control measures are, however, specific for different viruses. Infection by aphid-borne viruses mainly occurs late in the season and therefore affects late-flowering cultivars, whereas tobacco necrosis virus and tobacco rattle virus affect early-flowering ones, and the complex relation between virus, vector and tulip cultivar can be upset by choosing cultivars appropriate for the site and breaking the infection cycle.

C. *Iris* viruses

A "mosaic" disease of *Iris* has been known for over 40 years and occurs whenever bulbous irises are grown. There is some confusion in the literature because two *Iris* mosaic viruses frequently occur together. Iris mosaic virus (also called iris mild mosaic) is very prevalent, and, as the name suggests, causes a mild mosaic symptom on leaves and a slight flower break with darker blotches in blue- and white-flowered cultivars and irregularly-shaped streaks in yellow-flowered cultivars (Brunt, 1968).

Iris yellow mosaic (also called iris greys) causes severe yellow mosaic symptoms on leaves, an intense flower break, and serious stunting of shoots with an almost complete loss of crop in a few years if not controlled. Both viruses are aphid transmitted. The two viruses can be distinguished on the basis of particle length, iris mosaic virus particles are 750 nm whilst those of iris yellow mosaic are 850 nm long.

Iris mosaic virus is so very prevalent in *I. xiphium*, *I. danfordiae* and *I. reticulata* that it is unlikely that virus-free stocks can be established by selection and roguing.

Virus-free irises have been obtained by meristem-tip culture. Little information exists on other *Iris* viruses, but it is likely that there are others.

D. Lily viruses

Large-scale, commercial lily growing developed in Bermuda and flourished up to the turn of the century, but the industry there was wiped out by a virus disease called the "Bermuda lily disease".

Lily symptomless virus (a misnomer because it causes stunting) is now very widespread in lilies, and is responsible, when it occurs together with cucumber mosaic virus, for the necrotic fleck disease which is characterized by minute yellow or white flecking of fully-expanded leaves.

Lily mottle virus is identical with tulip-breaking virus, but several strains are recognized by American workers. Mottle symptoms occur early in the growing season when plants are small and temperatures low, but often disappear later. Lily rosette virus, causing the "yellow flat" disease, where the leaves curl downwards to form a basal rosette, is now rare.

As far as is known, all these viruses are spread by aphids, and the only control measure that can be advocated is a ruthless roguing combined with a system of selecting healthy, superior true-to-type bulbs and growing these apart from the main crop as a foundation stock (McWhorter and Allen, 1967). Many of the mid-century hybrids grown for cut flowers are at least partly resistant to virus disease because of their *L. tigrinum* ancestry.

Chapter 11

The future

". . . schedules for cultural treatment cannot at present be regarded as final and they may have to be modified to some extent in the interest, for instance of improved flower quality, of additional hardiness or disease resistance, or of solving the practical problems involved in large scale production."   O. N. Purvis, 1938

Chapter 1 included an account of the origins of bulbous plants, the way they had become impórtant as crop plants and how the various forms now widely grown had been developed. It would seem wrong not to attempt to look to the future to visualize the changes in the ornamental bulb plant which will be brought about by man's activity, and to attempt to describe the kind of plant which would, in the light of present experience, be desirable.

Much more attention will be paid in future to plant features other than appearance, although, obviously, colour, form and texture will remain important because of their visual impact. In bulbous ornamentals, unlike food plants, selection for yield has hardly been practised, although the observed range of flower and bulb yields between cultivars suggests that much natural variation awaits exploitation.

Considering bulb yield first, selection must be done in relation to planting density, and the successful crop ideotype must be a weak competitor which makes the minimum demand on external reserves per unit of harvested dry matter, a concept elaborated by Donald (1968) for wheat, but which is applicable, with modification, to many other crop plants. It is likely that planting systems will be evolved which will make more efficient use of land than the present-day ridges, yet will be fully mechanized to preserve efficient planting and lifting. Further, as the results of the spacing experiments indicate, densities higher than those commonly used now will be adopted.

Against this background the form of the plant of the future must be examined. For efficient light interception, the leaf arrangement must be

269

efficient, this is qualitatively so in tulips where the smallest, most erect leaves are in the upper part of the canopy with the largest leaves presented horizontally near soil level. Stem height determines canopy depth, but the stem is itself green and the dry matter in the stem is probably unimportant because it is self-maintaining. For *Narcissus*, more erect foliage which maintains this presentation throughout the growing season is important. Under high densities a mass of collapsed linear leaves is not the most efficient for light interception, and this is currently what occurs in the field. The importance of the upper membranous parts of scales in supporting the leaves has been overlooked as a factor influencing leaf presentation. For the other bulbous ornamentals the same criteria apply, with the additional factor of leaf number which must be related to the numbers of daughter bulbs which are present in the axils of the scales and leaves of the mother plant.

A large number of daughter bulbs gives a large potential number of growing points, so that sinks do not restrict productivity in good growing seasons. On the other hand, there is little value in large numbers of growing points per unit area of land if all these grow and result in a crop composed largely of small, worthless daughter bulbs. The number of active growing points can be affected both by changing planting density and by using plants where the number of growing points is low or high, and a sensible balance must be achieved between dry-matter production and sites for the acceptance of dry matter. It appears that some tulip cultivars have apical dominance developed such that there is some flexibility in the numbers of daughter bulbs which grow, and the result is that large numbers of small daughter bulbs never occur. Insufficient is known about this mechanism, but it has obvious advantages to the grower. There are also indications that such apical dominance mechanisms can be affected by storage treatments before planting to provide the required numbers of daughter bulbs of the correct grades, but further work is required to define these treatments more accurately.

One of the most important factors controlling yield in bulbous ornamentals is the time of senescence, which slows growth at a time of year which is extremely favourable for rapid growth in many of the bulb-growing areas of the world, and for many bulb crops. For these areas, the use of plants with poorly-developed summer dormancy would be of advantage in allowing a longer growing season and higher productivity. More information will first be required on senescence and summer dormancy in bulbous ornamentals before attempting to change the controlling mechanisms.

There are known to be considerable differences between cultivars in the numbers of flowers produced per large unit of bulbs, e.g. flowers ton^{-1}.

This must be related to the minimum bulb size (or weight) for flower initiation, but insufficient is known at present of the factors determining whether a bulb will flower or not, or why the critical size for flowering differs between closely-related cultivars. This is, however, an obvious means of increasing flower production without incurring extra costs. A further possible means of increasing flower production is to induce flowering by some as yet unknown treatment in bulbs which are too small to flower normally. The large amount of work in progress in this field leads to the hope that such a treatment could be discovered.

A feature of ornamental bulb flowers which has long been recognized is the long period of low temperature required for rapid extension growth in the spring or in the glasshouse. In recent years it has also become apparent that different cultivars have different low-temperature requirements although few cultivars have been examined in sufficient detail to indicate the likely range of variation. For very early forcing, it is clearly economic to use a cultivar with a short low-temperature requirement so that the bulbs can be transferred to the glasshouse at an early date. Only when the low-temperature requirements of individual cultivars are better understood will it be possible to have accurate "blueprints" for forcing and to eliminate the troubles that are still experienced by some growers relying on empirical methods. For lilies and *Iris* the considerations are somewhat different; early forcing of lilies is not so important as *Narcissus* and tulip, but the numerous recent attempts to develop programmes for forcing to meet the movable Easter market indicates a similar trend to accurate control of flowering.

Some species with very limited cold requirements are already grown in the field in areas where winters are sufficiently mild to allow flowering in late autumn and early winter (e.g. Brittany and the extreme south-west of England), but little use is made of these cultivars in glasshouse forcing, despite their obvious advantages.

It is important, however, that some low-temperature requirement be retained for *Narcissus* and tulip cultivars grown in the normal bulb-producing areas or the plants will grow in the autumn and flower outdoors as winter approaches, instead of in spring as required. The combination of a longer growing season for the sake of bulb yield and a shorter low-temperature requirement for flowering is probably the ideal to be aimed at, although there will doubtless be specialized growers who would wish to settle for some other combination.

If present trends continue, the temperature-treatment of bulbs will become even more sophisticated than at present, and with treatment more closely related to the bulb cultivar grown. It is likely that warm storage of bulbs after lifting will be better defined in terms of morphological development and in relation to soil temperatures experienced by the bulb before lifting. Low-temperature treatment will probably involve lower temperatures than are currently used and will be similar to those now used in Japan, particularly for early forcing. This, allied to lower low-temperature requirements will probably result in tulips being commonly grown for the Christmas market.

Increased specialization will result in fewer cultivars being important commercially; this has already occurred in Easter lilies in the U.S.A., to some extent with *Narcissus* in the U.K. and the Netherlands, and in *Iris* whose culture all over the world is largely a single cultivar. The state of tulip cultivar numbers is somewhat unsettled, partly because of the current boom in Darwin hybrids but this will probably be rationalized within a few years to a smaller number of standard cultivars, whose behaviour will be sufficiently predictable to allow very carefully programmed growing. It would be a pity, however, if this led to the loss of valuable genetic material in the hundreds of other cultivars which would become unavailable as growers concentrated on a few key cultivars, and some effort must be made to retain gene banks of cultivars for the future.

References

ABRAMOVA, S. N. (1968). [Biology of seed germination in some tulip species in Turkmenia.] *Bjull. glav. bot. Sada* **69**, 52–4.

ADELMAN, H., TAYAMA, H. K. and KIPLINGER, D. C. (1970). An exploratory study of the effects of phosfon on 'Ace' and 'Nellie White' Easter lilies. *Bull. Ohio Florists' Ass.* **484**, 8-9.

ALGERA, L. (1936). Concerning the influence of temperature-treatment on the carbohydrate metabolism, the respiration and the morphological development of the tulip I–III. *Proc. Sect. Sci. K. ned. Akad. Wet.* **39**, 846–75.

ALGERA, L. (1947). Over den invloed van de temperatuur op de koolhydraat-stofwisseling en ademhaling bij de tulp en de hyacinth en de beteekenis daarvan voor de ontwikkeling der plant. *Meded. LandbHoogesch. Wageningen* **48**, 87–183.

ALGERA, L. (1968). Topple disease of tulips. *Phytopath. Z.* **62**, 251–61.

ANON. (1935). Vernalization. *Bull. Dep. Agric. Bermuda* **14**, 21–3.

ANON. (1967). Teelt van bloembollen. *Tuinbouwgids 1967*, 293–7.

ANON. (1969). Lily. *Rep. Lee Vall. exp. Hort. Stn 1967–8*, 369–76.

ANON. (1970a). Narcissus in South West England. *Stn Leafl. Rosewarne exp. Hort. Stn* **4**, 1–44.

ANON. (1970b). Survey of nutrient levels in tulip leaf, bulb and soil in Lincs. (Holland). *Exps east. Reg. N.A.A.S. 1969*, 219.

AOBA, T. (1967). [Studies on bulb formation of bulbous-iris plant. (1) On the process of bulb formation and structural state of bulb.] *Bull. Yamagata Univ. (Ag. Sci.)* **5**, 111–20.

ARBER, A. (1925). "Monocotyledons, a Morphological Study". Cambridge University Press, Cambridge.

ASHBY, E. (1932). Studies in the inheritance of physiological characters. II. Further experiments upon the basis of hybrid vigour and upon the inheritance of efficiency index and respiration rate in maize. *Ann. Bot. O.S.* **46**, 1007–1032.

AUNG, L. H. and DE HERTOGH, A. A. (1967). The occurrence of gibberellin-like substances in tulip bulbs (*Tulipa* sp.) *Pl. Cell Physiol. Tokyo* **8**, 201–5.

AUNG, L. H. and DE HERTOGH, A. A. (1968). Gibberellin-like substances in non-cold and cold treated tulip bulbs (*Tulipa* sp.) *In* "Biochemistry and Physiology of Plant Growth Substances". (F. Wightman and G. Setterfield, eds.), pp. 943–56. Runge Press, Ottawa.

AUNG, L. H., DE HERTOGH, A. A. and STABY, G. L. (1969a). Gibberellin-like substances in bulb species. *Can. J. Bot.* **47**, 1817–19.

AUNG, L. H., DE HERTOGH, A. A. and STABY, G. L. (1969b). Temperature regulation of endogenous gibberellin activity and development of *Tulipa gesneriana* L. *Pl. Phys.* **44**, 403–6.

AUNG, L. H., DE HERTOGH, A. A. and STABY G. L. (1971a). Possible identification of gibberellins in *Tulipa gesneriana* by gas–liquid chromatography. *Phytochemistry* **10**, 215–17.

AUNG, L. H., DE HERTOGH, A. A. and STABY, G. L. (1971b). The alteration of bulb hormones by environmental stimuli. *In Proc. I Int. Symp. on Flowerbulbs*, Noordwijk/Lisse 1970. Wageningen, Centre for Agricultural Publishing & Documentation, pp. 156–61.

BAHADUR, R. and BLANEY, L. T. (1968). Influence of vernalization and long days on flowering of 'Ace' Easter Lily (*Lilium longiflorum*, Thunb.) *HortScience* **3**, 96.

BAKKER, M. (1970). Plantdichtheid van tulpen in een matig groeizaam seizoen. *Weekbl. BloembCult.* **81**, 87–8.

BARBER, J. T. and STEWARD, F. C. (1968). The proteins of *Tulipa* and their relation to morphogenesis. *Devl Biol.* **17**, 326–49.

BARTON-WRIGHT, E. C. and PRATT, M. C. (1931). The first sugar of carbon assimilation and the nature of carbohydrates in the narcissus leaf. *Biochem. J.* **24**, 1217–34.

BEIJER, J. J. (1936). De invloed van de schuurbehandeling op de bloemkwaliteit van de hyacinth. Extracts from *Weekbl. BloembCult.*, *Lab. BloembOnderz. Lisse Publ.* **53**, 1–32.

BEIJER, J. J. (1938). Preparatie van narcissen voor het zuidelijk halfrond. Extracts from *Weekbl. BloembCult.*, *Lab. BloembOnderz. Lisse Publ.* **61**, 1–6.

BEIJER, J. J. (1942). De terminologie van de bloemaanleg der bloembolgewassen. *Meded LandbHoogesch. Wageningen* **46**, (5), 1–17.

BEIJER, J. J. (1947). Het "spouwen" der hyacinten *Meded. LandbHoogesch. Wageningen* **48** (5), 185–225.

BEIJER, J. J. (1952). Experiments on the retardation of Dutch irises. *Acta bot. neerl.* **1**, 268–86.

BEIJER, J. J. (1955). The influence of normal and artificially created climatic conditions on the flowering of daffodils. *Rep. XIV Int. hort. Cong. 1955*, 188–95.

BEIJER, J. J. (1963). Het mechanisch spouwen van hyacinten. *Versl. Werkzaamh. Lab. BloembOnderz. Lisse 1963*, 27–8.

BENSCHOP, M. and DE HERTOGH, A. A. (1971). Post-Harvest development of cut tulip flowers. *In Proc. I Int. Symp. on Flowerbulbs*, Noordwijk/Lisse 1970. Wageningen, Centre for Agricultural Publishing & Documentation, pp. 121–6.

BERGMAN, B. H. H. and BEIJERSBERGEN, J. C. M. (1971). A possible explanation of variations in susceptibility of tulip bulbs to infection by *Fusarium oxysporum*. *In Proc. I Int. Symp. on Flowerbulbs*, Noordwijk/Lisse 1970. Wageningen, Centre for Agricultural Publishing & Documentation, pp. 225–9.

BERGMAN, B. H. H., BEIJERSBERGEN, J. C. M., KAMERBEEK, G. A. and SCHIPPER, J. A. (1968). Het gommen van tulpen. *Jversl. Lab. BloembOnderz. Lisse 1967–8*, 31–2.

BLAAUW, A. H. (1920). Over de periodiciteit van *Hyacinthus orientalis*. *Meded. LandbHoogesch. Wageningen* **18**, 1–82.

BLAAUW, A. H. (1924). The result of the temperature during flower formation of the whole hyacinth (2nd part). *Proc. Sect. Sci. K. ned. Akad. Wet.* **27** (9–10), 781–99.

BLAAUW, A. H. (1926). Rapid flowering of Darwin tulips I. *Proc. Sect. Sci. K. ned. Akad. Wet.* **29**, 1343–55.

BLAAUW, A. H. (1931). Orgaanvorming en periodiciteit van *Hippeastrum hybridum* Tweede gedeelte De periodiciteit van *Hippeastrum. Verh. K. Akad. Wet.* (*Sectie 2*) **29** (1), 1–90.

BLAAUW, A. H. (1934). De grenzen der bloeibaarheid bij bol-irissen 1. *Proc. Sect. Sci. K. ned. Akad. Wet.* **37**, 633–43.

BLAAUW, A. H. (1935). De periodieke ontwikkeling van een bol-iris (*Iris xiphium praecox* "Imperator". *Verh. K. Akad. Wet.* (*Sectie 2*) **34** (3), 1–90.

BLAAUW A. H. (1941). On the relation between flower formation and temperature. I–II. Bulbous irises. *Proc. Sect. Sci. K. ned. Akad. Wet.* **44**, 513–20, 684–9.

BLAAUW, A. H. and VERSLUYS, M. C. (1925). The result of the temperature treatment in summer for the Darwin-tulip (first part). *Proc. Sect. Sci. K. ned. Akad. Wet.* **28**, 717–31.

BLACKMAN, G. E. (1962). The limit of plant productivity. *Rep. E. Malling Res. Stn for 1961*, 39–50.

BLACKMAN, V. H. (1919). The compound interest law and plant growth. *Ann. Bot. O.S.* **33**, 353–60.

BLANEY, L. T. and ROBERTS, A. N. (1966a). Growth and development of the Easter lily bulb, *Lilium longiflorum* Thunb. 'Croft.' *Proc. Am. Soc. hort. Sci.* **89**, 643–50.

BLANEY, L. T. and ROBERTS, A. N. (1966b). The vernalizing effect of warm soil in late winter and spring on the Easter lily, *Lilium longiflorum. Proc. XVII Int. hort. Cong. 1966*, 229.

BLANEY, L. T. and ROBERTS, A. N. (1966c). Influence of harvest date and pre-cooling on leaf and stem elongation in the 'Croft' Easter lily (*Lilium longiflorum* Thunb.). *Proc. Am. Soc. hort. Sci.* **89**, 651–6.

BLEASDALE, J. K. A. and NELDER, J. A. (1960). Plant population and crop yield. *Nature, Lond.* **188**, 342.

BOOTH, V. H. (1957). β-Carotene in the flowers of *Narcissus. Biochem. J.* **65**, 660–3.

BOULD, C. (1939). Studies on the nutrition of tulips and narcissi. *J. Pomol.* **17**, 254–74.

BOX, C. O. (1963). Natural cooling of Georgia Easter lilies. *Bull. Miss. agric. Exp. Stn* **675**, 1–15.

BRAGT, J. VAN (1971). Effects of temperature, light, sugars and gibberellin A3 on growth in vitro of terminal buds of tulip. *In Proc. I Int. Symp. on Flowerbulbs*. Noordwijk/Lisse 1970. Wageningen, Centre for Agricultural Publishing & Documentation, pp. 429–34.

BRAGT, J. VAN and HOFF, T. VAN'T (1969). Effecten van CCC bij tulpen. *Meded. Dir. Tuinb.* **32**, 404–6.

BRAGT, J. VAN and ZIJLSTRA, F. A. (1971). Effects of gibberellins on flowering of tulip cv. 'Apeldoorn'. *Z. PflPhysiol.* **64**, 139–44.

BRIERLEY, P. (1941). Effect of cold storage of Easter lily bulbs on subsequent forcing performance. *J. agric. Res.* **62**, 317–35.

BRUNT, A. A. (1968). Some hosts and properties of bulbous iris mosaic virus. *Ann. appl. Biol.* **61**, 187–94.

BRUNT, A. A. (1970). Virus diseases of narcissus. *Daffodil Tulip Yb. 1971* **36**, 18–37.

BURNS, W. (1946). Corm and bulb formation with special reference to the Gramineae. *Trans. Proc. bot. Soc. Edinb.* **34**, 316–47.

BURTON, W. G. (1950). Studies on the dormancy and sprouting of potatoes. 1. The oxygen content of the potato tuber. *New Phytol.* **49**, 121–34.

CALDWELL, J. and WALLACE, T. J. (1955). *Narcissus pseudonarcissus* L. *J. Ecol.* **43**, 331–41.

CARLSON, W. H. and DE HERTOGH, A. A. (1967). A preliminary evaluation of various cooling techniques for forcing of 'Ace' lily bulbs. *Mich. Flor.* **441**, 21, 27.

CARR, J. and PATE, J. S. (1967). Ageing in the whole plant. *Symp. Soc. exp. Biol.* (*1967*) **21**, 559–99.

CHAN, T. T. (1952). The development of the narcissus plant. *Daffodil Tulip Yb.* **17**, 3–31.

CHEAL, W. F. and HEWITT, E. J. (1963). Effects of mineral nutrition on the production of tulip bulbs. *Ann. appl. Biol.* **52**, 493–502.

CHEAL, W. F. and WINSOR, G. W. (1966). The effects of nitrogen, phosphorus, potassium and magnesium on the growth of tulips during the second season of treatment and on the chemical composition of the bulbs. *Ann. appl. Biol.* **57**, 287–99.

CHEAL, W. F. and WINSOR, G. W. (1968). The response of tulips (variety Elmus) to nitrogen and potassium. Part I: Sand culture. *Expl Hort.* **18**, 88–100.

CHEN, S. (1966). Localization of starch in the base of narcissus leaves. *Ann. Bot.* **30**, 721–5.

CHEN, S. (1969a). Carbohydrate metabolism in the narcissus leaf. *J. exp. Bot.* **20**, 302–16.

CHEN, S. (1969b). The contractile roots of *Narcissus*. *Ann. Bot.* **33**, 421–6.

CHOUARD, P. (1926). Germination et formation des jeunes bulbes de quelques Liliiflores (*Endymion, Scilla, Narcissus*). *Annls Sci. nat. (Bot.) sér. 10* **8**, 299–353.

CHOUARD, P. (1931). Types de développement de l'appareil végétatif chez les Scillées. *Annls Sci. nat. (Bot.) sér. 10* **13**, 131–323.

CHOUARD, P. (1960). Vernalization and its relations to dormancy. *A. Rev. Pl. Physiol* **11**, 191–238.

CHURCH, A. H. (1908). "Types of floral Mechanism". Part I. Oxford University Press, Oxford.

CORNER, E. J. H. (1963). The tropical botanist. *Advmt Sci., Lond.* **20**, 328–34.

CULBERT, J. (1967). Preparation for the market. *In* "Easter Lilies" (D. C. Kiplinger and R. W. Langhans, eds.), pp. 137–140. New York and Ohio Lily Schools.

DE HERTOGH, A. A., and EINERT, A. E. (1969). The controlled temperature forcing (CTF) method for potted Easter lilies, its concept, results and commercial adaptation. *Florists' Rev.* **145**, 25–7, 70–3.

DE HERTOGH, A. A., CARLSON, W. H. and KAYS, S. (1969). Controlled temperature forcing of planted lily bulbs. *J. Am. Soc. hort. Sci.* **94**, 433–6.

DE HERTOGH, A. A., AUNG, L., CARLSON, W. and SLOOTWEG, A. F. G. (1967). "Bulb Forcers Handbook". Netherlands Flower-bulb Institute, New York.

DENNE, P. (1959). Leaf development in *Narcissus pseudonarcissus* L. I. The stem apex. *Ann. Bot.* **23**, 121–9.

DENNE, P. (1960). Leaf development in *Narcissus pseudonarcissus* L. II. The comparative development of scale and foliage leaves. *Ann. Bot.* **24**, 32–47.

DICKEY, R. D. (1954). Growing tulips in north Florida. *Proc. Fla St. hort. Soc.* **66**, 331–3.

DICKEY, R. D. (1957). Effects of storage treatment on growth and flowering of tulips in Florida. *Proc. Am. Soc. hort. Sci.* **70**, 461–77.

DIE, J. VAN, LEEUWANGH, P. and HOEKSTRA, S. M. R. (1970). Translocation of assimilates in *Fritillaria imperialis* L. I. The secretion of ^{14}C-labelled sugars by the nectaries in relation to phyllotaxis. *Acta bot. neerl.* **19**, 16–23.

DIMOCK, A. W. and TAMMEN, J. (1967). Diseases. In "Easter Lilies" (D. C. Kiplinger and R. W. Langhans, eds.), pp. 107–110. New York and Ohio Lily Schools.

DOLK, H. E. and SLOGTEREN, E. VAN (1930). Über die Atmung und die Absterbeerscheinungen bei Hyazinthen-Zwiebeln bei höheren Temperaturen im Zusammenhang mit der Bekämpfung der Gelbkrankheit. *Gartenbauwissenschaft* **4**, 113–58.

DONALD, C. M. (1968). The breeding of crop ideotypes. *Euphytica* **17**, 385–403.

DOORENBOS, J. (1954). Notes on the history of bulb breeding in the Netherlands. *Euphytica* **3**, 1–11.

DURIEUX, A. J. B. and PAGTER, J. A. W. DE (1967). Bloei van Hollandse iris gedurende het hele jaar. *Praktijkmededeling Lab. BloembOnderz. Lisse* **23**, 1–10.

DURKIN, D. and HILL, D. (1966). Effect of 70°F storage on response of vernalized 'Ace' lily bulbs. *Proc. XVII Int. hort. Cong.* 228–31.

EASTWOOD, T. (1952). Forcing Creole lilies at different levels of soil nitrate. *Proc. Am. Soc. hort. Sci.* **59**, 531–41.

EIJK, J. P. VAN and TOXOPEUS, S. J. (1968). The possibilities of early selection for forcing ability and productivity in tulips. *Euphytica* **17**, 277–83.

EINERT, A. E. and BOX, C. O. (1967). Effects of light intensity on flower bud abortion and plant growth of *Lilium longiflorum*. *Proc. Am. Soc. hort. Sci.* **90**, 427–32.

EINERT, A. E., BOX, C. O. and LANE, H. C. (1969). Quality of supplemental lighting and bulb planting depth on development of naturally cooled *Lilium longiflorum* Thunb. 'Harson'. *J. Am. Soc. hort. Sci.* **94**, 413–16.

EINERT, A. E., DE HERTOGH, A. A., RASMUSSEN, H. P. and SHULL, V. (1970). Scanning electron microscope studies of apices of *Lilium longiflorum* for determining floral initiation and differentiation. *J. Am. Soc. hort. Sci.* **95**, 5–8.

T

EMSWELLER, S. L. and PRYOR, R. L. (1943). Floral development in 'Creole' Easter lilies stored at various temperatures. *Proc. Am. Soc. hort. Sci.* **42**, 598–604.

FERNANDES, A. (1967). Contribution à la connaissance de la biosytématique de quelques espèces du genre *Narcissus* L. *Port. Acta biol.* (B) **9**, 1–44.

FORTANIER, E. J. (1971). Shortening the period from seed to a flowering bulb in tulip. *In Proc. I Int. Symp. on Flowerbulbs*, Noordwijk/Lisse 1970. Wageningen, Centre for Agricultural Publishing & Documentation, pp. 413–420.

FORWARD, D. F. (1960). Effect of temperature on respiration. *In* "Encyclopedia of Plant Physiology" (W. Ruhland, ed.), 12/2, 234–58. Springer-Verlag, Berlin.

FRITSCH, F. G. and SALISBURY, E. J. (1944). "Plant Form and Function". G. Bell and Sons Ltd., London.

FRY, B. M. (1967). The vase life of daffodils. *Gdnrs' Chron.* **161** (8), 11.

GALIL, J. (1961). [*Kinetics of geophytes*.] Hakibbutz Hameuchad Ltd., Tel-Aviv.

GALIL, J. (1965). Vegetative dispersal of *Allium ampeloprasum* L. I. Vegetative reproduction. *Israel J. Bot.* **14**, 135–40.

GALIL, J. (1967). On the dispersal of the bulbs of *Oxalis cernua* Thunb. by mole-rats (*Spalax ehrenbergi* Nehring). *J. Ecol.* **55**, 787–92.

GAY, M. J. (1858). Recherches sur la famille des Amaryllidaceae. *Annls Sci. nat.* (*Bot.*) *Sér. 4e* **10**, 75–109.

GERRITSEN, J. P. and KLOOT, W. G. VAN DER (1936). Verschillen in het bloemvormende vermogen van narcis en hyacinth. *Proc. Sect. Sci. K. ned. Akad. Wet.* **39**, (3), 404–13.

GIBSON, G. W. (1935). Some observations on the manuring of bulbs. *Scient. Hort.* **3**, 174–83.

GILL, D. L., BEIJER, J. J., STUART, N. W. and GOULD, C. J. (1957). Some effects of bulb storage temperatures and planting conditions on production of tulip flowers in the greenhouse and outside in southern Georgia. *Proc. Am. Soc. hort. Sci.* **70**, 451–60.

GODDEN, B. F. and WATSON, D. P. (1962). An anatomical study of the origin and development of the bulblets on the scale leaves of lily bulbs. *Q. Bull. Mich. State Univ.* **45**, 45–54.

GOEBEL, K. (1905). "Organography of Plants". Part II (English edition). Clarendon Press, Oxford.

GOOD, R. (1966). The botanical aspects of continental drift. *Sci. Prog. Oxf.* **54**, 315–24.

GOULD, C. J. (1950). Diseases of bulbous iris. *Bull. Wash. St. Coll. Ext. Serv.* 424.

GOULD, C. J. (1967). World production of bulbs. *Florists' Rev.* **140**, 14–16, 70–1.

GRAINGER, J. (1941). Food manufacture and flowering in the daffodil. *Herbertia* **8**, 134–45.

GRIFFITHS, D. (1936). Speeding up flowering in the daffodil and bulbous iris. *Circ. U.S. Dep. Agric.* **367**, 1–18.

HAGIYA, K. and AMAKI, W. (1959). [Studies on the dropper of tulip bulbs III

The influence of cultural conditions on the formation of droppers.] *J. hort. Ass. Japan* **28**, 130–8.

HAGIYA, K. and AMAKI, W. (1966). [Nutritional studies on tulips III Seasonal changes in the absorption of three major elements and water.] *J. Jap. Soc. hort. Sci.* **35**, 170–6.

HALEVY, A. H. (1962). Anthocyanins in petals of tulip var. President Eisenhower. *Biochem. J.* **83**, 637–9.

HALEVY, A. H. (1963). Metabolic changes in Wedgewood iris as influenced by storage temperature of bulbs. *Proc. XVI Int. hort. Cong. 1962*, 220–8.

HALEVY, A. H., MOR, J. and VALERSHTEIN, J. (1971). Endogenous gibberellin level in *Ornithogalum arabicum* and its relationship to storage temperatures of bulbs and to flower development. *In Proc. I Int. Symp. on Flowerbulbs*, Noordwijk/Lisse 1970. Wageningen, Centre for Agricultural Publishing & Documentation, pp. 82–7.

HALEVY, A. H. and SHOUB, J. (1964a). Changes in metabolic activity and composition of Wedgewood iris bulbs during maturation of bulbs. *Proc. Am. Soc. hort. Sci.* **85**, 605–10.

HALEVY, A. H. and SHOUB, J. (1964b). The effect of cold storage and treatment with gibberellic acid on flowering and bulb yields of Dutch iris. *J. hort. Sci.* **39**, 120–9.

HALEVY, A. H., SHOUB, J., RAKATI, D., PLESNER, O. and MONSELISE, S. P. (1963). Effects of storage temperature on development, respiration, carbohydrates content, catalase and peroxidase activity of Wedgewood iris plants. *Proc. Am. Soc. hort. Sci.* **83**, 786–97.

HALL, A. D. (1937). Polyploidy in *Tulipa*. *J. Linn. Soc. (Bot.)* **50**, N. 335–49.

HALL, A. D. (1940). "The genus Tulipa". The Royal Horticultural Society, London.

HARTSEMA, A. M. (1953). Storage of bulbs. *Bull. int. Inst. Refrig.* **7**, 1–7.

HARTSEMA, A. M. (1961). Influence of temperatures on flower formation and flowering of bulbous and tuberous plants. *In* "Encyclopedia of Plant Physiology". (W. Ruhland ed.), **16**, 123–61, Springer-Verlag, Berlin.

HARTSEMA, A. M. and BLAAUW, A. H. (1935). Verschuiving der periodiciteit door hooge temperaturen. Aanpassing en export voor het zuidelijk halfond II. *Proc. Sect. Sci. K. ned. Akad. Wet.* **38**, (7), 722–34.

HARTSEMA, A. M. and LUYTEN, I. (1938). Snelle bloei van de narcis (*Narcissus pseudonarcissus* 'King Alfred'). *Proc. Sect. Sci. K. ned. Akad. Wet.* **41** (6), 65.

HARTSEMA, A. M. and LUYTEN, I. (1940). Snelle bloei van iris Wedgwood. *Proc. Sect. Sci. K. ned. Akad. Wet.* **43** (7), 878–9.

HARTSEMA, A. M. and LUYTEN, I. (1950). Over het blindstoken van tulpen. *Meded. LandbHoogesch, Wageningen* **50**, 1–19.

HARTSEMA, A. M. and LUYTEN, I. (1955). Early flowering of Dutch Iris "Wedgwood". II. Influence of temperature and light. *Proc. K. ned. Akad. Wet. (Ser. C.)* **58**, 462–88.

HARTSEMA, A. M. and LUYTEN, I. (1961). Snelle bloei van iris Wedgwood. IIIA and IIIB. Invloed van temperatuur en licht. *Proc. K. ned. Akad. Wet. (Ser. C.)* **64** (5), 600–16, 617–29.

HARTSEMA, A. M. and LUYTEN, I. (1962). Snelle bloei van Hollandse irissen "Imperator" VIA and VIB. Lichtbehoefte na verschillende prepareerbehandelingen. *Proc. K. ned. Akad. Wet. (Ser. C.)* **65** (1), 1–21.

HARTSEMA, A. M., LUYTEN, I. and BLAAUW, A. H. (1936). De optimale temperatuur van bloemaanleg tot bloei (Snelle bloei van Darwin-tulpen II, var W. Copland). *Verh. K. Akad. Wet. (Sectie 2)*, **27** (1), 1–46.

HEATH, O. V. S. and HOLDSWORTH, M. (1948). Morphogenic factors as exemplified by the onion plant. *Symp. Soc. exp. Biol.* **2,** 326–50.

HEKSTRA, G. (1966). Houdbaarheid van tulpebloemen op water. *Practijkmededeling Lab. BloembOnderz. Lisse* **20.**

HEKSTRA, G. (1968). Selectieve teelt van tulpen gebaseerd op produktie-analyse. *Versl. landbouwk. Onderz.* 702.

HERKLOTZ, V. A. and WEHR, B. (1969). Uber die periodische Entwicklung von *Lilium candidum* L. *Gartenbauwissenschaft* **34,** 271–9.

HESLING, J. J. (1965). Narcissus eelworm—yesterday and today. *Daffodil Tulip Yb., 1966* **31,** 76–94.

HESLOP-HARRISON, J. (1970). Development, differentiation and yield. *In* "Physiological aspects of crop yield" (J. D. Eastins *et al.*, eds.), pp. 291–321. American Society of Agronomy and Crop Science Society of America, Madison, Wisconsin.

HIGUCHI, H. and SISA, M. (1967). [Serological analysis on the changes in scaly leaf tulip bulb caused by low-temperature treatment.] *J. Jap. Soc. hort. Sci.* **36,** 427–32.

HILL, L. L. and DURKIN, D. J. (1968). Vernalization of the growing Easter lily. *HortScience* **3,** 277.

HOLDSWORTH, M. (1961). The flowering of rain flowers. *Jl W. Afric. Sci. Ass.* **7,** 28–36.

HOLTTUM, R. E. (1955). Growth-habits of Monocotyledons—variations on a theme. *Phytomorphology* **5,** 399–413.

HOOGETERP, P. (1966). Richtlijnen voor het gebruik van bij 5°C gekoelde tulpen bij het forceren in de volle grond van warenhuizen en rolkassen. *Rapp. Lab. BloembOnderz. Lisse* **4.**

HOOGETERP, P. (1967). De vroege bloei (december) van tulpebollen die bij 5°C zijn gekoeld. *Praktijkmededeling Lab. BloembOnderz. Lisse* **21,** 1–13.

HOOGETERP, P. (1968). Nieuwe adviezen voor behandeling van vijf-graden-tulpen. *Weekbl. BloembCult.* **79,** 1217–20.

HOOGETERP, P. (1969a) De teelt van narcissen waarvan de bollen bij 5°C zijn gekoeld. *Weekbl. BloembCult.* **80,** 41–2.

HOOGETERP, P. (1969b). De invloed van een behandeling bij lage temperatuur op groei en bloei van tulpen en andere bolgewassen. *Jversl. Lab. Bloemb-Onderz. Lisse 1968/9,* 93–4.

HOOGETERP, P. (1970). Hoogeterp wil onrijp laten rooien. *Hobaho* **44** (12), 1–2.

HOSAKA, H. and YOKOI, M. (1959). [Studies on the scale propagation of lilies.] *Tech. Bull. Fac. Hort. Chiba Univ.* **7,** 45–54.

HOSAKA, H., YOKOI, M. and KOMATSUZAKI, M. (1962). [Storage studies with bulbs of *Lilium auratum* for export.] *Tech. Bull. Fac. Hort. Chiba Univ.* **10**, 89–102.

HUISMAN, E. and HARTSEMA, A. M. (1933). De periodieke ontwikkeling van *Narcissus pseudonarcissus* L. *Meded. LandbHoogesch. Wageningen* **37**, 3–54.

HUSSEY, N. W., READ, W. H. and HESLING, J. J. (1969). "The pests of protected cultivation". Edward Arnold Ltd., London.

ISAAC, W. E. and McGILLIVRAY, G. (1965). A note on the water-storing seeds of two species of *Crinum* and of some other South African Amaryllidaceae (sub-family Amaryllidoideae). *Ann. Bot.* **29**, 739–40.

JEFFERSON-BROWN, M. J. (1969). "Daffodils and Narcissi". Faber & Faber, London.

JONES, H. A. and MANN, L. K. (1963). "Onions and their Allies". Leonard Hill, London.

KALIN, E. W. (1954). Flower removal in the field and its effect on bulb production and forcing quality of *Narcissus pseudonarcissus* var. King Alfred. *Proc. Am. Soc. hort. Sci.* **63**, 473–87.

KALIN, E. W. (1956). Further studies on field cuttings and its influence on bulb production and forcing quality of King Alfred narcissus. *Proc. Am. Soc. hort. Sci.* **68**, 508–10.

KAMERBEEK, G. A. (1958). Het blauw groeien van tulpebollen. *Tijdschr. PlZiekt.* **64**, 463–9.

KAMERBEEK, G. A. (1962a). Respiration of the iris bulb in relation to the temperature and the growth of the primordia. *Acta bot. neerl.* **11**, 331–410.

KAMERBEEK, G. A. (1962b). The influence of light upon blueing of tulips bulbs, a disease of a physiological nature. *Tijdschr. PlZiekt.* **68**, 219–30.

KAMERBEEK, G. A. (1963). Vroege broei van iris 'Wedgwood'. *Versl. Werkzaamh. Lab. BloembOnderz., Lisse 1963* 17–19.

KAMERBEEK, G. A. (1965a). Temperature treatment of Dutch iris bulbs in relation to the development. *Rep. 1st. Int. Symp. Iris, Florence 1963,* 459–75.

KAMERBEEK, G. A. (1965b). Fysiologie en bloembollenteelt. *Meded. Dir. Tuinb.* **28**, 337–42.

KAMERBEEK, G. A. (1969a). Fysiologische afwijkingen bij bloembollen. *Meded. Dir. Tuinb.* **32**, 286–92.

KAMERBEEK, G. A. (1969b). A quantitative enhancement of the basic respiration in iris bulbs (cv. 'Wedgwood') by ethylene. *Abstracts XI Int. bot. Cong. Seattle:* 106.

KAMERBEEK, G. A. (1969c). Influence of light and temperature on flower-bud development in bulbous irises (*Iris* cv. 'Wedgwood') and lilies (*Lilium* cv. 'Enchantment'). *Acta Hort.* **14**, 175.

KAMERBEEK, G. A. and BEIJER, J. J. (1964). Vroege bloei van iris 'Wedgwood'. *Meded. Dir. Tuinb.* **27**, 598–604.

KAMERBEEK, G. A. and HOOGETERP, P. (1968). Bloeibeinvloeding bij bloembollen en de achtergronden daarvan. *Weekbl. BloembCult. Kerstnummer,* 552–3, 556.

KAMERBEEK, G. A. and MUNK, W. J. DE (1965). Kernrot in tulpen. *Jversl.
Lab. BloembOnderz. Lisse* 20–1.

KAYS, S., CARLSON, W., BLAKELY, N. and DE HERTOGH, A. A. (1971). Effect of
exogenous gibberellin on the development of *Lilium longiflorum* Thunb. 'Ace'.
J. Am. Soc. hort. Sci. **96**, 222–25.

KERLING, L. C. P. (1941). The gregarious flowering of *Zephyranthes rosea*
Lindl. *Ann. bot. Gdn. Buitenz.* **55**, 1–42.

KHO, Y. and BAËR, R. (1971). Incompatibility problems in species crosses of
tulips. *Euphytica* **20**, 30–5.

KIMURA, Y. (1967). Biochemical indicators of iris bulb maturity. *Circ. agric.
Exp. Stn Wash. St. Inst. agric. Sci.* **461**, 4.

KIPLINGER, D. C., TAYAMA, H. K. and MCDOWELL, T. C. (1969). Spacing,
storage and forcing temperature tests on Ace lilies 1967–1968 at Wooster.
Bull. Ohio Florists' Ass. **471**, 5–8.

KNIGHT, G. H. (1964). Some factors affecting the distribution of *Endymion
nonscriptus* (L.) Garcke in Warwickshire woods. *J. Ecol.* **52**, 405–21.

KOHL, H. C. (1967). Correlation between rate of leaf initiation and apex diameter of *Lilium longiflorum* cultivar 'Ace'. *HortScience* **2**, 15–16.

KOSUGI, K., YOKOI, M. and KATO, Y. (1968). Effects of cold storage treatment
on the growth and flowering of recently introduced tulips. *Tech. Bull. Fac.
Hort. Chiba Univ.* **16**, 17–21.

KOUKKARI, W. L. and HILLMAN, W. S. (1966). Phytochrome levels assayed by
in vivo spectrophotometry in modified underground stems and storage roots.
Physiologia Pl. **19**, 1073–8.

KRAAIJENGA, D. A. (1960). Groeimetingen bij de tulpebol. *Meded. Landb-
Hoogesch. Wageningen* **60** (8), 1–53.

KURKI, L. (1962). [Forcing of *Iris* × *hollandica* cv. Wedgwood during mid-
winter.] *Annls agric. Fenniae* **1**, 284–7.

KURKI, L. (1964). [Growth disturbances during the forcing of flower bulbs.]
Nord. JordbrForsk **8**, 311–13.

LAAN, G. J. VAN (1955). Correlation of enzyme activity with the early flowering
of cured, pre-cooled bulbs of *Iris tingitana* (Wedgwood) used for forcing.
Proc. Am. Soc. hort. Sci. **60**, 392–6.

LANG, A. (1952). Physiology of flowering. *A. Rev. Pl. Physiol.* **3**, 265–
306.

LANGHANS, R. W. and WEILER, T. (1967). Factors affecting flowering. *In*
"Easter Lilies" (D. C. Kiplinger and R. W. Langhans, eds.), pp. 37–46.
New York and Ohio Lily Schools.

LAST, F. T. and PRICE, D. (1969). Yeasts associated with living plants and their
environs. *In* "The Yeasts" (A. H. Rose and J. S. Harrison, eds.), vol. 1, pp.
183–218. Academic Press, London.

LEIVONEN, H. (1958). The effect of gibberellins and indole-3-acetic acid on the
root cells of *Narcissus tazetta* (L.). *Physiologia Pl.* **11**, 838–43.

LIEMBURG, J. (1960). Koelproeven met tulpenplantgoed 1958/9. *Weekbl.
BloembCult.* **70**, 590–1.

LUYTEN, I., JOUSTRA, G. and BLAAUW, A. H. (1926). The results of the temperature treatment in summer for the Darwin tulip (Second part). *Proc. Sect. Sci. K. ned. Akad. Wet.* **29**, (1) 113–26.

LUYTEN, I., VERSLUYS, M. C. and BLAAUW, A. H. (1932). De optimale temperatuur van bloemaanleg tot bloei voor *Hyacinthus orientalis*. *Verh. K. Akad. Wet.* (*Sectie 2*), **29** (5), 1–64.

MACARTHUR, M. (1941). Development of the lily. *Scient. Agric.* **22**, 104–7.

MASTALERZ, J. W. (1965). Bud blasting in *Lilium longiflorum*. *Proc. Am. Soc. hort. Sci.* **87**, 502–9.

McWHORTER, F. and ALLEN, T. (1967). Viruses. *In* "Easter Lilies" (D. C. Kiplinger and R. W. Langhans, eds.) pp. 111–18. New York and Ohio Lily Schools.

MILLER, R. O. and KIPLINGER, D. C. (1964). Response of Easter lilies to high temperature. *Ohio Fm Home Res.* **49**, 8–9, 15.

MILLER, R. O. and KIPLINGER, D. C. (1966a). Interaction of temperature and time of vernalization on Northwest Easter lilies. *Proc. Am. Soc. hort. Sci.* **88**, 635–45.

MILLER, R. O. and KIPLINGER, D. C. (1966b). Reversal of vernalization in Northwest Easter lilies. *Proc. Am. Soc. hort. Sci.* **88**, 646–50.

MILLER, R. O. and KIPLINGER, D. C. (1967). Experiments with garden lilies for pot plant culture. *Bull. Ohio. Florists' Ass.* **457**, 2–3.

MILLER, R. O. and KOFRANEK, A. M. (1966). Temperature studies of lilies. *Calif. Agric.* **20**, 2–3.

MILTHORPE, F. L. (1963). Some aspects of plant growth. An introductory survey. *In* "The Growth of the Potato" (J. D. Ivins and F. L. Milthorpe, eds.), pp. 3–16. Butterworths, London.

MOORE, W. C. (1939). Diseases of bulbs. *Bull. Minist. Agric. Fish. Fd, Lond.*, **117**.

MULDER, R. and LUYTEN, I. (1928). De periodieke ontwikkeling van de Darwintulp. *Verh. K. Akad. Wet.* (*Sectie 2*) **26** (3), 1–64.

MULLIN, M. (1970). Tissue culture of some monocotyledonous plants. *Aust. J. biol. Sci.* **23**, 473–7.

MUNK, W. J. DE (1971). Bud necrosis in tulips, a multifactorial disorder. *In Proc. I Int. Symp. on Flowerbulbs*, Noordwijk/Lisse 1970. Wageningen, Centre for Agricultural Publishing & Documentation, pp. 242–8.

MUNK, W. J. DE and ROOY, M. DE (1971). The influence of ethylene on the development of 5°C-pre-cooled 'Apeldoorn' tulips during forcing. *HortScience* **6**, 40–1.

NARD, M. LE and COHAT, J. (1968). Influence des températures de conservation sur l'élongation, la floraison et la bulbification de la tulipe (*Tulipa gesneriana* L.). *Annls Amel. Pl.* **18**, 181–215.

NAYLOR, E. E. (1940). Propagation of *Hyacinthus* by leaf cutting. *Bull. Torrey bot. Club.* **67**, 602–6.

NELDER, J. A. (1962). New kinds of systematic designs for spacing experiments. *Biometrics* **18**, 283–307.

NEZU, M. and OBATA, S. (1964). [Studies on the induction of bud sports in tulips by ionizing radiation. 1. Morphology and development of the bulbs.] *Jap. J. Genet.* **38**, 386–91.

OGURA, Y. (1952). Morphology of the subterranean organs of *Erythronium japonicum* and its allies. *Phytomorphology* **2**, 113–22.

OKADA, M. and MIWA, S. (1958). [Studies on the structure and life cycle of scaly bulb 1. On the trumpet narcissus.] *J. hort. Ass. Japan* **27**, 135–43.

OLDROYD, K. (1967). Shock treatment for tulips gives higher returns. *Grower* **67**, 1060–1.

PAPENDRACHT, G. (1955). De bewaartemperatuur van het tulpenplantgoed. *Meded Vereen. Proefstation Lisse* **18**, 41–56.

PARKIN, J. (1912). The carbohydrates of the foliage leaf of the snowdrop (*Galanthus nivalis*) and their bearing on the first sugar of photosynthesis. *Biochem. J.* **6**, 1–47.

PARSONS, C. S., ASEN, S. and STUART, N. W. (1967). Controlled-atmosphere storage of daffodil flowers. *Proc. Am. Soc. hort. Sci.* **90**, 506–14.

PAYNE, R. (1967). A progress report on the influence of 40° and 70°F storage temperatures on respiration and forcing in bulbs of *Lilium longiflorum*, cultivars Ace and Georgia. *Bull. Ohio Florists' Ass.* **458**, 5–7.

PAZOUREK, J. (1970). The effect of light intensity on stomatal frequency in leaves of *Iris hollandica* hort. var. Wedgwood. *Biologia Pl.* **12**, 208–15.

PEACE, T. R. and GILMOUR, J. S. L. (1949). The effect of picking on the flowering of bluebell, *Scilla non-scripta*. *New Phytol.* **48**, 115–17.

PEARSALL, W. H. and BILLIMORIA, M. C. (1938). Effects of age and season upon protein synthesis in detached leaves. *Ann. Bot.* **2**, 601–18.

PEARSALL, W. H. and BILLIMORIA, M. C. (1939). Influence of light upon nitrogen metabolism in detached leaves. *Ann. Bot.* **3**, 601–18.

PETROVA, T. F. and SILINA, Z. N. (1966). Hybridization and polyploidy among tulip varieties originating from wild central asian species. *Soviet Genetics* **2** (2), 66–73.

PFEIFER, N. E. (1935). Development of the floral axis and new bud in imported Easter lilies. *Contr. Boyce Thompson Inst. Pl. Res.* **7**, 311–21.

POPCOV, A. V. and BUČ, T. G. (1968). [The temperature conditions for tulip seed germination.] *Bjull. glav. bot. Sada* **69**, 48–52.

PREECE, T. F. and MORRISON, J. R. (1963). Growth stages of the narcissus flower within the bulb. Illustrations of the Beyer scale. *Pl. Path.* **12**, 145–6.

PRICE, D. (1970). Tulip fire caused by *Botrytis tulipae* (Lib.) Lind.; the leaf spotting phase. *J. hort. Sci.* **45**, 233–8.

PRIESTLEY, J. H. and SCOTT, L. T. (1950). "An Introduction to Botany". Longmans Green and Co. London.

PURVIS, O. N. (1938). Recent Dutch research on the growth and flowering of bulbs. II. The temperature requirements of tulips and daffodils. *Scient. Hort.* **6**, 160–77.

RASMUSSEN, E. (1963). Forsøg med forskellig opbevaringstemperatur til læggelog af tulipaner 1954–60. *Tidsskr. PlAvl* **66**, 848–61.

RASMUSSEN, E. (1964). Førsog med forskellig baeggeafstand til tulipaner. *Tidsskr. PlAvl* **67**, 797–814.

RASMUSSEN, E. (1965). Forsøg med tvungen nedvisning, forskellig optagningstid og særlig høj opbevaringstemperatur til tulipaner. *Tidsskr. PlAvl* **69**, 314–319.

REES, A. R. (1964). The apicial organization and phyllotaxis of the oil palm. *Ann. Bot.* **28**, 57–69.

REES, A. R. (1965). Potential rates of dry-matter production in southern England with special reference to the tulip. *Rep. Glasshouse Crops Res. Inst. 1964*, 132–8.

REES, A. R. (1966a). Dry-matter production by field-grown tulips. *J. hort. Sci.* **41**, 19–30.

REES, A. R. (1966b). Effects of infection with narcissus mosaic, narcissus yellow stripe and tobacco rattle viruses on the growth and flowering of narcissus cv. 'Minister Talma'. *Ann. appl. Biol.* **58**, 25–30.

REES, A. R. (1967). The effect of high-temperature treatment of tulip bulbs ("blindstoken") on flowering and bulb yield. *Rep. Glasshouse Crops Res. Inst. 1966* 126–9.

REES, A. R. (1968a). The initiation and growth of tulip bulbs. *Ann. Bot.* **32**, 69–77.

REES, A. R. (1968b). Bulb respiration rates. *Rep. Glasshouse Crops Res. Inst. 1967* 61–2.

REES, A. R. (1969a). Effects of duration of cold treatment on the subsequent flowering of tulips. *J. hort. Sci.* **44**, 27–36.

REES, A. R. (1969b). Effect of bulb size on the growth of tulips. *Ann. Bot.* **33**, 133–42.

REES, A. R. (1969c). The initiation and growth of *Narcissus* bulbs. *Ann. Bot.* **33**, 277–88.

REES, A. R. (1971). Factors affecting the growth of daughter bulbs in the tulip. *Ann. Bot.* **35**, 43–55.

REES, A. R. and TURQUAND, E. D. (1967a). Warm storage of narcissus bulbs in relation to growth, flowering and damage caused by hot-water treatment. *J. hort. Sci.* **42**, 307–17.

REES, A. R. and TURQUAND, E. D. (1967b). Effects of lifting date and warm storage on tulip flowering. *Expl Hort.* **17**, 78–81.

REES, A. R. and TURQUAND, E. D. (1969a). Effects of temperature and duration of cold treatment on the flowering of forced tulips. *Expl Hort.* **20**, 49–54.

REES, A. R. and TURQUAND, E. D. (1969b). Effect of planting density on bulb yield in the tulip. *J. Appl. Ecol.* **6**, 349–58.

REES, A. R. and WALLIS, L. W. (1970). Pre-cooling of narcissus bulbs for early flowering in the field. *Expl Hort.* **21**, 61–6.

REES, A. R., BLEASDALE, J. K. A. and WALLIS, L. W. (1968). Effects of spacing on flower and bulb yield in the narcissus. *J. hort. Sci.* **43**, 113–20.

RICHARDS, F. J. and TEMPLEMAN, W. G. (1936). Physiological studies in plant nutrition. IV. Nitrogen metabolism in relation to nutrient deficiency and age of leaves in barley. *Ann. Bot. O.S.* **50**, 367–402.

RIVIÈRE, S. (1963). Étude ontogénique du méristème végétative et de sa transformation lors de l'édification de l'inflorescence chez le *Lilium candidum* L. (Liliacées). *C. r. Séanc. Hebd. Acad. Sci, Paris* **257**, Groupe II, 1–3.

ROBB, S. (1957). The culture of excised tissue from bulb scales of *Lilium speciosum* Thun. *J. exp. Bot.* **8**, 348–52.

ROBERTS, A. N. and BLANEY, L. T. (1968). Effects of vernalization and partial defoliation on flowering and correlative relationships in *Lilium longiflorum*, Thunb. 'Croft'. *Proc. Am. Soc. hort Sci.* **92**, 646–64.

ROBERTSON, A. (1906). The "droppers" of *Tulipa* and *Erythronium*. *Ann. Bot.* **20**, 429–40.

RODRIGUES PEREIRA, A. S. (1962). Physiological experiments in connection with flower formation in Wedgwood iris (*Iris* cv. 'Wedgwood'). *Acta bot. neerl.* **11**, 97–138.

RODRIGUES PEREIRA, A. S. (1964). Endogenous growth factors and flower formation in Wedgwood iris bulbs. *Acta bot. neerl.* **13**, 302–21.

RODRIGUES PEREIRA, A. S. (1965). Physiological analysis of flower formation in Wedgwood iris. *J. exp. Bot.* **16**, 405–10.

RODRIGUES PEREIRA, A. S. (1966). Effect of 2-thiouracil and gibberellic acid on flower formation in Wedgwood iris. *Acta bot. neerl.* **15**, 215–23.

RODRIGUES PEREIRA, A. S. (1970). The effect of CCC on growth and endogenous growth substances in Wedgwood iris. *Acta bot. neerl.* **19**, 895–900.

SACHS, R. M. (1962). Gibberellin, auxin and growth retardant effects upon cell division and shoot histogenesis. *Adv. Chem. Ser.* **28**, 49–58.

SALISBURY, E. J. (1942). "The Living Garden". Second edition. Neill and Co. Ltd., Edinburgh.

SARGANT, E. (1903). A theory of the origin of Monocotyledons founded on the structures of their seedlings. *Ann. Bot. O.S.* **17**, 1–92.

SASS, J. E. (1944). The initiation and development of foliar and floral organs in the tulip. *Iowa St. Coll. J. Sci.* **18**, 447–56.

SAVOS'KIN, I. P. (1960). [Specific biological characteristics of bulbous geophytes as related to their past and present ecology.] *Bot. Zh.* **45**, 1073–8.

SCHENK, P. K. (1969). Geschiktheid van verschillende geografische gebieden voor de bloembollencultuur. *Meded. Dir. Tuinb.* **32**, 293–300.

SCHENK, P. K. and BOONTJES J. (1970). Lilies in the Netherlands. *Lily Yb.* *1970*, 47–57.

SCHMALFELD, H. W. and CAROLUS, R. L. (1965). Nutrient redistribution in the tulip. *Proc. Am. Soc. hort. Sci.* **86**, 701–7.

SCHUURMAN, J. J. (1971). Effect of size and shape of tulip bulbs on root development. *In Proc. I Int. Symp. on Flowerbulbs*, Noordwijk/Lisse 1970. Wageningen, Centre for Agricultural Publishing & Documentation, pp. 312–17.

SHAW, M. and MACLACHLAN, G. A. (1954). The physiology of stomata. 1. Carbon dioxide fixation in guard cells. *Can. J. Bot.* **32**, 784–94.

SHERIDAN, W. F. (1968). Tissue culture of the monocot *Lilium*. *Planta* **82**, 189.

SHYR, S.-Y. and BLANEY, L. T. (1968). Physiology of dormancy in *L. longiflorum*. *HortScience* **3**, 96.

SISA, M. and HIGUCHI, H. (1967a). [Studies on shortening the juvenile phase of tulips under controlled environments. I. On the germination of seed and growth of seedling.] *Jap. J. Breed.* **17**, 122–30.

SISA, M. and HIGUCHI, H. (1967b). [Studies on the shortening of the juvenile phase in tulips under controlled environment. II. On the thermoperiodicity of juvenile tulip.] *J. Jap. Soc. hort. Sci.* **36**, 52–62.

SLOGTEREN, D. H. M. VAN and ASJES, C. J. (1969). Virus diseases in tulips. *Daffodil Tulip Yb., 1970* **35**, 85–97.

SLOGTEREN, E. VAN (1936). The influence of climate and storing-conditions on the flowering of flower-bulbs. *Int. Congr. Refrig. Inds.* **7**, 3–23.

SLOGTEREN, E. VAN (1937). The influence of different temperatures on development, growth and flowering of hyacinths, tulips and daffodils. *Gartenbauwissenschaft* **11**, 17–34.

SLOGTEREN, E. VAN and BRUYN OUBOTER, M. P. DE (1941). Investigations on virus diseases of narcissus. *Meded. Inst. Phytopath. Lab. BloembOnderz. Lisse* **64**, 1–17.

SLOOTWEG, A. F. G. (1962). Hot-water treatment of daffodils. *Daffodil Tulip Yb. 1963* **28**, 82–7.

SLOOTWEG, A. F. G. (1968). Grondslagen van de tulpebroei. *Meded. Dir. Tuinb.* **31**, 140–2, 44.

SLOOTWEG, A. F. G. and HOOGETERP, P. (1965). Enkele richtlijnen voor proefsgewijze toepassing van de 5°C–behandeling van tulpen. *Rapp. Lab. BloembOnderz. Lisse* **3**, 1–15.

SMITH, D. R. (1963). "The influence of the environment upon initiation and development in *Lilium longiflorum* (Thunb.)". Ph.D. Thesis, Cornell University.

SMITH, D. R. and LANGHANS, R. W. (1961). Facts about Easter lilies. *Bull. N.Y. St. Flow. Grow.* **192**, 1–4.

SMITH, D. R. and LANGHANS, R. W. (1962). The influence of photoperiod on the growth and flowering of Easter lily (*Lilium longiflorum* Thunb. var. Croft). *Proc. Am. Soc. hort. Sci.* **80**, 599–604.

SMITH, W. H. and WALLIS, L. W. (1967). Use of low temperatures to intensify colour of cut blooms of narcissus 'Soleil d'Or'. *Expl Hort.* **17**, 21–6.

SOLECKA, M. (1967). [Anthocyanins in *Tulipa gesneriana* L. variety 'Bartigon' and its mutants.] *Acta agrobot.* **20**, 95–118.

SOMA, K. and BALL, E. (1963). Studies on the surface growth of the shoot apex of *Lupinus albus. Brookhaven Symp. Biol.* **16**, 13–45.

SOUTHERN, D. I. (1967). Species relationships in the genus *Tulipa. Chromosoma* **23**, 80–94.

STABY, G. L. and DE HERTOGH, A. A. (1970). The detection of ethylene in the internal atmosphere of bulbs. *HortScience* **5**, 399–400.

STANT, M. Y. (1954). The shoot apex of some Monocotyledons. II. Growth organization. *Ann. Bot.* **18**, 441–7.

STEWARD, F. C. and DURZAN, D. J. (1965). Metabolism of nitrogenous compounds *In* "Plant Physiology". (F. C. Steward, ed.) Vol. IVa, pp. 379–686. Academic Press, New York.

STEWARD, F. C. and MILLAR, F. K. (1954). Salt accumulation in plants. A reconsideration of the rate of growth and metabolism. *Symp. Soc. exp. Biol.* **8**, 367–406.

288 THE GROWTH OF BULBS

STEWARD, F. C. and SUTCLIFFE, J. F. (1959). Plants in relation to inorganic salt. *In* "Plant Physiology" (F. C. Steward, ed.), vol. II, pp. 253–478, Academic Press, New York.

STOFFERT, G. (1965). Der Einfluss von Zwiebelabstand, Kistentiefe und Substrat auf das Wachstum von Treibtulpen. *Gartenbauwissenschaft* **30,** 75–90.

STUART, N. W. (1943). The influence of storage temperature on forcing performance of Creole Easter lilies. *Proc. Am. Soc. hort. Sci.* **42,** 597.

STUART, N. W. (1946). The effect of storage temperature and length of storage on forcing Northwest lilies for Easter. *Florists' Rev.* **98,** 35–7.

STUART, N. W. (1953). Quick cooling of new-crop Easter lily bulbs permits same-year forcing for winter market. *Florists' Exch.* **121,** 20–1.

STUART, N. W. (1967). Present methods of handling bulbs. *In* "Easter Lilies" (D. C. Kiplinger and R. W. Langhans, eds.), pp. 47–58. New York and Ohio Lily Schools.

STUART, N. W. and GOULD, C. J. (1954). Wedgewood iris forcing in 1953–4. *Proc. Bulb Growers' Short Course Tacoma Wash.* 29–30.

STUART, N. W. and GOULD, C. J. (1967). New directions in forcing bulbous iris. *Md Flor.* **138,** 2–3.

STUART, N. W., ASEN, S. and GOULD, C. J. (1966). Accelerated flowering of bulbous iris after exposure to ethylene. *HortScience* **1,** 19–20.

STUART, N. W., GOULD, C. J. and EMSWELLER, S. L. (1949). After-harvest and pre-cooling temperature effects on the forcing of Wedgwood iris. *Florists' Exch.* **113,** 11–45.

STUART, N. W., GOULD, C. J. and GILL, D. L. (1955). Effect of temperature and other storage conditions on forcing behavior of Easter lilies, bulbous iris and tulips. *Rep. XIV Int. hort. Cong. 1955,* 173–87.

STUART, N. W., GOULD, C. J., VASSEY, W. E. and HICKMAN, M. (1963). Heat-curing, cool storing speed flowering of Wedgwood iris. *Florists' Rev.* **132,** 25.

SYTSEMA, W. (1965). Temperatuurbehandelingen van nerinebollen. *Jversl. Proefstn bloemisterij Aalsmeer 1965,* 94–5.

TIMMER, M. J. G. and KOSTER, J. (1969a). Invloed van temperatuur tijdens bewaring op groei van hoofdknop en bijknoppen bij tulpen. *Weekbl. Bloemb-Cult.* **80,** 420.

TIMMER, M. J. G. and KOSTER, J. (1969b). Kunstmatige bladbeschadiging en de opbrengst van tulpen. *Weekbl. BloembCult.* **80,** 453.

TOMLINSON, P. B. (1970). Monocotyledons—Towards an understanding of their morphology and anatomy. *In* "Advances in Botanical Research". (R. D. Preston, ed.), Vol. 3, pp. 207–92. Academic Press, London.

TOYODA, T. and NISHII, K. (1957). [Studies on high-temperature treatment of tulip bulbs to prevent flowering. I. Effects of date and length of treatment on flowering, growth and bulb production.] *J. hort. Ass. Japan* **26,** 243–50.

TOYODA, T. and NISHII, K. (1958). [Studies on high-temperature treatment of tulip bulbs to prevent flowering. II. Relation between degree of injury in the flower bud and the yield of new bulbs.] *J. hort. Ass. Japan* **27,** 63–7.

TSUKAMOTO, Y. (1971). Changes of endogenous growth substances in Easter lily as effected by cooling. *In Proc. I. Int. Symp. on Flowerbulbs,* Noordwijk/

Lisse 1970. Wageningen, Centre for Agricultural Publishing & Documentation, pp. 75–81.

TSUTSUI, K. and TOYODA, T. (1970). Effect of storage temperatures of seed bulbs on the dropper formation in tulips. *J. Jap. Soc. hort. Sci.* **39**, 85–92.

TURNER, A. (1967). "Morphogenesis of the shoot apex in *Endymion non-scriptus* (L.) Garcke and some aspects of its sensitivity to ionizing radiations and certain growth regulating substances". Ph.D. Thesis, University of Manchester.

TURQUAND, E. D. (1967). Bulbs. *Rep. Kirton exp. Hort. Stn 1965*, 12–56.

TURQUAND, E. D. (1968). Bulbs. *Rep. Kirton exp. Hort. Stn 1966*, 13–62.

TURQUAND, E. D. (1969). Weed control in bulbs: A summary of work at Kirton. *Proc. Br. Weed Control Conf. 1968*, 959–64.

TURQUAND, E. D. (1970). Bulbs. *Rep. Kirton exp. Hort. Stn 1967*, 5–72.

TURQUAND, E. D. and REES, A. R. (1968). Storage of narcissus bulbs. *Prog. Rep. exp. Husb. Fms exp. hort. Stns N.A.A.S. 1968*, **9**, 69–70.

UPCOTT, M. and LA COUR, L. (1936). The genetic structure of *Tulipa*. 1. A chromosome survey. *J. Genet.* **33**, 237–51.

VALK, G. G. M. VAN DER (1971). Frost injury to flowerbulb crops. *In Proc. I Int. Symp. on Flowerbulbs*, Noordwijk/Lisse 1970. Wageningen, Centre for Agricultural Publishing & Documentation, pp. 345–9.

VALK, G. G. M. VAN DER and HAAN, F. A. M. DE (1969). Gevolgen van bodemverdichting voor de produktie van bloembolgewassen. *Meded. Inst. CultTech. WatHuish.* **498**, 1–41.

VERSLUYS, M. C. (1927). Aanleg en groei der wortels van *Hyancinthus orientalis* gedurende het geheele jaar en onder verschillende omstandigheden. *Verh. K. Akad. Wet. Amsterdam (Sectie 2)*, **25** (4), 5–100.

VICKERY, H. B., PUCHER, G. W., WAKEMAN, A. J. and LEAVENWORTH, C. S. (1946). Chemical investigations of the metabolism of plants. 1. The nitrogen nutrition of *Narcissus poeticus*. *Bull. Conn. agric. Exp. Stn* **496**, 1–93.

VIGODSKY, H. (1970). Hardening of iris bulbs for hot-water treatment. *J. hort. Sci.* **45**, 87–97.

WAISTER, P. D. and JOY, P. J. (1968). Growth of tulips. *Rep. Scott. hort. Res. Inst. 1967*, 20.

WALLIS, L. W. (1965). Bulbs. *Rep. Rosewarne exp. Hort. Stn 1964*, 18–36.

WALLIS, L. W. (1966). Bulbs. Storage. *Rep. Rosewarne exp. Hort. Stn 1965*, 16–23.

WALLIS, L. W. (1967). Bulbs. *Rep. Rosewarne exp. Hort. Stn 1966*, 18–41.

WALLIS, L. W. (1968). Bulbs. *Rep. Rosewarne exp. Hort. Stn 1967*, 21–60.

WALLIS, L. W. (1969). Bulbs. *Rep. Rosewarne exp. Hort. Stn 1968*, 20–30.

WANG, S.-Y. (1969). Physiology of dormancy in *Lilium longiflorum* Thunb. *Diss. Abstr. B* **30**, 1428–9.

WANG, S.-Y., ROBERTS, A. N. and BLANEY, L. T. (1970). Relationship between length of vernalization, stem apex size and initiatory activity in *Lilium longiflorum* cv. 'Ace'. *HortScience* **5**, 113–14.

WANGERMAN, E. (1965). Longevity and ageing in plants and plant organs. *In*

"Encyclopedia of Plant Physiology" (W. Ruhland, ed.), **15**/2, 1026–57. Springer-Verlag, Berlin.

WASSINK, E. C. (1965). Light intensity effects in growth and development of tulips in comparison with those in gladiolus. *Meded. LandbHoogesch. Wageningen* **65** (15), 1–21.

WASSINK, E. C. (1969). Effects of light intensity on dry-matter production and morphogenesis of *Iris* 'Wedgwood', as compared with *Gladiolus* and tulip. *Meded. LandbHoogesch. Wageningen* **69** (20), 1–17.

WASSINK, E. C. and WASSINK-VAN LUMMEL, L. E. A. (1952). The action of light intensity and night temperature on flowering of bulbous irises (Wedgwood) and tulips. *Rep. XIII Int. hort. Cong. 1952*, 969–81.

WATERS, W. E. and WILKINS, H. F. (1966). Influence of light intensity and duration on growth and flowering of uncooled Easter lilies (*Lilium longiflorum* Thunb. var. Georgia). *Proc. XVII Int. hort. Cong. 1966*, 234.

WATERS, W. E. and WILKINS, H. F. (1967). Influence of intensity, duration and date of light on growth and flowering of uncooled Easter lily (*Lilium longiflorum* Thunb. 'Georgia'). *Proc. Am. Soc. hort. Sci.* **90**, 433–9.

WATERSCHOOT, H. F. (1927). Results of the temperature during flower formation for early *Hyacinthus*, 'L'Innocence' and 'La Victoire'. *Proc. Sect. Sci. K. ned. Akad. Wet.* **31** (1), 31–49.

WATSON, D. J. and HAYASHI, K.-I. (1965). Photosynthetic and respiratory components of the net assimilation rates of sugar beet and barley. *New Phytol.* **64**, 38–47.

WATSON, D. J. and WILSON, J. H. (1956). An analysis of the effects of infection with leaf-roll virus on the growth and yield of potato plants, and of its interaction with nutrient supply and shading. *Ann. appl. Biol.* **44**, 390–409.

WEILER, T. C. and LANGHANS, R. W. (1968a). Determination of vernalizing temperatures in the vernalization requirement of *Lilium longiflorum* (Thunb.) cv. 'Ace'. *Proc. Am. Soc. hort. Sci.* **93**, 623–9.

WEILER, T. C. and LANGHANS, R. W. (1968b). Effect of photoperiod on the vernalization requirement of *Lilium longiflorum* (Thunb.) cv. 'Ace'. *Proc. Am. Soc. hort. Sci.* **93**, 630–4.

WEILER, T. C. and LANGHANS, R. W. (1968c). A report on field vernalization and devernalization studies of Pacific Northwest-grown *Lilium longiflorum* cv. 'Ace'. *HortScience* **3**, 96.

WENT, F. W. (1948). Thermoperiodicity. *In* Vernalization and photoperiodism, a symposium. *Lotsya* **1**, 145–7.

WHITE, O. E. (1948). Fasciation. *Bot. Rev.* **14**, 319–58.

WIERSUM, L. K. (1971). Tulip root behaviour and aeration requirements. *In Proc. I Int. Symp. on Flowerbulbs*, Noordwijk/Lisse 1970. Wageningen, Centre for Agricultural Publishing & Documentation, pp. 318–25.

WILKINS, H. F., WATERS, W. E. and WIDMER, R. E. (1968). Influence of temperature and photoperiod on growth and flowering of Easter lilies (*Lilium longiflorum* Thunb. 'Georgia', 'Ace' and 'Nellie White'). *Proc. Am. Soc. hort. Sci.* **93**, 640–9.

WILKINS, H. F., WIDMER, R. E. and WATERS, W. E. (1968). The influence of carbon dioxide, photoperiod and temperature on growth and flowering of Easter lilies (*Lilium longiflorum* Thunb. 'Ace' and 'Nellie White'). *Proc. Am. Soc. hort. Sci.* **93,** 650–4.

WILSON, K. and HONEY, J. N. (1966). Root contraction in *Hyacinthus orientalis. Ann. Bot.* **30,** 47–61.

WINSOR, G. W. and CHEAL, W. F. (1969). Response of tulips (variety Elmus) to nitrogen and potassium. Part II, Field-grown crops. *Expl Hort.* **19,** 61–70.

WIT, C. T. DE (1959). Potential photosynthesis of crop surfaces. *Neth. J. agric. Sci.* **7,** 141–9.

WOOD, J. (1940). Experiments on hot-water treatment, 1937–39. *Rep. Bulb Exp. Kirton agric. Inst.* **7,** 24–33.

WOOD, J. (1944). Hot-water treatment of narcissus bulbs. *Jl R. hort. Soc.* **69,** 298–304.

YASUDA, I. and FUJI, H. (1963). [Re-rooting following the cutting off of new roots on some bulbs. II. In the case of iris and daffodil.] *Sci. Rep. Fac. Agric. Okayama* **21,** 41–7.

YOKOI, M. (1964). Analyses of quality and yield of cut flowers with particular reference to spacing of plants. III. Cut flower quality and yield of forced tulips in relation to planting density, nutrition and the use of bulbs produced from different soil texture in preceding generation. *Tech. Bull. Fac. Hort. Chiba Univ.* **12,** 37–44.

ZACHARIAS, J. T. and STEWARD, F. C. (1957). The nitrogen compounds and nitrogen metabolism in the Liliaceae. III. Changes in the soluble nitrogen compounds of the tulip and their relation to flower formation in the bulb. *Ann. Bot.* **21,** 193–201.

ZEILINGA, A. E. and SCHOUTEN, H. P. (1968). Polyploidy in garden tulips. 1. A survey of *Tulipa* varieties for polyploids. *Euphytica* **17,** 252–64.

Author Index

Subject Index

A

Abortion, 20, 92, 103, 179, 235, 239, 249, 257
Abscisic acid, 200, 223
Adventitious buds, 13
Aldrin, 254
Alicep, 249
Allium, 14, 40, 71, 79
Amaryllidaceae, 14, 230
Amaryllis, 97, 230
Androecium, 31
Anther, 31–3, 35–7, 100–1, 110, 225
Anthesis, 19–20, 24, 31, 42, 44, 107, 113, 117, 128, 132, 137, 146, 158, 161, 174
Apex 13, 20, 30, 37, 38, 101, 189
  activity, 134, 186, 192, 195
  damage, 76
  pre-floral, 25
  quiescent, 22, 24, 25, 29, 30, 44, 75, 101
  size, 30, 39, 110
  structure, 37–9
  reproductive, 34, 37, 102–3, 190–1, 218
  vegetative, 24, 25, 30, 37, 48, 218
Aphid, 256–7, 265, 266, 268
Apical dominance, 14, 34, 54, 74, 86, 93, 95, 144, 179, 254, 270
Arabis mosaic disease, 266
Arid climate, 15
Augusta disease, 267
Autopolypoloidy, 9
Auxin, 220–8, 221, 224

B

Bacterial soft rot, 262
Bacterium, 262, 263

Base plate, 39, 191, 202, 254
Beds, 60, 66
Bees, 32
Begonia, 1
Bellevalia, 40
Benlate, 226
Bermuda lily disease, 268
Bipolaris, 263
Black stem rot, 261
Blauwgroeien, 243–4
Blindstoken, 87, 143–5, 226
Bordeaux mixture, 259
Botrytis, 231, 259–60, 262, 264
Bract, 38
Branching system, 26, 27, 45
Breeding, 3
Brodiaea, 32
"Broken" tulip, 6, 267
Brunsvigia, 230
Bud, 14, 25, 31, 105
"Bud blasting", 248–9
Bulb,
  aerial, 22, 36, 37, 44, 71
  age, 27
  appearance, 92–3
  "curing", 115, 137, 187, 193
  daughter, 14, 15, 20, 22, 29, 34, 36, 40, 44, 73, 90, 93, 208, 219, 260, 270
  development, 214
  differentiation, 92
  diseases, 259–60
  dispersal, 70–1
  dissection, 100–1, 198
  double-nosed, 67
  drying, 93
  export, 3, 140
  "flat", 35, 140

Perianth, 31–3, 35–7, 100–1, 110, 127, 165, 209, 214, 237
Periodicity, 14, 22, 23, 39, 42–3, 44, 102
Petiole, 32, 36
Pheasants, 256
Phloem, 218
Phosfon, 226
Photoperiod, 41, 86, 102, 105, 174, 178, 181–2, 209, 213, 228
Photosynthesis, 15, 49, 53, 59, 85, 173, 204, 211, 212, 215, 248
Phytochrome, 226
Phytophthora, 264
Pigments, 209–11
Planting density, 46, 60–70
Plasmolysis, 40
Plasticity of plant form, 45
Plastochrone, 17, 38
Pollen, 225
Pollination, 32, 33, 229
Polyploidy, 5
Post-harvest physiology, 231–3
Pot plants, 11, 151, 163, 176, 227, 231
Pratylenchus, 253
Precooling, 119, 123, 124, 127, 128, 137, 147, 165, 168
"Preparation", 134
Primordium, 24, 30
   flower, 103, 110, 187
   leaf, 30, 37, 38, 44, 134, 187, 191
   scale, 30, 44
Profitability, 65, 70
Prometryne, 249
Propagation, 15, 36, 53, 93–4, 95, 97
Prophyll, 31, 38
Protein, 43, 209, 216
Pythium, 261, 262, 264

Q

Q_{10}, 87

R

Radiation, 15, 85, 203
Ramularia, 258
Rats, 256
Receptacle, 31, 32

Relative growth rate, 55–6, 73–89
Relative humidity, 95
Respiration, 134
   "basic", 187
   "developed", 187
   and ethylene, 199
   hyacinth, 195–6
   Iris, 79–81, 113, 136, 173–4, 185–200
   lily, 196
   Narcissus, 73–5, 199
   and substrates, 190
   tulip, 59, 77–8, 81–2, 87–8
Respiratory quotient, 190
Resting organs, 12
Retardants, 226–8
"Retarded" bulbs, 111, 136, 140, 184, 262
"Reversion", 239
Rhizoctonia, 261, 264
Rhizoglyphus, 242, 255
Rhizomes, 12
Ridges, 60, 66
Roguing, 257, 266
Root
   damage, 253
   emergence, 39, 148, 258, 263
   failure, 247
   growth, 44, 93, 96, 114, 141, 148, 152–3, 202, 219, 220
   hairs, 39, 201, 208, 225
   initiation, 39, 201, 253
   number, 39, 41, 201–2
   penetration, 39
   pressure, 247
   removal, 202
   rot, 253, 257, 259, 261, 264
Rooting period, 147
Rooting rooms, 148–51, 169
Roots, 12, 15, 39–40, 201
   adventitious, 13, 39
   basal, 36
   contractile, 13, 40
   Hippeastrum, 39
   hyacinth, 39, 247
   Iris, 39, 202, 219, 259
   lily, 39

310

SUBJECT INDEX

Tulip—*cont.*
'Krelage's Triumph', 203
'Merry Widow', 104, 125, 141
'Mme. Lefeber', 9
'Mozart', 219
'Murillo', 193
'Pandion', 90–1
'Paris', 141
'Paul Richter', 104, 125, 130, 141, 161, 164, 166, 182
'Peach Blossom', 143
'President Eisenhower', 209, 211
'Pride of Haarlem', 104–5, 109, 211
'Ralph', 219
'Red Matador', 132
'Rose Copland', 10, 22, 46, 48, 49, 55–7, 62–3, 81, 85, 86, 87–9, 125, 141, 143, 161, 181, 196, 201, 245
'Spring Song', 9
'Weber', 56–7, 82–3
"William Copland', 109, 157
'William Pitt', 10, 48, 49, 56–7, 141, 147, 152
'Zwaneburg', 219
daughter bulbs, 22–3, 41, 43, 44, 76–9, 81–7, 89, 91, 93–7
death, 43, 46
diploid, 5, 7
disease, 260–1
divisions,
Eriostemones, 7, 8
Leiostemones, 7
'droppers", 40
earlier flowering, 117
emergence, 46
extending growing season, 89
flower
growth, 114
initiation, 99–100, 103, 185
pigments, 209
storage, 232
structure, 32–3
forcing, 118, 125–31, 154, 157–8, 164, 167, 181–3, 219, 241

growth, 46–9, 211–12, 220
in ridges, 69–70
season, 51
"knuckling", 245
leaf area index, 46, 47, 62, 70
leaves, 212
low-temperature treatment, (*see* Temperature)
mineral nutrition, 204
periodicity, 42–4
polyploids, 7, 8
respiration, 59, 195
roots, 39, 201–2, 225, 236, 244, 259, 267
senescence, 46, 56
species
T. aleppensis, 9
T. chrysantha, 9, 41
T. clusiana, 9
T. edulis, 41
T. fosteriana, 7, 9
T. gesneriana, 228
T. greigii, 9
T. ingens, 9
T. kaufmanniana, 9
T. latifolia, 41
T. orphanidea, 9
T. praestans, 33, 227
T. saxatilis, 9
stomata, 204
structure aerial parts, 32–3
tetraploid, 5, 7
transpiration, 203
triploid, 5, 7
viruses, 266
warm storage, (*see* Temperature)
Tulipa, 14, 15
Tulipalin, 226
Tunic, 22, 23, 29, 35, 92, 93, 189, 198
Tyrophagus, 242

V

Value of crops, 3
Vascular tissue, 13, 41, 211
Vase life, 227, 231–3